Clarence
Kelly
Assit Coach

SO-BSV-736

Bobby Plump

Last of the Small Town Heroes

Co-Authors
Marty Pieratt
and
Ken Honeywell

Good Morning Publishing Co., Inc.
All Rights Reserved

Except for appropriate use in critical reviews, the reproduction or use of this work in any form or by any electronic, mechanical, or other means now known or hereafter invented by man, including photocopying and recording, and in any information storage and retrieval system, is forbidden without the written consent or permission of Good Morning Publishing Co., Inc., the publisher.

Good Morning Publishing Co., Inc., has made every effort to trace the ownership of all copyrighted material and to appropriately acknowledge such ownership. In the event of any question arising as to the use of any material, Good Morning Publishing Co., Inc., will gladly make changes in future printings at the expense of the ownership.

Printed in the United States of America.

Copyright ©1997

Copyright #TXU686-900, Volume #3346, Page 313 through 317—Volume #3346, Page 318 through 322.

Library of Congress Catalog Card No.: 97-72748
I.S.B.N.: 0-9636873-9-5

2 3 4 5 6 7 8 9 10

Cover and family photos: Sid Rust.
Cover design and layout: Roger Dobrovodsky.
Book design and layout: Roger Dobrovodsky and Wesley Press.
Proofreaders: Ken Honeywell and Wesley Press.

Good Morning Publishing Co., Inc.
P.O. Box 2366
Indianapolis, Indiana 46206-2366

DEDICATION

To my loyal friend and loving wife Jenine, who has stood by me through thick and thin and has always inspired me to never stop.

To my daughters, Tari and Kelli, and my son Jonathan and their spouses and all my grandchildren for their love and devotion.

To my father, Fredrick William George Lester Plump (deceased) and my mother, Mabel Mary Dilla Plump (deceased). I will always be grateful for the love and guidance they gave me and my sisters and brothers: Dorothea Mae Plump Sullender, Virginia Lee Plump Schwing, Eloise Esther Plump Heidorn, Wallace Loren Plump (deceased), and Lester Junior Plump (deceased). My brothers and sisters and your families: you are the greatest, and I am lucky to have been part of your lives. I want you to know how much I love you all.

And to my other families: Coach Marc Combs (deceased), Coach Herman Grinstead (deceased), Coach Marvin Wood, Coach Clarence Kelly, Coach Paul D. "Tony" Hinkle (deceased), and Coach Omar "Bud" Browning (deceased); and all my teammates, classmates, and friends for making it possible for me to carry out my life's ambitions and live the American Dream.

My eternal thanks,

Bobby

ACKNOWLEDGEMENT

Good Morning Publishing Co., Inc., would like to take this opportunity to thank each and every one of the people who helped us with research and granted interviews for what we believe is the greatest sports story ever told. We would love to recognize all of you be name, but, for fear of missing someone, we will just say thanks. You know who you are, and know how much your contribution is appreciated.

We would like to give special thanks to the following people who read our manuscript prior to publication and helped the book achieve its final form:

Angela Ambrasiani	Tim O'Neill
Carolyn Baldwin	Steve Phillips
Don Campbell	Jacqi Phillips
Steve Carroll	Marty Pieratt
Eva Combs	Bobby Plump
Marc Combs	Jenine Plump
Elizabeth Dein	Carol Purichia
Lloyd Freeman	Lynette Rayn
Virginia Herbst	Christine Rainey
Carolyn Keller	Betsy Roby
Joanne Kelly	Kelly Russell
Kathleen Kendall	Gwen Speck
Vicki Long	Chris Theofanis
Becky Matlock	George Theofanis
Joy May	George Thompson
Judith Mayhew	Amy Wagner
Dave McCollum	Melissa Warriner
Harlene McCollum	Jim Weinmann
Andrea McGordon	Doc Wilham
Forrest McLinn	Jim Wilham
Tom O'Brien	Kathy Wilhite

We are also very grateful to everyone who shared photographs, personal items, collections, and other information. Finally, we will always be thankful to Bobby Gene Plump and his teammates, classmates, teachers, coaches, and friends; and the Town of Milan and the people of Milan for accepting us into your homes, offices, and, in some cases, barns so that we could tell the real, untold story of Bobby Plump and the Milan Indians.

Joe Wolfla
Vice President, Sales & Marketing
Good Morning Publishing Co., Inc.

TABLE OF CONTENTS

FOREWORD

This is the greatest human interest story you will ever read.

This book is about a boy, a man, a father named Bobby Gene Plump, who just happens to have been the high school basketball player who in 1954 hit "the shot heard 'round the world. Bobby's shot brought a state basketball championship home to a tiny Southeastern Indiana town called Milan (population 1,100) and their little school that had an enrollment of just 161 students.

In the 1952-53 basketball season, the Indians made it to the Final Four of the Indiana High School Athletic Association boys' state basketball tournament, and everybody thought that it was a fluke, that the Cinderella team from Milan would not repeat. But the 1953-54 Indians not only made it to the Final Four, they were crowned state champions.

This Cinderella team from Milan and its star player Bobby Plump had their share of personal challenges that have never been revealed until now. There has been a lot written about the Milan Indians. But this book is the untold story of Bobby Plump, his eleven teammates, their head basketball coach, and his assistants.

For example, most people don't know that Bobby Plump never lived in Milan. He was born and raised in Pierceville, Indiana, population 45, along with three of this teammates on that 1954 state championship team. Pierceville is three-and-a-half miles west of Milan on State Road 350, and Bobby and his Pierceville buddies were the original Pierceville Alleycats, the kids from the other side of the tracks.

This book is not just about basketball. It's about a kid who didn't even have a name for the first five days of his life, until a country girl from down the road named him Bobby Gene, after a classmate she liked. Bobby's mother died at home when he was only five years old. His father raised the family, with the help of a devoted daughter who put the rest of her life on hold. Bobby's father never dated or remarried. He devoted the rest of his life to his family, friends, and church.

Bobby and his family have faced many obstacles, including cancer, open heart surgery, and the dark side of life's struggles. The Plumps' faith, love, and devotion to their friends and family have helped them overcome these and other obstacles and truly placed them in the circle of life's winners.

Good Morning Publishing Co., Inc., and its staff and friends are proud to share this story with you. We know you'll agree that this is one of the greatest stories ever told.

Marcia A. Wolfla
President
Good Morning Publishing Co., Inc.

THE VICTOR

If you think you are beaten, you are.
If you think you dare not, you don't.
If you like to win but think you can't,
It's almost a cinch you won't.
If you think you'll lose, you're lost,
For out in the world we find
Success begins with a fellow's will:
It's all in the state of mind.
If you think you are outclassed, you are.
You've got to think high to rise.
You've got to be sure of yourself before
You can ever win a prize.
Life's battles don't always go
To the stronger or faster man.
But sooner or later, the man who wins
Is the man who thinks he can.

— *C.W. Longenecker*

CHAPTER ONE

BASKETBALL HERO, INDIANA STYLE

Colorado has the Rocky Mountains. South Dakota has Mount Rushmore. Florida has sunshine. In Indiana, we have basketball. It is basketball that stands tallest here, basketball that lights up gymnasiums across the state through the long winter, basketball nearly every night, in every high school and junior high and elementary school and YMCA and CYO gym in the state. In this age of slam-dunk NBA millionaires and big-money college ball, it is still high school basketball that packs them in here. Fifteen of the sixteen largest high school gymnasiums in the world are in Indiana. In many small towns, someone has to die before you can get a season ticket, and that someone had better be a relative.

Basketball winds through Indiana like the Wabash River: from north to south, east to west. And Indiana basketball winds through practically any game played anywhere, sometimes in surprising ways. Take the 1995 NCAA Division I Tournament, for example. Indiana and Purdue and Ball State had bowed out early, and Notre Dame, Butler, Evansville, Indiana State, and Valparaiso had failed to make the Division I field (although the University of Southern Indiana not only qualified for the Division II tournament, they won it, 71-63 over California Riverside after charging back from an early 22-point deficit). But there in the stands, cheering his UCLA Bruins on to victory against defending champion Arkansas, sat John Wooden. The legendary coach evokes memories of Lew Alcindor (Kareem Abdul-Jabbar) and Bill Walton, of UCLA teams so good that, for an entire decade, the rest of the nation's colleges were playing for second place. But before his coaching days, before his ten national championships, John Wooden was an Indiana high school star at Martinsville, a college star at Purdue, and a coach at South Bend Central High School and Indiana State University. An Indiana connection to the biggest college game of the year.

It's often been that way. The State of North Carolina, for example has had plenty of basketball championships with the University of North Carolina and North Carolina State and Duke, but Indiana players and coaches such as Vic Bubas, Everett Case, Sammy Ranzino, Monty Towe, Norm Sloan, Rick Fox, and Eric Montross have played key roles in the Tarheel State's runs at basketball glory. At one time, all of Michigan State's starters were from Indiana. Bobby White, a high school star at Jasper, Indiana, once recalled a game between Vanderbilt and Mississippi in which 12 of the 20 players hailed from a 50-mile radius of Southern Indiana. Back in 1938, seven of the ten players on the University of Southern California team were Hoosiers. When they played at home, the USC band played "Back Home Again In Indiana."

And the Indiana connection at the 1995 tournament was not on the basketball floor. Because if you were watching at home, you probably noticed a series of television commercials for long-distance giant AT&T. The commercials featured Georgetown coach John Thompson competing with a fictional college coach played by Ernie Lively for the favor of a small-town high school hardwood phenom. The kid was played by Tony Staley, a senior at Taft High School in Cincinnati. His high school coach in the commercials was a veteran Hollywood character actor named Bill Jordan, who just happened to have a pretty good basketball resume: he was a backup guard on an Indiana high school championship team back in 1954.

And the connection doesn't end here, because this was not just any team, nor was this commercial filmed in just any small town. In one spot, you may have noticed a shot of the town's water tower. It reads: "Milan, 1954 State Champs." And if you live in Colorado or South Dakota or Florida, that sign may have meant nothing at all to you. But if you live in Indiana, you know better. You know that this tiny town in the rolling hills of Southeast Indiana is the epicenter of Indiana basketball, and by logical extension, the epicenter of basketball, period. You know that, were we to build a Mount Rushmore to basketball, we would have to locate it in Ripley County, Indiana. And we would argue mightily if you asked us to restrict our monument to just four famous faces. Who could we possibly leave off? Not John Wooden or Bob Knight or Gene Keady or Tony Hinkle or Angus Nicson. Not Rick Mount or Damon Bailey or Steve Alford or Scott Skiles. Certainly not Oscar Robertson or Jimmy Rayl or George McGinnis or Larry Bird. Glenn Robinson? Shawn Kemp? The Van Arsdale twins? Bill, Billy, and Dave Shephard?

But there would be no question as to one of the faces. It would belong on our monument the way basketball belongs in Indiana. Young and old across the state would recognize the face and the name. It's a name that stands for more than Indiana high school basketball, more than a small-town team winning over big-time odds, more even than one of the greatest sports stories ever told. It stands for every underdog who ever looked a giant in the eye and refused to flinch. And that name sounds uncommonly like the sound a basketball makes as it swishes through the iron and catches in the net, just for an instant, before dropping through:

Plump.

Bobby Gene Plump was the best player on the most famous schoolboy basketball team of all time. Bobby Plump hit "the shot heard 'round the world," the biggest shot in the greatest game in the history of high school basketball — the last-second shot that gave the 1954 Indiana high school basketball title to the Milan Indians, 32-30, over heavily-favored Muncie Central. It was a shot that completed the story that inspired a town, a state, and a whole way of life — not to mention an award-winning movie. It was a shot that has, in many subtle ways, changed the game of basketball forever. It was a shot that people across the state of Indiana still talk about nearly half a century after it happened.

How big was that one shot? In this day and age of hundreds of channels of TV programming, it is perhaps unfathomable to imagine that an estimated 90 percent of all the families in Indiana were watching or listening to that game on March 20, 1954. Butler Fieldhouse at Butler University in Indianapolis was jammed beyond its 15,000 capacity — to roughly a million people, if you believe everyone who'll tell you he saw the shot in person. People in Indiana remember where they were when Bobby Plump made The Shot the way they remember where they were when President Kennedy was shot in Dallas, or when Neil Armstrong walked on the moon.

It was not the first time a small-town team had ever won a state championship against a much larger foe. To the west in Illinois, the little town of Hebron, with a tiny high school enrollment and a gym only 74' by 34' — that's eight feet narrower than a regular court — had surprised everyone in the state with a championship just a couple of years earlier. To the south in Kentucky, small schools often captured the hearts of fans — most notably, Carr Creek, who chose their team from only 18 boys in the school and stormed through the regular season without a loss before bowing to Ashland in five overtimes in the 1928 state championship. Throughout the Midwest, fans lived and died with their local teams. Even an early-round tournament victory — even a close defeat — by a small town team was good for decades of local memories. So why aren't these stories as big as the Milan story? Why is Milan the name basketball fans across the nation associate with a miraculous small-town victory?

More than anything because it happened in Indiana. Hoosiers know that Abraham Lincoln was born in Kentucky, but really spent his formative years north of the Ohio River in Indiana. Similarly, Indiana was not the birthplace of basketball, but it was certainly the place it was raised to adulthood. Dr. James Naismith invented the game in Springfield, Massachusetts, in 1891. But, just two years later, a Presbyterian minister named Nicholas McKay picked up the game from Dr. Naismith's YMCA camp and brought it to Indiana.

We take our basketball seriously in the Hoosier State. For example, legend has it that, one night in 1927, McCordsville High School beat Hancock County neighbor Fortville High School in a game at Fortville. That same night, McCordsville High School mysteriously burned to the ground. Without pointing any fingers, let it be noted that McCordsville and Fortville never played each other again — and that people from one town were never again welcome in the other.

We stick by our hometown teams, too. The story is told of a time in the mid-50s when a staunch Anderson Indians supporter drove his family to Butler Fieldhouse to watch the local boys take on the Indianapolis Crispus Attucks Flying Tigers in a regional tournament game. The Tigers had lost only one game all year. But the father was confident.

His young son wasn't so sure. He told his dad he was looking forward to seeing Oscar Robertson, "the greatest ballplayer in the world."

The man snorted and told his son he'd been taken in by the Indianapolis press. Everybody knew they exaggerated. This Oscar was probably good. But he wasn't that special.

That afternoon, Oscar Robertson and his Flying Tigers proceeded to demolish the Anderson Indians. The game wasn't close, and the man was in no mood for idle chatter on the ride home. So when his son brought up the conversation they'd had on the way to the game, the man barked, "You little smart-aleck. You just be quiet. You're just like your mother."

Basketball in Indiana can be serious business, no matter what town you're from. Herschel K. "Doc" Sloan, who played for Gosport back in the early 1920s, tells the story of a teammate whose girlfriend Edna was sitting courtside one game. The teammate dribbled down the floor, looked over at his girl, and asked, "How am I doing, Edna?"

"Coach yanked him out of the game, and he never got in again," said Sloan.

It was a different game back in Doc Sloan's day, with a center jump after every basket. Each team had a designated free throw shooter; no matter who you fouled, the same player went to the line. Most important, basketball was the only game in town. Sloan's Gosport team was one of 16 teams in the Martinsville sectional, where they packed more than the 5,200 capacity into the gym to watch the games. (In 1924, Gosport handled Ellettsville and Stinesville before falling to Monrovia, whose star forward was future Indiana University Coach Branch McCracken. Officiating the tournament was Birch Bayh, Sr., whose son and namesake was a U.S. senator, and whose grandson became Governor of Indiana.)

The first Indiana boys' high school tournament happened in 1911 and set the standard for tournaments for the rest of the nation. Even back in the early days, it was unusual for a small team to win it all. But Milan proved it could be done. And while almost every other state in the union adopted a multi-class system for their high school basketball tournaments — that is, several state tournaments for schools of different sizes rather than a single tournament — Indiana held doggedly to its single-class system. Until 1996, only three other states still had single-class basketball tournaments. Two of them, Delaware and Hawaii, have so few high schools that a multi-class tournament doesn't make sense. The other, Kentucky, still has a year-end, single-class tournament, but gives smaller teams a chance to compete among themselves in an earlier tournament.

It would not be out of line to say that Indiana's tournament remained as it had for so many years because of the shot that Bobby

Plump made. The tournament still had a mystique and an importance in Indiana that simply doesn't exist anywhere else. High school coaches who have won championships in other states have said that it's a more impressive and memorable achievement to win a sectional or regional tournament in Indiana.

Nor would it be out of line to suggest that the Indiana tournament was the model for today's NCAA tournament. Terms such as "Sweet Sixteen," "Final Four," and "March Madness," now common in the NCAA tournament, were first applied to the tournament in Indiana. And the tournaments' structures are incredibly similar: both take place over four weekends of play. Indiana has 64 sectional sites and produces 64 champions who advance to the regional round; the NCAA tournament begins with 64 teams. The 16 Indiana regional winners move on to four semistate sites; the NCAA's Sweet Sixteen move to four regional sites. The biggest difference between the two tournaments is that not everybody gets to play in the NCAA tournament. "Indiana has the only tournament for everybody," said John Wooden. "I wish the NCAA would do that and allow all the Division I teams in the tournament."

How big is Bobby Plump in Indiana? As a basketball player, his name is still at the top of the list when it comes to picking all-time high school all-star teams. He was the first — and for many years, the only — player in Indiana history to win the state title, the prestigious Trester Award for mental attitude and scholarship, and the coveted Mr. Basketball crown. Since 1954, only two other players — Marion's Dave Colescott in 1976 and Bedford North Lawrence's Damon Bailey in 1990 — have garnered all three honors.

In the intervening years, the shine has hardly begun to fade from Bobby Plump's star. A recent survey suggested that Bobby Plump is the fifth most-recognized name in the state, trailing only then-Governor Evan Bayh, Indiana Coach Bob Knight, Purdue Coach Gene Keady, and the Indianapolis Motor Speedway's Tony Hulman George — and those are names that people across the nation see in the news often and Hoosiers see virtually every day. Bobby Plump is still a sought-after speaker. Kids still surround him with pens and autograph books at his many school and club engagements. The *Chicago Tribune, Washington*

Post, USA Today, and ESPN, among many others, still seek his opinion.

How big was that shot, that game, that team? In 1996, the Hoosier Lottery released a video presentation of the ten greatest Indiana sports stories of the past 100 years. They included the story of Larry Bird and Indiana State, Damon Bailey's leading Bedford-North Lawrence to a state championship, the stories of John Wooden and Oscar Robertson, the Colts moving from Baltimore to Indianapolis, Indiana University's Mark Spitz shattering the Olympic swimming record book, A.J. Foyt winning his fourth Indianapolis 500, and Marion High School's three consecutive state championships. IU's 1975-76 NCAA championship team that finished the season 32-0 was the number two story. The number one story, by a wide margin, was Bobby Plump and the 1954 Milan Indians' run for the state basketball championship.

Rewind about a year from that NCAA title game in 1995, to July 4, 1994, in Milan — in many ways, the same town it was 40 years earlier, when the Milan Indians marched off to Indianapolis to meet their destiny on the Butler Fieldhouse hardwood, and 50 years earlier, when their friends and neighbors and older brothers marched off to war. On this hot summer day, the veterans and basketball players are marching side by side in the Milan Independence Day Parade. The years have made it more difficult than ever to tell the ballplayers from the soldiers; there is more gray hair, more lines on the faces, children and grandchildren.

But the Ripley County faithful know. They know the faces, and they know the names. The players: Ray Craft. Bob Engel. Gene White. Ronnie Truitt. Roger Schroder. Rollin Cutter. Ken Wendelman. Glen Butte. Bill Jordan. Ken Delap and Bob Wichman. The coaches: Marvin Wood. Clarence Kelly. Marc Combs. Even the cheerleaders, Marjorie Ent, Virginia Voss, and Pat Bohlke, and the student managers, Oliver Jones and Fred Busching, are part of the legend. These players and cheerleaders and managers are leading the parade, ahead of the politicians, the bands, the tractors, even the World War II veterans. Not that the veterans minded. They'd defeated Hitler and won their war. But the 1954 Milan Indians had been bigger underdogs; in fact, a study by the Indiana Basketball Hall of Fame showed that the Indians had a tougher road to the finals than any other champion in IHSAA tournament history.

And there on the firetruck with his teammates and coaches and managers and cheerleaders from that dream team is Bobby Gene Plump, smiling and waving, as broadly and happily as if he'd just cut down the nets in victory, as if the twine were still around his neck. That image — the 1954 Milan Indians, with their burr-headed captain Bobby Plump wearing the net around his neck — is preserved in a photograph that today hangs in Springfield, Massachusetts, at the James Naismith National Basketball Hall of Fame. One just like it — and many others — grace the Indiana Basketball Hall of Fame in New Castle.

If Bobby Plump never did anything but hit the biggest shot in the biggest game in high school basketball history, his story would be worth telling. In fact, Bobby Plump's last shot and the Milan Indians' stunning victory over Muncie Central has already inspired not only a veritable mountain range of Hoosier folklore, but the movie *Hoosiers* (wherein the Bobby Plump character's name is Jimmy Chitwood, which looks rural enough, but sounds disconcertingly like the metallic ringing of a ball flying through an urban chain net).

But there is much more to the Bobby Plump story. It is a story of small-town roots and big dreams. . .of triumph over tragedy. . .of not just a single shot or a single game, but of one of the great high school athletic careers of all time. It was a career that continued through college and into the ranks of professional basketball. And it is a story that carries through to the present day and beyond.

Fast-forward now, to 1996. Bobby Plump sits in his restaurant in Indianapolis's Broad Ripple district, a long three-pointer from Hinkle Fieldhouse, preaching basketball purity, Indiana-style, to an attentive crowd. Not that the crowd will let him forget The Shot. Nor would he want them to. To Bobby Plump, it is a symbol of everything that's right about Indiana high school basketball.

And it's in jeopardy. After 86 years, Indiana is on the verge of throwing over its vaunted single-class basketball tournament and adopting a multi-class system. Bobby has been one of the most prominent and vocal opponents of the change. It matters little to him that such a move would only make his own legend more secure. It's simply not the way the tournament was meant to be played, at least not here in Indiana.

Here inside the restaurant, Bobby's love of the game is impossible to ignore. Here is a section of the old gym floor from Milan High School; there is a giant blow-up of young Bobby Plump hitting the shot that changed his life and the lives of countless Hoosiers from North Vernon in the south to South Bend in the north. Newspaper clippings, magazine covers, team photos, honors and accolades cover the walls. Even the Muncie Central fans — perhaps the only people in Indiana to have been dismayed with the outcome of that fateful game — have contributed to the restaurant's memorabilia. But then, the folks in Muncie have had eight state championships to crow about in the past 40 years. One loss in 1954 can almost be forgiven.

People come from all over the state and across the nation to eat at the restaurant and share in the Indiana high school basketball nostalgia. Young and old alike argue about the greatest games and the best teams and the finest players. More than a few have been known to leave their sentiments on napkins. An example: "My dad (Delphi High School '61) thought you were the greatest. I told him that I came to your bar to drink and he sent me a check for $100.00 and said go spend this at Bobby Plump's bar. Bobby Plump was his hero as a kid."

Bobby Plump has been a hero. He has been a basketball legend, baseball star, businessman, husband, father, and grandfather. He has been and continues to be a passionate advocate for the game he loves. Through it all, and above all, he has been a gentleman. Now a youthful 60, Bobby has joined his son Jonathan in the new challenge of becoming a successful restaurateur.

The name of the restaurant? "Plump's Last Shot."

Don't bet on it. The facts of Bobby Plump's life suggest that he probably still has a few shots left.

CHAPTER TWO

THE PLUMPS
OF PIERCEVILLE

In the story of Bobby Plump and the 1954 Milan Indians, two ironies stand out. The first is that one of the most recognizable names in Hoosier sports history was known only as "the baby" for the first five days of his life. The second is that Bobby Plump wasn't from Milan.

Bobby was part of the fourth generation in his family to grow up around Pierceville, Indiana, a village three-and-a-half miles northwest of Milan on State Road 350 in the heart of Ripley County, Indiana. Like most American families, the Plumps can trace their ancestry to a number of foreign lands; one set of Bobby's great-great grandparents came from Ireland and settled in Cincinnati, just 35 miles east. Another pair of great-great grandparents emigrated from the Alsace Lorraine region of France. But, like a majority of families in Southern Indiana, most of the Plumps' ancestors came from Germany.

Fredrick Dilla, one of Bobby's great grandfathers on his mother's side, was born in Hanover, Germany, where he married Isabell Berger of Scrottinghomer. They settled in Central City, Illinois in 1868 before buying a farm just north of Milan in 1870.

On his father's side of the family, Bobby's great-great grandparents Henry and Loiesa Hulke also emigrated from Hanover, settling at Stumpke's Corner in Ripley County. Their daughter Dora married another German immigrant, William Jordan, who bought a Ripley County farm after leaving Germany to escape the draft. Family lore has it that Jordan bribed a ship's captain to smuggle him to America. Henry Plump and Harmon Nieman, Bobby's other great-great grandfathers, were also born in Hanover.

Southern Indiana is still thick with German heritage. You can see it not only in the names of Southern Indiana families, but in the names of the towns themselves: Weisburg. Oldenburg. New Frankfort. Hanover. Darmstadt. These are the kinds of towns where you'll still find Bierstubes and Oktoberfests, where local celebrations still feature men in lederhosen, where bratwurst is a fat and spicy sausage, not the pale, thin wiener found in supermarkets in much of the rest of the country.

Perhaps the German immigrants settled in Southern Indiana because the gentle, rolling hills and rich farmland reminded them of home. Perhaps it was the rugged four-season climate. There is a long-standing joke in Indiana that if you don't like the weather, you can wait about five minutes, and it'll change. Winters can be snowy and bitterly cold. Summers are almost invariably hot and muggy. It certainly isn't for everyone; although Abe Lincoln spent his boyhood just 150 miles down the road from Pierceville in Spencer County, Richard Nixon's family packed up and left nearby Jennings County for Yorba Linda, California, before the future president was born. But while winter and summer can be extreme, the spring and autumn months in Southern Indiana are among the most beautiful in the world, and the German families would have felt right at home in the complex terrain and the changeable weather of the Ohio River Valley.

Bobby Plump's father, Frederick William George Lester Plump, was born on a farm near Pierceville in 1898, the son of John and Louisa Plump. He attended Prattsburg school and graduated from Milan High School with the Class of 1916. After high school, Lester attended nearby Moores Hill College, then Central Normal in Danville, Indiana, and returned home for classes at Hanover College. He served in the army for a brief time near the end of World War I, but never saw combat. In 1920, shortly after his soldiering days were through, he married Mabel Mary Dilla.

Mabel Dilla — which, around Ripley County, is pronounced "dilly" — was born near Versailles — which, around Ripley County, is pronounced "ver-SALES" — in 1903. (Milan, let it be noted, is pronounced "MY-lan" — not "muh-LAHN," as it would be pronounced on the Continent.) She attended Sligo School and Versailles High School and was just 17 when she married Lester Plump.

The Plumps didn't have much, but neither did most people around Pierceville in those days. Lester was a hard worker. His college degree allowed him to teach at a one- or two-room schoolhouse, which was plenty of qualification for most of the schools in Ripley County. Each day, Lester walked four miles along dirt roads and across fields and pastures from his Pierceville home to the one-room Behlmer's Corner schoolhouse. When he was finished teaching every day, he worked his second job — in the same building, as the janitor — before making the long trek home. Lester worked as a teacher for seventeen years at a succession of tiny Southern Indiana schools, including schools in Dover, Prattsburg, and the little schoolhouse in Pierceville. Today, a lot of senior Ripley County residents still remember the lessons taught to them by this kind, gentle, patient man.

In 1921, Lester and Mabel Plump had a daughter, Dorothea Mae Plump, whom they called Dot. Now that they had a child, the Plumps needed a place to raise their family. So, just a few short months after Dot's arrival, the Plumps bought a wooden-frame house on a side street in Pierceville, near the railroad tracks that ran through town. The house had a big kitchen and living room and a bedroom for Lester and Mabel downstairs, and a couple of bedrooms on the second floor. What it didn't have was electricity or an indoor bathroom facility. But there was a smokehouse out back, and lots of trees on the two-acre lot, and an outbuilding for pigs and chickens and plenty of space for a garden to raise vegetables.

There was also plenty of space to raise children. The Plumps' first son, Wallace Loren "Bill" Plump, was born in 1923. Lester Junior Plump was born in 1927. Four years later, in 1931, the Plumps had another girl, Virginia Lee "Ginny" Plump. Eloise Esther Plump arrived in 1933. The Plumps were a virtual population explosion in the sleepy little town of Pierceville. With seven people in the family, they comprised 16 percent of the town's whole population of 45 citizens.

On September 9, 1936, the Plumps had their sixth child. Dot, who was 15 at the time, remembers that all the Plump children were upstairs waiting for the baby's arrival. "We were congregated around a heat register in one of the bedrooms. When Dad finally told us to come down, there was the baby. He was a cute little thing."

And "the baby" was all anybody called him for five days. "I was the last of six children, and I think they must have run out of names when they got to me," Bobby laughed. "So instead of thinking up another one, they went to a neighbor."

Helen Dunn was a schoolgirl who lived down the road from the Plumps. "As the story goes, Helen liked the name of a boy in her class: Bobby Gene. That was her suggestion, that's what the family went with, and that's been my name ever since," Bobby said.

The Plump children loved to dote on their new baby brother. And it often seemed he needed special care. Sister Esther, who was only three years older than Bobby, remembers him as a sickly child, most likely because he contracted Rocky Mountain spotted fever, a difficult and potentially fatal infectious disease carried by ticks, when he was four years old. In cases of Rocky Mountain spotted fever, tiny organisms invade the cells lining the blood vessels, causing blood clots. Bobby developed a fever and a pinkish rash that turned a deep brown as it spread across his body. "We made a bed for him on the porch, because it was cooler out there," Esther said. The cool weather must have been good therapy. Bobby was back to his rambunctious four-year-old ways in a couple of weeks.

But life was changing in the Plump household. With all those mouths to feed, Lester's teaching salary was spread too thin. Like a lot of rural Indiana men in those days, Lester sometimes relied on hunting to put meat on the table. But his family's needs went beyond extra food. Lester decided to leave the teaching profession he loved so much because he simply couldn't provide for his family the way he wanted to.

First, Lester came upon the idea of selling farm-fresh products to folks in the big city. He made a deal with local farmers, buying their eggs and chickens and driving them 35 miles to Cincinnati to sell in neighborhoods such as Price Hill and St. Bernard. Lester also hung bittersweet vines off the sides the old huckster truck he drove to the city. These were big sellers, too.

But in the end, the chicken and egg route didn't pay the bills either. Lester eventually took a job making pallets at the A.D. Cook Pump Company in Lawrenceburg. He worked at A.D. Cook until he retired.

Back in the late 1930s and early 1940s, the world was changing rapidly. It seemed to be getting smaller and more dangerous every day. The nation was still trying to pull itself out of the Great Depression. A strange little man named Adolph Hitler had risen to power in Germany and was stirring an intense nationalism that eventually exploded into world war. But in Ripley County, Indiana, the world made sense. Most of the time, the events of the world barely reached into rural Indiana. Even the Japanese bombing of the U.S. Pacific Fleet at Pearl Harbor in December of 1941 seemed impossibly far away.

Later that same month, however, tragedy struck closer to home. Suddenly all was not well at the Plump home in Pierceville. Mabel Plump's uterus began to hemorrhage.

Dot remembers Lester Plump, obviously frightened, bravely carrying his wife downstairs. "He told us she was pretty bad. He thought it was a miscarriage, but Momma told me it wasn't. She knew it was something terrible."

Although no one knows for certain what happened to Mabel Plump, it's possible that doctors today would have diagnosed what's known as a molar pregnancy — a pregnancy that usually produces no fetus, but only placental tissue. Molar pregnancies are not uncommon in older women. Today, doctors can usually remove the tissue quickly and easily. But years ago, women often bled to death as a result of molar pregnancies.

No one had much time to figure out what was wrong with Mabel Plump. Lester put her in bed and made her as comfortable as possible. But within 24 hours of the onset of bleeding, a blood clot formed and traveled to her heart.

"I remember taking one step into Mom and Dad's room," Dot said. "She took two deep breaths. And that was it. I couldn't believe she was gone."

Pierceville was too small to support a funeral home. So Lester carefully placed the body of his beautiful wife, his best friend and the mother of his six children, in the back of his car and drove to Milan. Mabel Mary Plump was laid in the simple casket Lester picked out and returned to Pierceville for the viewing.

The whole town mourned the passing of Mabel Mary Plump. Pierceville neighbor Al Busching said, "They laid Mrs. Plump out in the house. We all felt sorry for them. They were a nice family."

Bobby's future mother-in-law, Marie Ford, remembers reading of Mabel's death in the local newspaper. "I wondered how Lester would manage with six children" she said.

"Bobby was just a little guy. He was so small, he didn't know what was going on," said Al Busching.

But Bobby Plump remembers.

"I remember Dad running down the stairs, shouting. And I remember being led up to her casket to kiss her goodbye. I'll remember that moment for the rest of my life. Even today, I have trouble at funerals. I won't look in a casket. I'll walk by, but I'll never linger."

Bobby's other memories of his mother are few and precious. "I remember one time sitting on her lap when my brothers and sisters had gone off to school, listening to the Lone Ranger on the radio. And I have a memory of standing next to Mom on a little stool, helping her dry dishes. But I don't remember much more."

Mabel's passing left Lester Plump with an awesome responsibility. It would no longer be enough to hold down a job to keep his children fed. Lester Plump had a whole family to raise, all by himself. Dot was a responsible young woman of 20, and Bill and Les were in their teens — old enough to help, and young enough to still need the care and protection of their father. Ginny and Esther were still in elementary school. And little Bobby was only five. Now more than ever, in more ways than ever before, Lester Plump's industrious nature would be put to the test.

CHAPTER THREE

PIERCEVILLE DAYS

It's not difficult to drive past Pierceville, Indiana, 1996, and not give it a second look. It's just a few old buildings along the side of State Road 350; in fact, unless you live in Pierceville, there's little reason to venture into the tiny town at all.

But Pierceville, 1941, was different. SR 350 didn't shoot past Pierceville, but wound through it, attracting passersby to stop and shop at its inviting stores and have a cold drink at its taverns. The National Limited passenger train came through twice a day and, at one time, Pierceville was the biggest milk pickup point on the B&O Railroad between Cincinnati and St. Louis. Every day, old Snowbird Falis hung the mailpouch on the pole near the track for someone on the train to snag with a hook. That same someone would throw the incoming mail out of the train. Snowbird would pick up the sack and bring it to Schroder's store, which was also Pierceville's post office.

"Snowbird still lived with his mother," recalled Pierceville resident Lloyd Freeman, one of Bobby's boyhood friends, "and Carl Schroder gave him the job of hanging out the mail. He was sort of a happy, unambitious guy. I think the hardest work he ever did was holding a lantern for his mother while she chopped the wood."

Pierceville may have been a bit livelier in 1941. But the town was tiny even then. Still, for Bobby Plump and his family, it may as well have been the whole universe.

"We never got to Milan too much," Bobby's sister Dot said. "We had a church and Schroder's store, and a couple of other stores. We'd get to Milan maybe on Saturday night and do some grocery shopping. We called it 'trading.'"

Gene White, Bobby's boyhood pal and Milan teammate, grew up on a farm just outside of Pierceville. He said the 1940s and 50s were a better time. "It was community-oriented. We didn't know or care about what was going on in Indianapolis or Cincinnati, outside of following the Reds, anyway. It was an easier world to live in — maybe not financially for Mom and Dad. But we kids all ate well enough."

Glen Butte, another Pierceville native and Milan High School basketball star, agreed. "We didn't know there was another world at that particular time."

And why would they have? You could buy groceries and hardware and appliances and gasoline at Schroder's. Frosty Cornett sold gasoline, too, from an old-fashioned gas pump outside his ice cream stand, where you could also buy soda pop and candy. Gus Kanucky, an old German who didn't speak much English, had a blacksmith shop in town, and there was a tavern called the Blue Goose where some of the men gathered for beer and card games. There was a feed store at the elevator (later owned by Gene White's family) where you could buy farm supplies, and fertilizer for your garden. There was a Methodist church right down the street. What else did you need but a roof over your head, and blue sky, and trees to climb and a field and a creek to run through? If you were short of cash, you could usually help out one of the local farmers for a bit of food or spending money. If you needed a bit of extra meat for your table, you could hunt squirrels and rabbits, of which there seemed to be a never-ending supply.

Pierceville was a tightly knit community, and Schroder's was the center of the town. Not only could you buy practically anything you needed there, you could also have your doctoring needs attended to; old Bein Whitlatch and his brother Alsidoe, who later started the Whitlatch Clinic in Milan, had an office over the store. There were always meetings going on at Schroder's, too, not to mention plays and even movies. "They'd hang a sheet and charge a dime for the show," Bobby said.

The Pierceville neighbors looked out for one another. "I had to count heads at mealtime to see how many plates to put on the table," said Helen Schroder, who ran the store in Pierceville with her husband Carl. "We were one, big, happy family. We all loved each other."

"Everybody knew everybody," Carl Schroder said. "If you needed help, you could always count on your neighbors."

One reason the Pierceville folks stuck together was that they didn't have much choice. There weren't many cars along the dirt roads leading into and out of Pierceville. Most people still got around on horseback or shank's mare. But Lester Plump had an old Dodge that worked most of the time, although the heater didn't. Cold weather meant blankets — or lots of warm bodies — to make auto travel bearable. Every once in a while, usually on the weekend, the family would make the bumpy three-and-a-half mile drive into Milan.

Saturday night was the night to be in Milan. To the folks from

Pierceville, Milan was among the more glamorous places in the world. "At one time, it was the darnedest place you ever saw on Saturday nights," said Lloyd Freeman. "All the stores were open. You could hardly find a place to walk on the sidewalk."

"Winter's store was a gathering place," Dot said. "It was always full of people on Saturday night."

While the grown-ups were trading in Milan, the kids would walk around town. Sometimes, particularly when there was a meeting at the Oddfellows' Lodge, Lester Plump would give each of his children a dime for a movie and an extra nickel for popcorn. It was one of the luxuries they could take advantage of in the big city.

And, as small a town as Milan was, it was indeed the big city to Lester Plump's children. "When Chris Volz opened his auto dealership in Milan in 1947, I can remember that I didn't want to go. Milan was just too big. I didn't think the Milan people liked us," Bobby said.

Once when Bobby was young, he got separated from his family on a trip to Milan. Bobby thought he was hopelessly lost. He wandered forlornly through the streets of Milan until local businessman Bill Thompson, whose family owned the Thompson Furniture Company, spotted him.

"Aren't you Lester Plump's boy?" Thompson asked.

Bobby nodded. "And I don't know the way back to Pierceville," he cried.

Thompson made sure little Bobby Plump found his way home to Pierceville, and the wooden house that still didn't have electricity or indoor plumbing or a telephone. "We were all pretty naive, but we enjoyed it," said Bobby's pal Roger Schroder, whose parents owned the store in town. "We didn't have much of anything else to compare it to."

Bobby's sister Dot did, though. At 20, she was working in Lawrenceburg as a babysitter and housekeeper for the Barretts, who owned the Aurora Casket Company. She stayed with the Barretts during the week, sometimes even going with them on vacation to their summer cottage in Michigan, and came home to Pierceville on weekends. But with Mabel Plump's passing, Dot decided Lester could use a helping hand.

"It was hard to believe that Mom was gone and wouldn't be here anymore. I quit my job in Lawrenceburg right away to come home and help Daddy with the kids," Dot said.

Little Bobby became more like a son than a brother to Dot. Decades later, she would still feel especially close to him.

"He still seems like a little kid to me. I still worry about him that way. He was so much younger than the others, he always seemed like my own son," Dot said.

Like her father, Dot was a hard worker. She did all of the cooking on the Plumps' woodburning stove. She canned vegetables from the family garden. She washed the clothes in a gasoline-powered Maytag wringer washer and did all the ironing with six cold irons. She kept the Plump home tidy and neat, and worked three other jobs, besides: cleaning house for the Buttes; working the counter at Busching's hardware store; and even delivering newspapers.

Effectively, Dot Plump put her life on hold for 20 years to help her family. "I always kind of thought of Dot as my mother," Bobby said. "Even today, I'll ask her for advice. I respect her greatly, and I know I'll never be able to repay her for what she did for me."

"I never thought anything about it," Dot said. "I just knew it was the right thing to do."

Even though Dot was there to help, the responsibility for the Plump family was still Lester's. Particularly in this time when millions of people were depending upon the government for survival, when Franklin Delano Roosevelt's alphabet soup of government programs was making work for people struggling to pull themselves out of the Great Depression, Lester Plump kept working, quietly and steadily providing for his family. He worked hard at his jobs all week long. On Sundays, he attended St. Paul's Lutheran Church in Stumpke's Corner, where he taught Sunday school. But like most of the kids in Pierceville, the Plump children went to Sunday school at the Methodist church in Pierceville. There, they were taught by Eva Ruggles, Geneva Freeman, Leona Busching, and Lester Plump's good friend Leo "Pop" Dunn and his sister Zuma.

"Dad would often stay up late studying the Bible. But he never wore it on his wrist. He never forced anything on us. He used to wake us up and ask us to go to church. But he didn't make us go," Bobby said.

Making his children do things just wasn't Lester Plump's style. He led by example. And his children took his example to heart — not just in the area of religious values, but in a strong work ethic, as well. For 25 years, the Plump children had a paper route, delivering the *Times-Star* and the *Cincinnati Post* in Pierceville and the surrounding countryside. Bill Plump had the route first. He passed it down to Les. Dot, Virginia, and Esther each took a turn with the route before Bobby had it. It became a Plump family tradition to deliver the papers every afternoon and collect on Saturdays. Because money was scarce in Pierceville, sometimes the collections were weeks behind. But the route taught the Plump children the value of hard work. And the paper route was profitable in other ways, too; Dot Plump met her future husband, Carl Sullender, while helping Bobby with the route.

Bobby said his father was a man of few words.

"I don't remember Dad ever spanking any of us, or even yelling at us. He never raised his voice. Even when once after Les wrecked a car, and even a couple of times when Bill came home after having quite a bit to drink, he never cussed or raised his voice. What he said was right to the point, so when he spoke, you listened. You knew he meant what he was saying."

Lester Plump also knew the value of time away from work. Every summer, he'd pack his family into the Dodge, hitch the trailer to the back, and head out for a two-week-long vacation at Versailles State Park. Today, a lake covers the area where the Plumps rented a cabin near the pump house. "Cabin" is perhaps being too kind; "shack" is probably a more appropriate term for the tiny structure that was known as the "Haven of Rest."

It may have been tiny and cramped. But to Bobby, it was paradise: two weeks of swimming and fishing and baseball and playing cards and seeing how many eggs they could eat every morning, nothing to do but relax and play with the gang from Pierceville, who were all there with their families, too: Glen Butte, Roger Schroder, Fred Busching, Sonny Pilz, Lloyd Freeman, Pop Dunn, and others. The long summer days stretched on forever. "All the woman had to leave at sundown. The men usually slept in the cabin, and we boys slept in the truck or out under the stars. I always looked forward to those days," Bobby said.

Things were serene in Ripley County, Indiana, in the '40s. But they were becoming more and more unsettled in the rest of the world. Back in Pierceville, at the Plumps' house by the railroad tracks, Bobby and his sisters stood out in back and waved to the troop trains on their way to Indianapolis. One day, one of the boys they waved to was brother Bill. He fought in the Pacific theater and was wounded in Okinawa, and carried the shrapnel in his arm until the day he died to prove it. Bill was awarded the Purple Heart for his service. And he wasn't the only Plump boy to serve overseas. Several years later, it was Les who rode away to serve in occupied Germany, and again later in Korea.

But Bobby was still too young to go to war. Bobby anxiously followed the war every night on the radio, listening for news of troop movements and Allied victories. Europe and Asia were strange, faraway places. But every morning, Bobby himself was going to a big, strange, faraway place: elementary school in Milan.

"I thought it was the most humongous place I'd ever seen," said Bobby of his school. In fact, it seemed so big that Bobby got lost on his first day of school.

Being a Pierceville kid made Bobby feel like an outsider in Milan. The behavior of some of his schoolmates didn't help, either. "One winter, Dot made me a beautiful snow suit — pants, jacket, even a cap. I thought I looked great. I was so proud of wearing it to school. But the Milan kids thought differently. They made fun of me and pushed me down and rubbed my face in the snow. I didn't much care to wear my beautiful new snowsuit after that."

Bobby may have been intimidated by some of the kids, but it didn't show in the classroom. Bobby's Milan elementary school teachers, including first grade teacher Geneva Wildman Myers and fourth grade teacher Kathryn Turner, remember him as a nice boy and a good student.

"Bless his heart. He was a wonderful boy. A very good student, and very cooperative. He was a good leader among his peers. He wasn't a mouse, but he wasn't boisterous, either. All the kids in that class wanted to learn. And they all got along so well," Turner said.

That they did. The Pierceville boys — Bobby and Gene White and Roger Schroder and Glen Butte and others — stuck together at school and at home and on the bus that took them back and forth, where they proved being good boys didn't mean you had to be angels. Like Lester Plump's old Dodge, the school bus didn't produce much heat in the winter. So Bobby and his buddies sometimes built a fire on the floor to keep warm. Bus driver Harry Jordan would stop the bus and stomp back to the rear to put out the fire. But more often than not, one of the Pierceville boys would light it again.

Heating the bus in this unorthodox fashion wasn't the only prank the boys pulled, either. Lloyd Freeman, who was several years older than Bobby and his friends, was often the catalyst for such mischief as overturning outhouses. "It was sort of a Halloween tradition to tip outhouses," Bobby said. "In fact, you had to go around with a crowd just to make sure yours didn't get tipped over."

One outhouse in Old Milan presented a particular challenge. "There was a guy in town named Rodman who bragged that there was no one who could tip over his outhouse. He'd built it with four-by-fours at the corners and drove them deep into the ground, and he also surrounded the place with a fence. Not only that, he let it be known that he sat in his field with a shotgun, just waiting for someone to try and tip his outhouse," said Bobby.

How could the Pierceville gang resist? A group of boys — Bobby, Lloyd Freeman, Bob Crockston, Noble Kern, Frank Lewis, Roger Schroder, Fred Busching, and Rodney Brandes among them — decided Rodman's outhouse was going down. "We made a battleplan — had it all mapped out," Bobby said.

The boys decided their best bet was to run at the outhouse, figuring that, together, they'd be able to tip it — and that if Mr. Rodman happened to be guarding it, his shotgun blast wouldn't be able to hit all of them. Hiding at the bottom of an embankment below the outhouse, they waited until everything was quiet. Then they charged.

The "untippable" outhouse wasn't quite so permanent, after all. The force of the charging boys pulled the four-by-fours right out of the ground and sent the outhouse tumbling. The raid was not without its casualties, though: Bob Crockston's momentum carried him right into the pit.

And, as it turned out, Rodman *was* watching with shotgun in hand. Upon seeing the outhouse fall, he fired at the boys as they scampered away.

This wasn't the only time the Pierceville boys' pranks prompted a shotgun blast. Another came as the result of a "tick tack" incident. "We'd get a can and fill it with rocks, then get a long string and tie the can to someone's doorknob. We'd take the other end of the string way across the street and hide in the bushes, then pull the string. It made an awful racket.

"Once when we did it, the guy who owned the house came out and shot his shotgun over our heads. He didn't see us, so we really weren't in much danger. But this guy had a tin roof, so the next thing we did was get our slingshots and shoot his roof. We probably drove him crazy," Bobby said.

"Bobby was usually the one to hang the tick tack," said Lloyd Freeman. "That kid had guts. He wasn't afraid of anything. He was also younger than us, so we could usually get him to do it."

Once a young father in town was so upset by the boys' tick tack prank that he charged out his front door with a knife. "I think he'd probably had enough of the baby crying, and our noise made things worse," Bobby said. The kids scattered. Bobby and Roger Schroder circled back and inside Schroder's store just as the irate young man entered.

"I knew you kids wouldn't have anything to do with that," he said.

But, the fact was, those kids had something to do with most of the mischief in town. And some of it was incredibly inventive. One favorite trick was to coat a doorknob with stinky limburger cheese, then hang the tick tack or otherwise induce the homeowner to open the door. Just about the time the homeowner finally got the smell off his hands, he's discover that the motor in his car had been treated with the smelly stuff, too.

Passing motorists were also victims of the boys' pranks. Sometimes, they'd string together empty oil cans nicked from Frosty Cornett's store, hide on either side of the road, and hook the cans to the bumpers of cars zooming through town. Other times, they'd attached a line to a purse or wallet and place it in the middle of the road. When the driver would spot the purse and stop, he would find, much to his surprise, that the purse had vanished — yanked into the bushes or up in a tree by a hidden boy.

Bobby and his friends had some fun with Lloyd Freeman's car, too.

"Sneaking into the drive-in movie was a favorite pastime. But if you hid in the trunk, you'd get caught when you had to open the trunk to get out. So we rigged Lloyd's car so the back seat came out and we could climb through from the trunk. We never had to get out of the car at all," said Bobby.

One of the town's most famous tricks was the handiwork not of Bobby, but of his brother, Les. "There was a farmer named Meacham Peters — wonderful man. I think we all worked for him at one time or another. Well, once Les and Al Busching took Mr. Peters' wagon apart and reassembled it — on top of his barn!"

Les didn't spare his baby brother from his pranks, either. "Once when I was really little, Les took me out to the garden and hooked me up to the plow. I guess I did his work for him, but I thought it was great fun," Bobby said.

These and other pranks were rarely mean-spirited. "Usually, people took them in stride. It was actually kind of an honor to have someone take so much time to play a joke on you," Bobby said.

Of course, practical jokes weren't the only things the boys did. Marbles was a big game, and comic books filled the quieter moments. The kids could always hang around Schroder's or Frosty Cornett's place, where they bought RC Cola and peanuts whenever they could scrape together a nickel. "You got twice as much RC — 12 ounces — for your nickel," said Lloyd Freeman. "We'd stuff the peanuts in the pop bottle to fizz it up. That was our official drink."

Frosty also served French Bower ice cream. "I thought it came from Paris," said Bobby.

Hide and seek was a popular summer game, too, "although I never understood what happened to some of the older boys and girls in that game. They'd go hide, and then they wouldn't ever come out — not even when it was free," Bobby said.

It was a colorful — and, sometimes, a bit dangerous — time to be a kid in rural Indiana. "We had to manufacture our own fun," said Roger Schroder.

The Pierceville gang was obviously good at that. Just how good they were would become even more apparent in just a few years.

CHAPTER FOUR

PLAY BALL!

If Pierceville had been big enough to support a high school in 1954, it may have made a solid run for the IHSAA boys' basketball title. Four of the 12 players from that storied Milan team, including two of the starters, actually came from the little village: Bobby Plump, Gene White, Glen Butte, and Roger Schroder.

And, had there been an Indiana state baseball tournament back in those days, this fictional Pierceville High may have made a run for that title, too.

For the Pierceville boys, summer meant working on area farms. Pierceville neighbor Al Busching, whose little brother Fred was the student manager of the 1954 Milan Indians and one of Bobby Plump's best friends, says the kids who eventually became basketball stars were hard workers. "They were a great bunch of boys. I had 30 acres of tomatoes one summer, and they all worked in the fields for me, first hoeing, then picking," he said.

But after work, there were ballgames. "We'd do our chores or work on a farm, then play baseball until dark. At night, we played basketball," said Bobby.

The boys played hard. Most important, they played purely for the love of playing. "We never played to try to get anything out of it. It was just fun — pure fun," Bobby said.

Bobby's organized sports career began not on the hardwood, but the baseball diamond. "We loved our baseball in Pierceville. Schroders always had the Reds game on the radio, and they always kept the boxscore. The first sports heroes I can remember were baseball players — Grady Hatton, Roy McMillan, Gus Bell, Ewell Blackwell, Ted Kluszewski, and other Reds," said Bobby.

Bobby may even have had a local sports hero. Vern "Tuck" Tucker, a Pierceville kid and Milan High School graduate, was regarded as one of the best semi-pro righthanders in Southern Indiana. In 1929, he was signed by Miller Huggins and had a tryout with the New York Yankees — a team that included Babe Ruth and Lou Gehrig. Tucker never made it to the big leagues, though. He played for the minor league St. Paul Saints for a while before moving back home.

When the Reds were on the radio, the boys congregated at Schroders'. But as soon as the game was over, it was off to the field to emulate their heroes. The Pierceville boys played every chance they got, with as many players as they had. Sometimes, they'd play with only two or three on a side. Sometimes, Bobby and Glen Butte would play all by themselves, with a ball that had been punished for so long it was held together with black electrician's tape.

Frosty Cornett loved his baseball, too. Frosty was a Pierceville fixture, an Air Force veteran who had lost an eye in the war. At his little ice cream store, he'd listen to the Pierceville boys talk about playing ball. When Bobby was 12, Frosty decided to organize a Knothole team. Roger Schroder's dad Carl provided the uniforms for the team, which was known as Schroder's All-Stars. The boys from Pierceville looked great in their pinstripes and caps. And they had plenty of action out of town. For road games, Buck Hempfling would pile the team into the back of his pickup, and off they'd ride to Milan or Osgood, Holton on Versailles, Elrod or Aurora or Lawrenceburg.

The team also got to Cincinnati occasionally, to see their heroes the Reds at the special Knothole games at Crosley Field. Horace Lee White, Gene's dad, would drive the team in his school bus. Bobby remembers that one time, Horace Lee got most of the way home without one of the Pierceville Knothole kids.

"He called names to make sure everyone was on the bus, and I know I answered twice — once for Glen Butte and once for myself. I thought I'd heard my name called, and then I heard it again. I was too embarrassed to say anything. So we left Glen at the ballpark. Eventually, we turned around and got him. It was really an honest mistake," said Bobby, "but I never told Glen about it."

As much as the Pierceville boys loved playing ball, they didn't have a real ball diamond to host home games. Then, one day, an official baseball diamond appeared in the middle of a cornfield, as if it had materialized directly from *Field Of Dreams*. Somehow, the bumpy field had been graded and was ready for action. Perhaps the county road grader that folks had seen parked along Highway 350 near Pierceville had something to do with it?

Decades later, the truth can be told. Lloyd Freeman, who was a teenager at the time, borrowed the grader late one night. "The highway department kept it parked under an old gumball tree. It was an old 1020 tractor, and I knew how to drive it, because my dad had a 1020. So I went down and got it, graded down our new Pierceville baseball diamond, then parked her again. I made only one mistake: I forgot to take off the emergency brake. I burned it clear off," he said.

The highway department either didn't know or didn't care about the midnight requisition. So the Pierceville nine had a place to play. And they used it to their full advantage. To hear Gene White tell it, baseball may actually have been their better sport. Years later, when the Pierceville boys combined with other ballplayers from Milan, they had the pitching and the firepower at the plate to beat anyone they faced.

"Baseball didn't have the emphasis that basketball had. Basketball was everything in Southern Indiana. But we loved baseball, too. I know we never lost a game in our conference when we were in high school. We may have lost to Aurora one year, and Lawrenceburg may have beaten us once — they always had good baseball teams. But we never went into any game thinking we were going to get beat," White said.

One summer, the Pierceville and Milan boys combined to play Bentley Post, a two-time national champion American Legion team from Cincinnati. Bentley Post featured a tough kid named Russ Nixon, who would go on to play 12 seasons in the major leagues, batting .268 lifetime for Cleveland, Boston, and Minnesota and managing the Cincinnati Reds from 1982-83. The Indiana boys and Bentley Post battled fiercely and ended up splitting the two-game series. The Pierceville/Milan squad rode the strong right arm of another Pierceville kid, Wayne Smith, who could bring the heat. "He was the best I ever caught," said Gene White. In fact, Smith played at Indiana University, where he also played trumpet in the Marching 100. He gave up baseball, much to the chagrin of major league scouts, because of nagging back problems.

Bobby Plump did a little pitching himself, and played shortstop. He would play baseball all through high school and throughout his college career, and may have been good enough to attract some major league attention himself. But Pierceville, after all, is in Southern Indiana. And Southern Indiana is basketball country.

The first place that most of the Pierceville boys played basketball was the second floor of Schroder's barn, where the goal was a peach basket. "It was just like those original basketball games back in Springfield, Massachusetts. That's how we were still playing in Pierceville in the 1940s," Bobby said.

Schroder's barn was great for cold-weather games. But the boys preferred playing outside. And Bobby Plump had the first outdoor goal in the neighborhood.

Lester Plump knew a little bit about basketball. One year while he was teaching, his school wanted to start a basketball team but didn't have a coach. So Lester volunteered. He found a rule book and soon was teaching his young team the game of basketball.

In December, 1944, Lester Plump was still working at A.D. Cook in Lawrenceburg. That job gave Lester the means to give eight-year-old Bobby his most memorable Christmas present ever. When he came downstairs on Christmas morning, Bobby Plump found a round package with his name on it under the tree. Tearing the paper off, he found his very own basketball. And that was only half the present.

"Dad had made a backboard and fastened a rim to it. He hid it out in the smokehouse. It was the greatest Christmas present I ever got," Bobby said.

Soon, the homemade rim was not inside the smokehouse, but on it. (Today, Lester Plump's Christmas gift to his son is on display at the Indiana State Museum in Indianapolis.) "I guess it was nine feet and change — the highest we could get it on the smokehouse. If you stood underneath it, you could see that it sort of sloped down," said Bobby. The court was dirt, terribly uneven, with rocks and a pile of ashes to one side. But it was the first outdoor court in town. And the Pierceville boys took to it right away.

"Actually, my brothers took to it," Bobby laughed. "It was a while before I got to play — and it was my rim and my ball!"

But when Bobby finally did get to play, it was hard to stop him. He played every chance he got, even through the hard winters, when the weather was so cold, the skin on his fingers would crack. He would tape them to keep them from bleeding, and just keep playing.

Bobby didn't stop playing when he got inside the house, either. He drove his sisters crazy shooting his basketball through the transoms over the doorways inside the house. "A ball would just fit through. The shot had to be perfect, " he said. No doubt shooting through transoms helped Bobby Plump develop his accuracy, especially at the free throw line. Years later, during his career at Butler University, he was one of the best free throw shooters in the nation, finishing third in free throw percentage in NCAA Division I his senior year. He still holds Butler's single-game consecutive free throw record (17).

Soon, there were other basketball courts in Pierceville. Glen Butte had a basket on his garage. Carl Schroder made a court behind his store for Roger and his friends. All in all, Schroder's was a better court than Plump's or Butte's. But it had one major hazard: a huge manure pile off to one side. One off-balance shot or hard foul, and you could end up smelling like the business end of a cow. Of course, there was a certain advantage to smelling bad: the guys on the other team didn't care to guard you very closely after you fell in the manure pile.

Fouls, actually, were hard to come by. "Just going into the manure pile wasn't a foul," Bobby said. "You could always try to claim a foul, but you always got outvoted. If you didn't have to be carried off, you didn't get to shoot. You could even be bleeding, and you wouldn't get the foul. I never shot a free throw, I know that."

It wasn't for lack of toughness. The Pierceville kids who played in those outdoor games at Schroder's and Plump's and Butte's remember Bobby Plump as a kid who could take just about anything they could dish out. You could hack him, shove him, elbow him in the stomach, knock him down, and push him in the manure. Not only would he not complain, he'd hit the bucket.

Lloyd Freeman remembers that, even in his elementary school days, he could tell the Plump kid was a player. "He jumped like a kangaroo. There was a guy named Dave Giltner who could jump, too. But Bobby was quicker. His timing on rebounding was terrific. He just had some kind of knack, some special kind of perception. He could tell how the ball was going to come off the goal the minute it left your hand."

It was on these outdoor courts in Pierceville that the mystery and majesty of the Indiana high school tournament first took hold of Bobby and his friends. They weren't just the Pierceville kids anymore. They were the Pierceville Alleycats, the roughest, toughest, sharp-shootingest bunch of basketball players ever to play in Southern

Indiana. And they were falling in love with the high school game. Out at the smokehouse, Bobby positioned a radio so he and Glen Butte could listen to the 1949 final game between Leo "Cabby" O'Neill's Jasper Wildcats and Dee Monroe's nearby Madison Cubs. (Years later, Bobby became friends with Cabby's nephew Tim O'Neill. Tim set up an annual golf outing in Jasper in which he, Joe Wolfla, and Bobby would play with Cabby and Ray Crowe, former coach of the Crispus Attucks Tigers. For four years, local newspapers and radio stations interviewed the players, and Cabby always referred to Bobby as "that kid who held the ball." "I don't think Cabby ever called me by my name," Bobby said.) The boys tried to play along with the game, Bobby pretending to be Jasper, Glen playing Madison. The game turned out to be the greatest upset the tournament had ever seen, with Jasper, who entered post-season play with a mediocre 11-9 record, getting the 62-61 victory. Madison would bounce back to win the 1950 title.

All that practice on less-than-perfect courts paid off when the Alleycats got inside a gym. "It was level," Bobby said. "There wasn't any grass or bumps or rocks." Not to mention ash heaps or manure piles.

CHAPTER FIVE

BASKETBALL BEGINNINGS

To people in other parts of the world, we Americans sometimes seem silly, crude, and unsophisticated. In New York or Boston, people from Indiana are often thought to be slow and dumb, hillbillies and hayseeds. The people who live in Jeffersonville may seem backward to the people in Indianapolis, and the people in Milan can't possibly be as sophisticated as the people in Jeffersonville. Which just goes to show that where you are and how you look at the world is all pretty subjective. And that, if you hail from Pierceville, Indiana, people from the big town of Milan might be hesitant to claim you as their own.

Bobby Plump was the only one of Lester Plump's children to attend school in Milan from first grade through high school; the others spent part or all of their school days in Pierceville. At times, Bobby and the other Pierceville kids felt as though they were from the wrong side of the tracks, that they weren't good enough to really be part of Milan. It took Bobby years to feel like he belonged there. Even after the Milan Miracle and the state championship in 1954, there were times when the old insecurities nagged at him.

Bobby's insecurity may have kept him off the first basketball team he had a chance to make at Milan Junior High. He and the rest of his Pierceville Alleycat buddies tried out for the team, but they didn't make it, although a couple of tough kids from Milan, Bob Engel and Ronnie Truitt, did make the team. Bobby was heartbroken. It was tough to spend the winter sitting and watching his buddies play ball with a real team on a real indoor court against real opponents. But he didn't give up. Instead, Bobby went to work at the homemade goal on the smokehouse, handling the ball, shooting, taping his fingers against the cold.

The next year, Bobby again felt some trepidation as he walked into the gym to try out for the junior high Milan Indians. "I remember sitting on the stage waiting for the tryouts to begin, looking at some big, rough eighth grader from Milan and wondering if I could really do this. But Roger Schroder said, 'Ah, you're better than him,' and, while I'm not sure I totally believed him, it gave me some confidence," Bobby said.

It was true: Bobby Plump was good enough to make the team. The late Marc Combs, who coached the Milan Junior High teams, remembered Bobby and his friends as special kids.

"I'll never forget those kids. Bobby especially. He's given more back to the game than any fellow I know of," Combs said.

The kids he coached will say the same about Marc Combs. (In fact, when Coach Combs died in December of 1996, most of his former players from the 1954 championship team attended the funeral and served as pallbearers: Bobby Plump, Gene White, Ray Craft, Roger Schroder, Glen Butte, Ken Wendelman, and Rollin Cutter, along with Coach Marvin Wood. He was laid to rest with his championship ring on his finger and a photo of the team in his casket.) They credit him with much of their success in their development as basketball players. He drilled them incessantly in basketball fundamentals: shooting, passing, blocking out, rebounding, defense, moving without the ball. Coach Combs would blindfold his players and have them dribble around chairs he'd set up on the gym floor to teach them the importance of keeping their heads up, not watching their dribble. Every practice, they played hard, worked on their passing, developed the feel for each other that would be so important to their success in the years to come.

Coach Combs was also interested in keeping the kids' heads up in another, more important way. "I used to sit them down at the end of every day at practice and talk to them, and tell them they could be anything they wanted to be. I told them they were as good as anybody, and maybe better than most. But the difference was their desire. If they really wanted to be the best, they could be," he said.

Combs had lived in Milan since his grade school days, when his parents moved north from Kentucky. He graduated from Milan High School in 1933, then spent the next two years in college at Morehead State. When his mother died the next year, Combs came home to Milan. He went to Hanover in the fall term to get his teaching license, and later attended Central Normal, where Lester Plump had gone to school. "I never intended to be a teacher all my life. I thought I'd just do it for a while and move on. But when I saw the looks on the faces of those kids in the classroom, I knew they really needed someone to talk to, someone who might be able to inspire them and help them along in life," Combs said.

Combs started his teaching and coaching career in Aurora, where the superintendent was Will Wilson. "He got a job at Milan and asked me if I'd go there with him. I told him I had a contract at Aurora, but I'd be happy to go if he could get me out of it."

Wilson struck the deal, and Marc Combs went to teach and coach in his home town. He also spent a good deal of his free time watching basketball games. "I picked up a lot of things I taught the boys," he said, among them the one-handed shot. He also developed an unusual full-court 1-3-1 zone defense he taught the boys. Combs had never seen a zone like it — but basketball fans around the nation have seen it many times since, employed by such successful collegiate basketball programs as Kentucky and Cincinnati.

"Marc Combs may have actually invented that zone," Bobby said. "We were certainly the first ones I ever knew of who played it."

Mostly, though, Coach Combs taught fundamentals. Bobby Plump was an attentive student. Through the first part of his seventh grade season, he watched and learned. About halfway through the season, he started to see more action. Soon, it became clear to Marc Combs that this seventh grader from Pierceville belonged in the starting lineup. In fact, it was clear to Combs that he had the makings of a very special team. "I knew in junior high that they would be capable of contending for a state championship, if they had the proper coaching and didn't neglect the fundamentals. You could see they had excellent characteristics — good body work, but good brain work, too," Combs said.

That season, the seventh graders regularly beat their eighth grade teammates in scrimmage games. Next season, they were beating everyone on their schedule. The kids from Pierceville — Bobby Plump, Roger Schroder, Gene White, and Glen Butte — were starting to gel with Milan kids Bob Engel and Ron Truitt and a couple of farm kids, Ray Craft and Ken Wendelman, whose brother Jim had played with them the year before and was now a freshman at Milan High School. The eighth grade Milan Indians swept through the 1949-50 season without a loss, and entered the county tournament against the Osgood Cowboys — a team they'd already beaten twice — brimming with confidence.

Maybe too much confidence. The game was an unqualified disaster. The Cowboys played furious defense and doubled the score on the Indians. "It was devastating," said Bobby. "We sat in the locker room, crying our eyes out. The world had come to an end."

It was Coach Combs who put the loss in perspective for the no-longer-cocky young Indians. He told them in no uncertain terms that this loss was not the end of the world. And he said something else that stuck with them for years to come.

"He told us we should take it as a lesson that you have to play every game. You can't get caught up in your own press clippings and act as if you've won the game before it starts. It was a crushing blow. But in the long run, it was a good thing. I never took an opponent for granted, ever again," Bobby said.

Though they had made an early exit from the county tournament, the eighth grade Indians had sparked a lot of interest in the community — especially in Milan High School basketball coach Herman "Snort" Grinstead. Snort could see he had a bunch of kids with a lot of potential, and he wanted to move them into his program as quickly as their development would permit.

Grinstead had already made an impression on Bobby. "Mr. Grinstead is the only person who ever laid a hand on me," Bobby said.

One afternoon after a seventh grade game, Bobby and his teammates were horsing around in the locker room when Snort Grinstead happened to come through. Snort told the boys firmly to settle down. But a few of the boys kept right on goofing around with their friends.

"I don't remember exactly what happened. I think Mr. Grinstead said something about someone being a smart aleck, and I said, 'Yeh, like you.' I wasn't saying it to Mr. Grinstead, but he must have thought I was. I was still just fooling around, trying to be one of the guys. But the next thing I knew, I was on the floor," Bobby said. Snort Grinstead had smacked him — something even his father had never done.

Snort Grinstead was not the type of man to be sassed. At 6'2", he was an imposing figure, a big, good-looking man the people of Milan loved. Grinstead coached basketball, baseball, and track at Milan High School. He lived in town with his wife, Lotta, who ran a beauty parlor out of their home. He was also known to drive out to Pierceville for an occasional beer and a game of cards at Chub Richardson's farm, and sometimes stopped in town to visit with Lester Plump, Pop Dunn, and some of the other men. He had a temper, as one might expect from a man named

Snort. But he was usually fair. "If Mr. Grinstead told you to do something, you did it. You knew he wasn't fooling around," said Bobby.

Grinstead certainly didn't fool around when it came to sports. He was a good basketball fundamentalist. And he didn't care where he found his talent.

"Before Snort came along, we kids from Pierceville didn't think we'd ever have much of a chance to play. But he took a chance on us and put us in the game. Snort used all the talent he had," said Lloyd Freeman, who played three years of baseball for Grinstead.

Grinstead obviously found a lot of basketball talent in Pierceville, too. He knew all about the Pierceville Alleycats — Bobby and Glen and Roger and Gene, the kids who played rough-and-tumble, anything-goes ball behind Schroder's store, whose skills had already been shaped and sharpened under Marc Combs. And he knew he had a leader in Bobby Plump. As a freshman, Bobby played on the reserve team, starting every game and impressing the Milan faithful with his ball handling and his shooting touch. But Bobby himself was impressed with the style of a varsity player named Bill Gorman.

"I saw him shooting a jump shot. Nobody shot jump shots back then. I remember thinking that it would be awfully hard to defend, so I started copying it."

He started getting good at it, too — so good that, by the end of his freshman year, Snort Grinstead took him into the gym at Milan High and told him how he could make the varsity the next year. Grinstead told Bobby to practice dribbling to the free throw line, stopping, and shooting the jump shot. "Do it from both sides," he said, "and you'll be able to play for me next year."

That was all the encouragement Bobby needed. He practiced his jump shot day and night, in the gym, at Schroder's, at Butte's, back at the smokehouse, through the transoms, and in his mind. He took jumpshots in his sleep, just as Coach Grinstead had suggested, from both sides of the free throw line. With all the work, the promising little jump shot soon became virtually unstoppable.

And Coach Grinstead was as good as his word. In the fall of 1951, Bobby Plump was again starting for the reserve squad. Coach Grinstead also had Bobby dressing for the varsity games. And Bobby started seeing a lot of playing time with the varsity. The Indians were big and experienced that year, with seven seniors. The folks in Milan — in particular, the men of the Downtown Coaches Club, who held court at Arkenberg's Restaurant or the drug store — weren't so impressed as to be thinking about a state championship, but they figured their Indians to be one of the favorites in the sectional come tournament time.

Trouble was, Snort Grinstead wasn't as impressed with his Indians as everyone else was. He didn't like the attitude or the work ethic of his senior players. Early in the season, he found an opportunity to shake things up — and open the door for Bobby Plump and his younger teammates to take their game to a whole new level.

That fall, the Indians were shellacked by their arch rivals, the Osgood Cowboys. "It was terrible," said Kenny Bergman, one of the seven seniors on the Milan team. "We couldn't do anything right in Osgood's little crackerbox gym."

Rodney Brandes, another of the seniors, concurred. "Osgood was hitting everything they threw up. They were knocking our socks off. At halftime, Snort said that if we couldn't play any better than that, he'd take away our uniforms."

The second half was no better than the first. The Indians suffered a humiliating 82-40 defeat.

In the locker room after the game, Snort Grinstead raged. He stomped and yelled and pounded on the lockers. "I was cringing. It was awful," Bobby said.

Then Snort Grinstead made the move he'd wanted to make for weeks. He made good on his threat to take the uniforms away from his seniors. Kenny Bergman, Rodney Brandes, Hiram Poore, Louis Ferringer, Tom Clapp, Denny North, and Raymond Shelp were kicked off the team.

Kenny Bergman was devastated. He'd been playing organized basketball since the sixth grade. "Jim Nagel gave me a pair of shoes so I could play on the seventh and eighth grade team," he said. Kenny had played with the varsity since he was a freshman, and had overcome many difficulties to do so. The Bergman family was poor, and Kenny's mother had a nervous breakdown that kept her institutionalized for many years.

The following Monday, all the seniors, Kenny Bergman and

Rodney Brandes included, decided it might be too embarrassing to show up at school. They planned to do some rabbit hunting instead. Kenny was waiting at home for Rodney to pick him up so they could join the other guys. What he didn't expect was for Rodney to arrive in Coach Grinstead's car.

Grinstead had decided he didn't want to lose *all* of his seniors. Brandes and Bergman had been long-time starters. In Grinstead's mind, his younger players still needed some experienced leadership. So Grinstead found a substitute teacher to watch his class and went out to find his players, stopping first at Brandes's house.

Rodney was there. "I said, 'None of us are coming back unless we all come back.' We had all agreed to that. So Snort and I went out to where the other guys were hunting and he told us he'd take us all back."

Next, they stopped at Kenny Bergman's house. "Snort came in and asked me why I wasn't at school, and I told him I was going rabbit hunting. He told me he thought I'd better go to school. So I changed my clothes and went with them. When we got there, he took Rodney and me down to the dressing room and told us he wanted us back — just us. Not the rest of the team," Bergman said.

The other seniors were upset, and felt betrayed by Rodney and Kenny. "But I wanted to play ball," Bergman said. "That was the most important thing to me. The seniors who were kicked off were good boys, but they weren't good basketball players. We were a better team without them."

The young Indians would be tested immediately. Their first game without the seniors was against the Batesville Bulldogs, the biggest, toughest team in Ripley County. Batesville was the powerhouse in the region. Unlike the other Ripley County teams, they wore slick warm-up pants and jackets. Also unlike the other Ripley County schools, Batesville never participated in the county tournament. They were nearly a write-in as sectional champions. And with good reason. In the late '40s and early '50s, Batesville had such players as Paul "Ham" Wernke, who later played at Florida State; Louie Dickman, a collegiate star at North Carolina State; Tom "Ace" Moorman, who played ball at Cincinnati; Milt Baas, who went on to play at Hanover; and Herm Struewing, who played at Ball State.

The season before, in the spring of 1951, Batesville had gone to the Elite Eight. "Batesville dominated," said Ham Wernke, a star of that 1951 team. "We were the biggest school in Ripley County. We were all city kids. We had the numbers to work with. We had good coaches."

And Milan was putting a new, inexperienced lineup on the floor. Joining Rodney Brandes and Kenny Bergman, the two seniors who had survived the wrath of Snort Grinstead, were junior Jim Wendelman and two sophomores: Bob Engel and Bobby Plump. The game had all the makings of a blow-out.

Instead, the fans got a shocker: the Indians beat their bigger, more experienced Batesville foes by one point.

It was a game Kenny Bergman will never forget. "It was amazing. This was a team that went to the last game of the semistate the year before. I had been sorry to see my friends leave the team. But after that game, I knew we had a better team with the sophomores."

Bobby Plump remembers the game as a turning point. "We proved to ourselves that we could play with anybody in the county."

And the insecure kid from Pierceville was starting to be recognized. The day after the game, Bobby walked into his class a couple of minutes late. As he entered the room, everyone in the class stood and clapped. "It was one of the greatest feelings I ever had," he said.

The Milan Indians stirred a lot of interest that year. They won the county tournament. They even beat Osgood, the team that had embarrassed them earlier in the season. "In fact, we beat them easily. I don't think they ever beat us again while I was there," Bobby said.

So when it was time for the 1952 sectional, Milan was thinking like a winner. The Indians had already beaten Batesville once. And in the months since that shocking win, they'd only gotten better.

That night, the fans were out in force, screaming for the Milan Indians, the boys in black. They knew their young squad had the right stuff to beat the Bulldogs. If anyone in Ripley County could do it, the Indians could.

It was not to be. On the night the Batesville Bulldogs met the Milan Indians at the 1952 Versailles Sectional, Bobby Plump was at home in Pierceville, where Dr. Henry Conrad was giving him shots of penicillin for a terrible case of the flu. Bob Engel and Kenny Bergman were sick with the flu, too, but felt strong enough to play. It wasn't enough; Batesville beat the Indians by nine, and would go on to win their fourth consecutive sectional crown with a crushing 54-37 victory over Osgood. That year, the Bulldogs would make it all the way to the Sweet Sixteen before being beaten by Shelbyville.

"If we'd have had ol' Bobby, I think we would have beaten them," said Kenny Bergman. "He was our set-up man, and a great team player. We missed him."

But Kenny Bergman's long high school basketball career was over. "I always wanted to play at Butler Fieldhouse, but I never made it."

The 1951-52 season had come to a close. But the stage was set. Bobby Plump and his teammates would be back, with enough experience to match up against the toughest opponents and just enough of a taste of success to know they wanted more.

Unfortunately for Snort Grinstead, he would not be with them.

CHAPTER SIX

THE NEW COACH

In the fall of 1952, there was a political debate raging across the land. American voters had a clear choice for President: Adlai Stevenson, the intellectual Democrat from Illinois, or Dwight D. Eisenhower, Republican hero of World War II. All sorts of remarkable things were happening in the world. You could buy a 10-inch round-screen RCA television set at Schroder's store in Pierceville for about $150, or a big 20-inch console unit for about $300. You could already watch Howdy Doody and Uncle Miltie in millions of American homes, and that number was increasing dramatically every year. Impressive new highways were being built across the nation. If you planned to take advantage of them, you could buy a Chevy coupe with an automatic transmission for $1,250, or a Ford station wagon for just under $2,000. New houses in the suburbs could be purchased for between $4,000 and $8,000. Gas grills and power lawn mowers were making suburban life easy.

Even with all these changes, things weren't much different at the Plumps' family home in Pierceville. By this time, the Plumps had electricity. But there was still no indoor plumbing, no phone, no television, no gas grill. Clothes were still washed in the gas-powered Maytag. Bobby and his friends watched TV through the window of Schroder's store. The lawn mower worked off of muscle power.

However, there was something remarkable happening around Milan. The whole town was abuzz with talk of a genuine basketball contender at Milan High School. Bobby Plump and Bob Engel and all the rest of those gifted sophomores would be back. Snort Grinstead was proclaiming to anyone who'd listen — and practically everyone in Milan would — that this was a team that could make it to the Sweet Sixteen.

That would be a tall order, indeed, and an unusual accomplishment for a team from Milan. Milan had first played in the fourth state tournament in 1914, losing to eventual champion Wingate. Way back then, the finals had been held at Indiana University in Bloomington — not at Butler (later Hinkle) Fieldhouse in Indianapolis. In the first local tournament known as a sectional, held in 1916, the Indians lost to host Seymour, 37-19. By 1952, Milan had won only four sectional titles — in 1932, 1935, 1936, and 1946 — and all of those teams had lost their first games in the regional tournament.

In other words, in the modern basketball era, Milan had never advanced to the final 32 teams, let alone the Sweet Sixteen. The only players on the team who had ever so much as seen the inside of Butler Fieldhouse were Bob Engel and Ronnie Truitt, who'd seen the Lawrenceberg Tigers play in the semistate tournament in 1949; and Bobby Plump, whose sister Ginny and her husband Bill Schwing had taken him to see that same game. "Bill lived in Lawrenceberg and was a big basketball fan. That was the first time I was ever in Indianapolis," Bobby said.

On the other hand, the Indians had proven they could beat Batesville, the four-time defending sectional champ. So confidence was high in Milan. Fans figured the Indians would surprise a lot of people in 1952 and 1953. But the first big surprise happened before the season even started. In fact, it happened before the 1952 school year even ended.

Snort Grinstead was rapidly becoming an institution in Milan, having coached the Indians for four interesting, moderately successful years. The people of Milan loved him. And he loved the celebrity status of a high school basketball coach in small-town Indiana, and could be seen almost nightly at Arkenberg's Restaurant or the corner barbershop giving the townfolk the benefit of all the basketball knowledge he'd accumulated in his 50-plus years.

But Grinstead's celebrity didn't hold much water with school superintendent Bill "The Bug" Franklin and the Milan school board — Freda Whitlatch, Lawrence "Bud" Jordan, and Arthur "Coon" Frolks. Perhaps they were upset about Grinstead's treatment of his senior players after the Osgood blowout — although, given the Indians' improved performance with the sophomores in the lineup, too much anger would have been hard to fathom. "Everybody liked the fact that Snort won with the sophomores. But some folks didn't care for the way he dumped the seniors. They thought he should never have taken them in the first place, and since he did, he should have stuck with them," said Lloyd Freeman.

Some other small town politics may have come into play, as well. According to Marc Combs, "We often had to play kids whose fathers were influential, at the expense of some kids who were better ballplayers. I remember kids who had dead hands and dead feet. It was really a disservice to them to have them on the floor. But the pressure was there. Snort didn't go for that stuff. He played the best ballplayers."

Perhaps there were other personality conflicts; Grinstead and Franklin had apparently not gotten along too well when they'd worked together previously at Aurora. But the last straw was the new basketball uniforms Coach Grinstead ordered for his team just before the state tournament — without the knowledge or approval of the school board. Back in those days, athletic salesmen called directly on the coaches and athletic directors (and Grinstead was both). But Grinstead didn't have the authority to purchase anything without the approval of the superintendent.

He bought them anyway. Superintendent Franklin got a bill for the uniforms, "and that was when the crap hit the fan," said Betty Dobson, Franklin's secretary.

The school board didn't want to let the players have the new uniforms. But the players had already seen them. They were so upset about not getting to wear them that they staged a protest. Finally, the board relented.

"We didn't have the money to pay for them," Betty Dobson said. "One of our board members had to take out a personal loan at the bank to pay for those uniforms."

Actually, Grinstead offered to pay for the uniforms out of his own pocket. The uniforms had been a gamble, but he was used to gambling. Snort Grinstead had gambled when he kicked the seniors off the team. He'd gambled by playing Pierceville kids on the Milan team. But now it seemed he'd rolled the dice once too often. If his star sophomore guard hadn't gotten sick with the flu, maybe things would have been different. But now Franklin wanted Grinstead's head. Just weeks after a flu bug had been the only thing standing between Snort Grinstead and a sectional championship, he was stripped of his position as teacher and coach at Milan High School.

"He came stomping up to me, all red-faced and looking terrible," said Marc Combs. "He said, 'You knew I was going to be fired. Why didn't you tell me?' I told him I hadn't known at all. I didn't know until he told me just then."

Soon, all of Milan knew. Word of Snort's dismissal swept through town like a summer thunderstorm. The town was in an uproar. Bobby Plump said, "My initial reaction was disappointment. I knew I could play for Mr. Grinstead. I felt like I had to start all over again. Most of the people I talked to were disappointed and angry."

"I think the Downtown Coaches were ready to lynch the school board," agreed Lloyd Freeman. They stopped short of the noose. But they did let the ax fall again. The town was in such an uproar over Snort's firing that Bill "The Bug" Franklin was fired as superintendent a short time later.

But that didn't bring back Grinstead. Soon after losing his job at Milan, he took a position as head basketball coach at nearby Gilford, a smaller school than Milan, where he coached for a year before moving just down the road from Milan to coach at Moores Hill. (His players never forgot him; in fact, years later, when Bobby and Ray Craft were in college, they traveled to Moores Hill to help their old coach learn the offensive strategies Milan had used so effectively.)

So the Indians needed a new head coach, and one thing was certain: whoever came in to replace Snort Grinstead already had one strike against him, as far as the Milan faithful were concerned.

It probably didn't help that the coach who arrived was as different from Snort Grinstead as Pierceville was from New York City. He wasn't a big, blustering, 52-year-old, old-fashioned crowd-pleaser. He was smaller, soft-spoken, a family man, just 24 years old. He wasn't comfortable in the sometimes-harsh spotlight of celebrity. And he had his own ideas about how to run a basketball team.

His name was Marvin Wood. His experience: three years as a player for Tony Hinkle at Butler University, two seasons as coach at French Lick, the high school in the small Southern Indiana town that would, years later, produce the great Larry Bird. He moved to Milan with his wife Mary Lou, his two young children, Doug and Dee, a lifetime .500 record as a coach, and absolutely no knowledge of the controversy surrounding his position.

Wood didn't exactly want to come to Milan. In fact, it was his third choice.

"I really wanted to stay at French Lick. After our season, I asked them for a $200 raise. The board offered me $50 — a buck a week. I took that as a sign that it was okay with them for me to look elsewhere."

Meanwhile, Bloomfield High School came looking for Wood. "They called the board and asked if they could talk to me, and the board said they could. Well, they didn't want to pay me any more than I was making at French Lick. But I figured that if Bloomfield was interested in me, someone else might be, too.

"My old high school coach, Gerl Furr, was working at Brownstown then," Wood said. "He was scouting a team that was playing Milan. Later, he called me and told me they had some trouble down there, and were looking for a new coach. Said they had a lot of talent there just looking for a young coach to make a name for himself. I never dreamed the talent could have been as good as it was."

Wood paid Milan a visit. "They'd just had a town clean-up day, and it was the prettiest little town I'd ever seen. Mary Lou and I fell in love with it."

Still, Milan High School was only half the size of French Lick, and Wood wasn't sure he wanted to go to a smaller school. And Milan didn't want to pay Wood's asking price, either — a whopping $4,000 for coaching basketball and baseball and teaching biology and driver education.

Soon after his interview, though, Superintendent Franklin called. "He told me I'd be a very poor businessman to come here for less than I could get somewhere else. Milan said they'd pay my asking price." So Wood was off to Milan, a little uncertain about the size of the school, but curious about the talent there. He figured he could always move on to bigger and better things. He could never have imagined the big things that lay just ahead.

"Actually, if I'd known about all the controversy, I'd probably never have taken the job," he said.

But Marvin Wood had plans. He knew the Tony Hinkle offensive system. He was devoted to aggressive man-to-man defense. And he was particularly intrigued by a slow-down, four-corner offense known as "cat and mouse."

These plans would take some getting used to. Under Snort Grinstead, the Indians played a freelance game, the kind of game made popular — and successful — by Indiana University Coach Branch

McCracken. Wood's style was more controlled, more oriented toward running patterns and working the ball inside and out for high-percentage shots.

Looking back, Bobby Plump gives Marvin Wood much of the credit for Milan's rise to prominence. "He polished our fundamentals and brought the innovations we would need."

And Coach Wood had a lot to work with — in terms of both talent and sheer numbers. In October of 1952, Wood arrived at his gym to find 58 boys prepared to try out for the team — 58 out of only 73 boys in the entire school. "Almost every one of them had some talent to contribute to a basketball program. It was difficult to eliminate them, especially as a first-year coach. That's always the most difficult part of coaching, though," Wood said.

Initially, Wood coached not only the varsity, but the junior varsity and the freshman team. He was told he'd get an assistant, but didn't have one at the start of the season. Fortunately, Wood could rely on the advice of Marc Combs, the coach who had helped develop Bobby Plump and company into a solid unit in junior high.

After his team was set, Coach Wood did something that alienated the Downtown Coaches Club — as if daring to try filling Snort Grinstead's ample shoes wasn't enough. He closed practices. The people of Milan were appalled. For years, many in the community had stopped to watch the Indians' after-school drills. But not this year. Wood's team had work to do.

They very nearly had to do it without Bobby Plump.

One cool, crisp October night, Bobby and three friends, Bill Raynor, Gladys Lattire, and Bernice Bentley, were out making preparations for the school Halloween Dance. They piled in Bernice's father's car to pick up some jugs of apple cider. Bill drove, never suspecting the danger that lay ahead.

The trip out was uneventful. But on the way home, the car loaded with cider, the kids having fun and looking forward to the dance, Bill failed to notice a hump on a curve in the road.

Suddenly, the car was in the air and turning over.

"I remember that so clearly," Bobby said. "Time seemed to stand still. It was as if the whole thing was happening in slow motion."

While the car was rolling, the back seat hit Bobby in the back, briefly knocking him unconscious. The car spilled off the road and tumbled into a ditch, throwing out teenagers and cider jugs as it spun.

Bobby awoke in a daze, half in, half out of the car. Miraculously, he was unharmed. The others were lucky, too. Bill and Gladys had some minor bruises. Bernice had cuts on her face that required several stitches.

The car was another story. Roof, hood, and side panels had all been horribly crushed. Upon inspection, the insurance company totaled the vehicle.

"We went down to Chris Volz's garage the next day to look at the car. It was a twisted-up mess. It was truly a miracle that anyone walked away from that accident," Bobby said.

Milan's rising star narrowly escaped tragedy. And the marriage between Coach Marvin Wood and the town of Milan was already off to a rocky start. But it's always difficult to be pessimistic at the beginning of basketball season in Indiana — especially when you have high hopes for your team. In the words of Tiny Hunt, sportswriter for the *Versailles Republican* and *Osgood Journal*:

> When old Mother Nature sends little Jack Frost to turn the leaves from green to golden brown and there is frost on the pumpkin, and the fodder is in the shock, we Hoosiers realize that it is basketball season in Ripley County.

Tiny Hunt was anything but tiny. He stood well over six feet tall and tipped the scales at more than 300 pounds. The Milan players used to joke that you could tell Tiny was on his way down the road when you saw his car's frame was nearly scraping pavement on the driver's side. "That's true," said Tootie Herbst, Arky Arkenberg's sister and a waitress at the Milan restaurant. "Tiny's car really did sag on the driver's side."

Tiny would cover the Milan Indians like a blanket for the next two years, reveling in this small-town Indiana success story, selling its glory to big-city sportswriters such as Bob Williams, *The Indianapolis Star's* top high school basketball writer. "Tiny was a great basketball fan. He got a real kick out of the Milan story," Williams said. "And he was definitely a big guy. He used to joke that the IHSAA had to give him two seats for games."

But even Tiny Hunt had no idea what lay ahead for the Milan Indians. In October, 1952, he wrote:

> The Milan Indians will open their season under their new Coach Marvin Wood with the Sunman Tigers. Both ball clubs have many lettermen back from last year and this should be a good ball game.

He wasn't even close. Milan blew away Sunman, 62-38. Bobby Plump led all scorers with 17 points. The starting lineup: 5'10" Pierceville's own Bobby Plump at one guard, 6'1" Bob Engel at the other. Senior Jim Wendelman used his 6'4" height and 210-pound frame to dominate the center position. At the forward positions were 6'2" Ron Truitt and 5'11" Pierceville native Gene White. Tough little Ray Craft, at 5'8", brought quickness and a deft shooting touch off the bench.

Next up was Rising Sun. The Shiners proved to be a tougher opponent, giving the Indians fits in the first half with an efficient offensive scheme and tough defense. At halftime, Marvin Wood was stumped. He had always sworn that, as long as he was a head basketball coach, he would never play a zone defense. But the man-to-man wasn't working. He didn't really know how to play a zone. But he knew someone who did: Marc Combs.

"Marvin came to me and said, 'Marc, I've only been doing this for a couple of years, and I'm not too proud to ask for help. Let's talk about playing a zone.' I told him, 'Coach, these kids already know how to play it,'" Combs said. It was an early form of the suffocating match-up zone popular today, and the Milan Indians had been playing it since their junior high days. They were already experts at chasing the ball, cutting off the passing lanes, and forcing the ball down and either inside or outside, depending on their opponent's strength. In other words, they knew how to play the match-up zone to perfection.

The second half made a believer of Marvin Wood. The zone worked, and Bobby Plump scored 32 — half of Milan's total offense — in the 64-43 victory.

Milan fans were getting their first good looks at Coach Marvin Wood's system. And they liked what they saw. Gone was Snort Grinstead's run-and-gun offense. In its place, Coach Wood installed Tony Hinkle's continuity offense, the same offense he'd used as a player at Butler, a fluid, motion-oriented offense designed to create high-percentage shots. If the Indians had no clear break for the bucket, the guards, Bobby Plump and Bob Engel, would slow down and set up a play. On the other side of the ball, the Indians were making the switch from the in-your-face, man-to-man defense Marvin Wood preferred to a zone defense that Wood, with the help of Marc Combs, was developing especially for them.

But as nicely as things started for Coach Wood and the Indians, they came unraveled in the season's third game against Vevay. Down seven in the first half, the Indians came storming back to take a 45-44 fourth quarter lead. But it didn't last. Vevay handed the Indians their first defeat of the season, behind Newell Fox's 27-point performance.

The Downtown Coaches were in an uproar. First closed practices. Then an odd, fancy new offense. Then a loss to Vevay. Who did this Marvin Wood character think he was, anyway? With Wood, maybe all the preseason excitement about the Milan Indians was just false hope.

Hardly. The Indians put together a six-game winning streak, beginning with a huge 55-43 win over Batesville. Ace Moorman poured in 23 for the Bulldogs, but he was no match for Milan's backcourt duo of Plump and Engel, who combined for 39 points. In rapid succession, the Indians disposed of Osgood (55-47), North Madison (72-45), Holton (41-35), Brookville (72-48), and Hanover (75-58).

Bobby Plump was emerging as a leader. Through the streak, he averaged 15 points a game — in spite of scoring only six in limited action against Hanover. He missed most of that game with an ailing back. "I hurt it playing ping pong," he said. "I went for a slam and wrenched my back. Bob Engel, who also had a bad back, and I went to a chiropractor in Aurora. My back got better. His never did." In fact, Engel's back problems would intensify and eventually force him to give up the game he loved.

But in 1952, Bob Engel and Bobby Plump were becoming recognized as one of the elite back court combinations in the state. "We were really starting to blend as a team," Marvin Wood said. "Everything fit: the players, the coach, the system. It was all coming together."

Around this time, Coach Wood was given his long-promised assistant: Clarence Kelly, a young graduate of Lafayette Jefferson High School and Purdue University who had recently been discharged from the United States Army after serving in Korea. Kelly would handle the freshmen, the reserve squad, and, come playoff time, the scouting duties for the Indians. He was also coach of the Milan track team, on which a lot of the Milan basketball players competed in the spring.

Interestingly enough, it was Bill "The Bug" Franklin who was responsible for Kelly finding the job at Milan. Kelly's father, Clarence Kelly, Sr., was the principal at Lafayette Jeff. Upon returning from the war, the junior Kelly labored in a series of menial jobs before his father told him about a placement service for teachers where Franklin had landed after being fired at Milan. Franklin, of course, knew all about the positions open at Milan. Kelly interviewed with Milan principal Richard Brollier and was hired. For his services, Kelly paid The Bug $35, never knowing he'd been dealing with the recently deposed Milan school superintendent.

At 8-1, the Indians were confident going into the toughest part of their schedule, a swing into Dearborn County. Their next opponent was Aurora, a team that many thought could win a state championship in the years ahead. Aurora had been loaded with talent in 1951-52, with seniors John Rahe, Jerry Ruble, Bobby Green, Eddie Satchwill, and Walter Johnson providing a balanced attack. That spring, Aurora won their sectional. Only a freak accident kept them from winning the Rushville Regional; star player Jerry Ruble cut his knee badly when he ran into a soft drink vendor while chasing a bad pass out of bounds.

The Milan/Aurora tilt was billed as a big game. And it didn't disappoint anyone. After leading for most of the contest, the Indians finally succumbed to a brutal scoring assault from Aurora's Gary Lyon, who connected for 21. Lyon, who later starred as a baseball player at Miami of Ohio, was hitting from the cheap seats, and the stingy Aurora defense was forcing the Indians to shoot from even farther back. Bobby scored 10 and Bob Engel added 11, but it wasn't enough. The Indians suffered their second loss of the year, 51-40.

Next, Milan traveled down the road to Lawrenceburg, another perennially tough foe. Back in the '40s, the Tigers had won four straight regional titles (1946-49). Lawrenceburg had talent: Larry Liddle, who later coached at Milan and long-time power Marion; Bill Wullner, who became a top collegiate official; and Bucky Dennis. Dennis lived with relatives and went to school in Lawrenceburg, but his parents actually lived in Milan for a time. He considered moving back with his parents and playing for the Indians, but ended up staying in Lawrenceburg.

But on this night, it was another Tiger, Jerry Horn, who stopped the Indians cold. Horn pumped in 20, and the Tigers led from the opening tip. Bobby's team-leading 12 points weren't nearly enough to stop Lawrenceburg from cruising to a 56-44 victory.

The Downtown Coaches were rumbling again. "I was beginning to realize that I had the boys' confidence. I felt I'd won them over during baseball season. But the town of Milan was not quite on my side yet. My landlord, Bob Peak, lived across the street from me, and I just couldn't get away from him. He'd be over at my house every evening, asking me if I'd thought of this or that. Mary Lou said he'd even come over at noon. I always thought it was just him. But now I know it was the Downtown Coaches who were making their suggestions through Peak," said Wood.

But Woody wasn't fazed. Unlike Snort Grinstead, he didn't hang out at Arkenberg's, and didn't let the boys hang out there, either. "I didn't listen to the gossip, so it never bothered me much," Wood said.

The Indians had lost two in a row. And their schedule wasn't getting much easier. Next up was Versailles. Along with Batesville, the Lions were one of the best teams in Ripley County. A lot of the Milan kids knew the Versailles kids very well. Elmer Pollard, one of the Lions' stars, lived in Milan until the sixth grade, when his family moved to a farm about a mile outside of Pierceville, just inside the Versailles school district. He and Bobby were good friends; years later, Bobby was the best man at Pollard's wedding. Ralph Ruggles, who lived across the road from Pollard, lived just inside the Napoleon boundary line. Needless to say, the boys from all three schools played a lot of ball together, especially during the summer months.

The Milan/Versailles game was part of a doubleheader at Tyson Auditorium in Versailles, the second game featuring the Osgood Cowboys and Rising Sun Shiners. Although Milan and Versailles were playing each other, it was like a home game for both teams. The Indians played most of their home games at Tyson, which held many more fans than the Milan gym.

This night, it appeared as though the Indians were back on track. Bobby scored 20, and the Indians won handily, 66-54. So 1952 ended with the Indians at 9-3. The 1953 portion of the season would determine whether they really had what it took to be champions.

It didn't begin very well. On New Year's Eve, Coach Wood gave his team a one a.m. curfew. He figured he was being lenient. Curfew was usually 10 p.m. on weekdays and midnight on weekends. Wood warned his team that he'd be driving by their houses to check up on them.

That night, Bobby was double-dating with classmate Bill Raynor. According to Bobby, the two couples were on their way home when they had a flat tire.

It is at this crucial point that Coach Wood's and Bobby's stories diverge. "I think it's the only mistake he ever made as a coach," Bobby said, tongue planted firmly in cheek. "I was home by one. We just happened to be outside."

That isn't how Marvin Wood remembers the story.

"I had told the boys that day to synchronize their watches with mine, because mine was the only one in town with the right time. That night, my landlord Bob Peak and I went out to check on the boys. We drove to Pierceville first. I never figured we'd have any trouble. I thought that basketball meant so much to the boys, they'd all be in by one."

So he was quite surprised when he saw a car speeding over the railroad tracks toward the Plump residence. "I think all four tires were off the ground," Wood laughed. "I told Peak, 'I believe those are the boys we're looking for.'"

Bobby protested, but Wood held firm. "We go by my watch, and my watch says five after one," he said. The five minute violation was good for a three-game suspension.

Bobby was devastated. At the next game, against Napoleon, Bobby couldn't dress or sit on the bench with his teammates. He cried in shame, feeling stupid sitting up in the stands, nowhere near the team. But he felt a little better when Jim Wendelman joined him up in the bleachers. He had been out past curfew, too — and in Wendelman's case, there was no argument. He'd missed the deadline by more than a few minutes. "As we were leaving Pierceville, I saw Jim's car speeding down the road. We stopped him and suspended him, too," said Wood.

The coach suspected he had one more offender that night. "The garage door was open at Ralph Preble's house, and his car was gone. He hadn't showed up by three in the morning, and I gave up on him. I knew he wasn't there. But I couldn't prove it. I thought I should punish him, but I didn't know how I could," Wood said.

As it turned out, he didn't have to. During warm-ups, Preble twisted an ankle. As Coach Wood took him to the dressing room to have it wrapped, he twisted the other one walking down the steps. "I didn't have to do anything with Ralph. He took care of himself for that game," Wood said.

The New Year's Eve offenders watched Gene White pace Milan to a 64-52 victory.

"We wanted them to win. We just wanted it to be closer than 12 points," Bobby joked. "Although Gene thought it would be good if we'd sit up in the stands every game."

Bobby and Jim got out of the remaining two games of their suspension by running a hundred laps around the Milan gym. Team manager and Pierceville pal Fred Busching counted each lap for Coach Wood, clicking them off on the scoreboard. "I think he kind of enjoyed watching us," Bobby said.

He was right. "Actually, I never intended to keep them out for three games. Maybe three days — Saturday, Sunday, and Monday," Wood laughed.

Bobby was ready to play again. Next game, he picked up right where he'd left off, scoring 27 in a convincing 81-60 win over Rising Sun. Elmer Strautman, who later played alongside Gene White, Roger Schroder, and Ken Wendelman at Franklin College and went on to become a member of the Indiana High School Athletic Association Board, scored 22 for the Shiners.

Next came one of the biggest events of the year: the county tournament. It was a gigantic affair in the early '50s, even bigger than the sectional in terms of generating local excitement. After all, Batesville dominated the sectional. But Batesville didn't play in the county tournament. (Depending on who you ask, they either weren't invited or didn't think it was worth their time.) So all of the eight remaining Ripley County teams thought they had a chance.

Not, as it turned out, against the Indians. Bobby, Gene White, and Ronnie Truitt each stood out as Milan demolished Napoleon, 51-33; Sunman, 59-30, and Versailles, 68-45. Elmer Pollard scored 16 for the Lions and, as usual, was assigned the unenviable task of guarding Bobby.

"He was no fun to guard. Bobby was a hard man to pin down. You couldn't hold him over a complete game, and Milan's type of offense made it tough to stay with your man. It was always a privilege to play Milan. It was dog-eat-dog, but we respected each other," Pollard said.

Now 13-3, the Indians had a two-and-half week layoff. Their first game after the break was against Versailles again. This time, Milan looked a little rusty. Jim Gabbard scored a game-high 18 for the Lions. But Bobby's 17 helped paced Milan to a 62-51 victory.

Next came a trip west to Jennings County and North Vernon. The Indians played well and led most of the way. But the North Vernon Panthers were persistent. Bob Engel pumped in 20 and Bobby added 17, but North Vernon took the match 60-57.

A temporary setback, thought the home crowd. At 14-4, the Indians were looking more and more like a sectional favorite. The folks over in Holton weren't too impressed, though. Although they had a weaker schedule, the Warhorses had posted an excellent 13-3 record. But they were no match for the Indians. Milan gave the Warhorses an 84-47 spanking, scoring 22 points in each of the first and fourth quarters, the last 22 using all subs after leading 62-32 at the end of three. All five Milan starters scored in double figures, led by Bob Engel's 25. In fact, Engel was on something of a scoring tear since he had his hair cut in a burr, the style favored by Bobby and some of the other Indians. "We called him 'Curly,'" Bobby said. "Actually, I really did have curly hair, but nobody ever knew it because I always had a burr cut."

Milan finished the regular season with a 37-15 trouncing of

Osgood. The win elevated their record to 16-4. More important, it was at this game that Coach Wood chose to unveil the cat and mouse offense the team had been practicing.

As is apparent from the scores during the season, the Indians were a high-scoring bunch. It wasn't unusual for them to score in the 70s or even the 80s. Teams tried playing a slow-down game against them, which may have given Coach Wood the idea for what would become his most infamous and deadly weapon.

Actually, he'd learned it the same place he'd learned the continuity offense that had been working so well: at Butler University, from Tony Hinkle.

This was the offense people remember from Milan, an offense designed for a different era, before shot clocks and five-second calls, to pull the other team out of their zone. The play would begin with Bobby Plump holding the ball at the top of the key, with the other four players spread out to the four corners on their end of the court: Wendelman and White on the base line, Truitt and Engel at half court. Bobby's job was to hold the ball until he had an open pass to one of the corners, then cut to the basket for a return pass and a shot. If he wasn't open, he would take a corner and the play would start all over again. "It wasn't really a slow-down game. We used the cat and mouse as an offensive weapon," Wood said.

"I thought we had the personnel to make it work. You have to have quick, unselfish guards who are good ballhandlers. They have to be able to score, but they have to be able to give it up, too. When the defense came at us, they gave us scoring opportunities like you wouldn't believe. If they didn't come at us, we just held the ball. We worked on it in practice to the point that, as soon as there was a double-team, we could get the ball to the open man," said Wood.

Wood thought the Osgood game would be the perfect time to put his new offensive weapon into practice. The Indians had already beaten Osgood earlier in the season. But the Cowboys had a tough team, with big, experienced players including Jack Bradshaw, John Henry Wolford, and Rom Schroder. "We were playing in their tiny little gym, and I didn't want those big horses banging our kids into the walls. We thought a delay tactic might make the game less physical," Wood said.

As it happened, the game was moved to Tyson Auditorium in Versailles at the last minute. But Coach Wood decided he wanted to see the cat and mouse, anyway.

The Indians took a commanding 26-10 lead in the first quarter, but the game was getting a little too rough for Marvin Wood. He called time out and told them to run the cat and mouse.

It worked better than anyone ever expected. The Cowboys touched the ball just three times in the entire third quarter. The Indians won handily, and the Osgood fans were livid. But there was nothing illegal or underhanded about the cat and mouse. The Milan Indians had a dangerous new trick in their bag.

Things had changed dramatically in Milan in just a few months. The fans were ready for the state tournament. The Downtown Coaches Club, so skeptical of Coach Marvin Wood at the start of the season, were on the verge of becoming true believers. But no one could have prepared them for the dose of Hoosier Hysteria that lay just ahead.

And, for the second year in a row, the Milan Indians nearly had to play in the tournament without their star, Bobby Plump. But this year, it wasn't the flu that threatened to keep Bobby away. It was love.

CHAPTER SEVEN

THE ROAD
TO INDIANAPOLIS

Before the Astrodome, before the Superdome, before the Kingdome and Skydome and Market Square Arena and the RCA Dome, there was Butler Fieldhouse. When it was constructed in 1928, Butler Fieldhouse was not just the largest basketball venue in Indiana, but the largest indoor arena in the world.

Even with the likes of Indiana and Purdue and Notre Dame in the state, the "Big Barn" at Butler University in Indianapolis had a mystique all its own. Some Indianapolis teams were used to playing there. But, come tournament time, Butler Fieldhouse was different and special. Playing as a high schooler at Butler meant you had arrived in the big time, whether you were playing in a sectional, regional, or semistate tournament. And if you made it all the way to the Final Four, playing at Butler meant that your team was one of the best of the 755 high school varsity basketball teams in the state.

For the Milan Indians, Butler meant getting to at least the Sweet Sixteen and the semistate tournament. Which meant getting to the regional tournament in Rushville. Which meant first getting out of the tough Versailles Sectional. Which meant making sure all of their stars — including Bobby Plump — were aboard.

That was not, as the saying goes, a slam dunk. Bobby Plump was having girl troubles that made basketball seem trivial.

Although Bobby was a leader on the basketball floor, he had always been bashful around girls. But that changed when he met Jo Anne Steinmetz, whose father Harold was a dentist in Milan, in his sophomore year. "Ronnie Truitt told me he thought she'd like to have a date with me, so I asked her out," Bobby said. "Sure enough, Ronnie was right — much to my surprise."

The two became inseparable. Bobby and Jo Anne dated seriously for more than a year, and Bobby was as deeply in love as a 17-year-old boy could be. "We were going to get married. Everybody told us so, anyway," he said.

Apparently, Jo Anne wasn't quite so certain. She decided she wanted to date other boys — one boy in particular, who just happened to be a star player on the Aurora basketball team. Bobby was crushed, and it showed in practice.

"I could see Bobby was hurting," said Coach Clarence Kelly. "He wasn't smiling. He was moping around, just going through the motions. That was not the Bobby Plump we knew — certainly not the Bobby Plump we needed for the tournament."

Kelly had a sharp eye for such details. Unlike a lot of other folks in Southern Indiana, the 26-year-old assistant's first love was not basketball. He was primarily a track coach, who later that year actually built a track at Milan High School so his team could compete. But Kelly was an excellent scout. Every week, he'd prepare his reserve squad to scrimmage in the style of the varsity Indians' upcoming opponent. More than one Milan player has remarked that the reason the team was so good was that it practiced against the second best team in the county — one that was always prepared to give the varsity a tough challenge.

Prior to the tournament, Coach Kelly concentrated on helping big Jim Wendelman toughen up for the opponents he'd face. "Jim was a big, powerful farm boy who was terribly tender-hearted. I tried to turn him into an animal," Kelly said. He succeeded, at least partially; in that year's tournament, big Jim crashed the boards like a madman.

But it was Kelly's scouting sense that noticed Bobby's funk. He decided he and the Indians' star guard needed to have a talk. He called Bobby aside, and the two walked up into the stands and sat down. What he found was that Bobby wasn't just depressed about the state of his relationship with Jo Anne Steinmetz: he was actually ready to quit the team.

Kelly wouldn't hear of it. "I told him that if he quit, Milan wouldn't go very far in the tournament, and he'd be just another clodbuster — another nobody from nowhere. But if he took the team and led them, they might actually have a chance to do something great."

Bobby took the talk to heart. "Coach Kelly let me know it wasn't worth quitting the team over a girl. I guess it kind of woke me up," Bobby said.

With Bobby back in form, the team was ready to go. They had their innovative new cat-and-mouse offense. And they had some new defensive tricks, too.

Marvin Wood had discovered the zone defense. And he had taken it in entirely new directions. Building on the zone he learned from

Marc Combs, Wood created full court and half court zone traps that stifled opposing offenses.

"From Marc Combs, I learned that you can do lots of different things with zones. In most zones, all five players guard the ball. But I learned that you could play zones where you guarded the player in your area, kind of a man-to-man within a zone.

"And a coach has to dream. You think about your players and what they can do, and you try to design a game plan that capitalizes on their strengths. I thought of the zone traps based on what we could do. You have to be quick and aggressive up front, and you have to have guys who can make good, intelligent reads in the back. We had both," Wood said.

The Indians worked hard on their "double up and cover up" trapping defense. "They liked it, and they were darn good at it," Wood said.

Milan also had another secret weapon, and Marc Combs had something to do with this one, too. Often, noisy partisan basketball crowds are referred to as the team's "sixth man." If that is true, Combs was Milan's "seventh man."

"We used to have Marc sit down at the other end of the gym, opposite the bench. This way, we could have coaches at both ends of the floor," Wood said.

Emotions — and expectations — were running high in Milan. Were the Indians good enough to bury the ghosts of sectionals past and move to the next level?

Of the nine teams competing in the Versailles Sectional in 1953, only Milan and Batesville remain today. The others — the Napoleon Bearcats, New Marion Panthers, Cross Plains Wildcats, Holton Warhorses, Osgood Cowboys, Sunman Tigers, and Versailles Lions — are only memories, victims of school consolidations that created schools with such prosaic names as South Ripley, Jac-Cen-Del, and East Central. But these schools were very real in 1953, and filled with fresh-faced, cleared-eyed young men, all of whom dreamt of hitting a winning shot, of cutting down the nets in victory to the delight of a capacity crowd of screaming fans.

For most of them, the dream met a steamroller named Milan. In a two-day span, Coach Wood's boys used their new cat-and-mouse offense to flatten three good opponents, holding them to an average of just 20 points a game.

First up was Holton. The Warhorses tried to turn the tables on the Indians, and came out holding the ball successfully for four minutes. "Teams started to do that. They figured if they kept it close, they had a chance to beat us," Bobby said.

Not on this night. The Indians played cat and mouse to perfection and handled the Warhorses 27-15.

The next afternoon, Milan met Osgood again. The Cowboys had been the very first victims of Milan's stall tactics. They figured they knew how to defense it this time around. They figured wrong. The Indians picked apart the Osgood defense with their four-corner play and led 30-16 before shifting into high gear. Milan 51, Osgood 23.

The victory set up the match everyone expected that evening: The upstart Indians versus the long-time champion Batesville Bulldogs. For three years in a row, Milan had lost to Batesville in the sectional tournament. This year, it was a different story. Bobby Plump led the way as the Indians built a ten-point lead, then pulled out the cat and mouse to shut down the Bulldogs in the fourth quarter. Milan won handily, 42-27.

The Milan fans were ecstatic. Coach Wood and the boys had done what only one other Milan team had done since 1936: they'd won the Versailles Sectional and were on their way to Rushville. And, although they had never won a game in the regional tournament, their chances looked awfully good in 1953. In the first round, Milan drew tiny Morton Memorial, a school for orphans in northern Rush County with a total enrollment of fewer than 100 students. Suddenly, Milan found itself in the uncharacteristic role of "the big school."

The Morton Memorial Tigers had never won a sectional championship before. This was not going to be the night they would win their first regional game, either. But they probably should have. For years afterward, the Indians would be chastised for "cheating those poor orphans." Here's how it happened:

The gym at Rushville High School was filled with Morton Memorial rooters that night. The plucky Tigers kept the game close for three quarters. When they took a one-point lead into the final quarter, the crowd went wild.

And Plump and Company went cold. With 1:55 to play, the Tigers were up by nine, 45-36. It looked as though the Indians would keep their perfect, never-winning regional record intact.

About this time, Bobby Plump was at the free throw line. He hit one of his two shots to cut the Tiger lead to eight.

To get more quickness on the floor, Coach Wood substituted Ray Craft for senior Ralph Preble. The Indians' full-court, double-teaming press was on.

Unfortunately for the Tigers, the clock was not.

Bobby remembers the crowd, and even the Morton Memorial coaches and players, screaming. But he didn't know why. It might well have been because of the Indians' trapping defense, he figured. Their full-court pressing defense was unusual in the early '50s. Maybe the fans had never seen anything like it before. In any case, Bobby didn't realize that the Rushville High School official game clock hadn't started.

The clock may not have been working. But the Milan trap worked to perfection. Bobby stole the ball, was fouled, and hit both free throws. Morton 45, Milan 39.

Finally, after hearing the Tiger fans and coaches and reserve players on the sidelines going crazy trying to attract an official's attention, the official timer realized that the game clock wasn't working. The plug had apparently been kicked out of its socket. People estimated that about 20 seconds of playing time had elapsed while the clock stood still. The Morton Memorial coaches threw a fit, arguing with the referees for nearly 15 minutes. But, because the officials hadn't noted the time, there was nothing anyone could do but start the clock again. The Tigers had most certainly been gypped, and their fans kept the uproar at fever pitch for the less than two minutes remaining in the game.

The referee blew his whistle to start the game. Much to the fans' indignant delight, the clock started, as well. Milan put on the press. This time, Gene White intercepted a pass and found Bobby open down the floor. Bobby hit a short jump shot. Morton 45, Milan 41, with 1:35 on the clock.

The Indians' defense was really starting to rattle the Tigers. They turned the ball over on a traveling violation. Ray Craft sliced through the lane for a bucket to cut the lead to two. At the other end, Morton's King answered with two free throws. Bobby responded with another basket. And again, Morton responded. Roy Wheeler hit two free throws. Morton 49, Milan 45, with less than a minute remaining.

Then the Tigers' Glen Stouder made a calculated move. He fouled Milan guard Bill Jordan — probably the least experienced free throw shooter on the floor — with 25 seconds on the clock.

The pressure was incredible. But Jordan was its equal. Carefully, he eyed the bucket. He shot.

Good.

Again, Jordan lined up for his shot. Again, he hit. The Morton Memorial lead was only two.

Now the fans were on their feet. The Tigers needed only to hold the ball to give their school the biggest victory in its history. But as the final seconds ticked, Gene White stole the ball. He quickly passed to Ray Craft, whose shot at the buzzer tied the game 49-49 at the end of regulation play.

In overtime, the Indians went to the cat and mouse. Bobby and his teammates held the ball for four minutes before finding Ray Craft for an easy basket. At the other end of the floor, King hit two clutch free throws for the Tigers. The overtime period ended with the score tied again, this time at 51-51.

According to IHSAA rules, the second overtime would be sudden death. The first team to score two points would win. Obviously, controlling the tip was critical.

Jim Wendelman, adrenaline pumping, went high in the air and tipped the ball to Bobby. Bobby held it for 1:45, looking for an opening. He made his move for the bucket and was fouled going up for the shot.

First free throw: swish. Now the crowd was on its feet again, and you could have heard a pin drop. It was Bobby's twentieth point of the afternoon. Just one more would make the difference.

Cool as a cucumber, Bobby put it up and through. Milan had won its first-ever regional game with a full-court press, mental toughness, cool shooting, and a little bit of extraordinary luck.

And it was only the beginning of a wild and wooly day at Rushville. In the second game, Connersville, ranked sixth in the state, beat Aurora, one of only four teams that had defeated Milan all year.

The Spartans had a "beautiful" team, according to Marvin Wood. And the Connersville fans smelled blood. Surely, this team that, but for a twist of fate should have lost to a bunch of orphans were no match for their Spartans. The Spartan fans began filling up the Rushville gym early that evening, in spite of the late winter storm that was covering the area with a heavy blanket of snow and ice. They didn't care. After all, they were on their way to the Big Barn, Butler Fieldhouse.

There was just one problem: they would first have to go through Marvin Wood and his Milan Indians. Milan came out in the first quarter and immediately employed the cat and mouse offense. During one stretch, Bobby held the ball for four minutes. Milan led 8-4 at the buzzer.

The second quarter brought more of the same. After a missed shot by Connersville, Bobby held the ball for nearly the entire period. The Indians stood in their corners. Engel and Truitt and the rest of the Indians waved their arms just to keep them loose.

"We were just doing what Coach Wood told us to do. He was calm. He figured if we could keep them from running, we could win. It was one of the few times we actually just stood there, without moving," Bobby said.

The Connersville fans were as irate as the Morton Memorial fans had been earlier in the day. They screamed. They spit. They threw paper, coins, and anything else they had in their pockets. "If I'm not mistaken, Ronnie Truitt took home some spending money from his forward position," Bobby joked.

Finally, just before the half, Bobby found a lane to the basket and scored. At the intermission, Milan lead, 10-4. The Indians exited the floor quickly and ran to the locker room under a hail of debris and a chorus of boos and name-calling by the crowd from Connersville.

In the third quarter, the Spartans found some success. The quarter ended with Milan ahead by only two, 17-15.

The Indians played cat and mouse with renewed vigor in the fourth. But the Spartans were relentless. Their press forced some poor decision-making by the Indians, and a see-saw battle ensued. After six lead changes, with little more than two minutes to play, the Spartans held the ball and a slim 22-20 lead.

But Milan would not be denied. Bob Engel stole the ball to get it back in the Indians' hands. Ray Craft hit a shot from far outside to tie the game. At the other end, Ron Truitt snagged a rebound and again found Ray Craft open for a pass. Craft buried a shot from the base line to give the Indians a 24-22 lead. Those two baskets were Craft's only points of the night. As it turned out, they were plenty.

There was still a lot of time left for Connersville to come back. But a missed shot and another Ronnie Truitt rebound sealed the Milan victory. Bobby Plump tied for game-high scoring honors with Larry Alexander of Connersville, who would be his future teammate at Butler University.

The crowd erupted, Milan fans in delight, Connersville fans in disgust. The Indians celebrated all the way to the showers. Tom Kohlmeier and Bill Steinmetz, who starred for Milan's 1946 sectional championship squad, joined the boys in the shower with their suits on. "They were just grinning," Bobby said. "We were all as happy as we could be."

Back home, the fans who couldn't make it to the game had braved the cold to listen to the radio broadcast through loudspeakers in downtown Milan. After the victory, they organized two bonfires to celebrate. Most of the returning fans and players never saw those bonfires. By the time they found their way home from Rushville through the snowstorm, it was two a.m.

Not to worry. The entire week would be one big party. The local newspaper called it "Milan's greatest week since being founded in 1854." The other newspapers in the region sat up and took notice, too. Soon Milan was being invaded by the *The Indianapolis Star* and *News, The Cincinnati Enquirer* and *Post* and *Times-Star,* and *The Louisville Courier-Journal,* all asking the same question: Who was this upstart giant-killer with the unusual four-corner offense?

They were the Milan Indians. They had made their way through a tough sectional and an even tougher regional. Now they were going to the Big City to compete with the Big Boys at the Big Barn.

CHAPTER EIGHT

THE BIG BARN

Bobby Plump will never forget his first trip to Butler Fieldhouse with the Milan Indians. It seemed huge, with 15,000 empty seats reaching upward in all directions, so high you could hardly see the top. "Most of the guys had never even been to Indianapolis before. We went up there for practice on a Friday. We were just in awe when we walked in. Finally, one of the guys on the team said, 'You could put a lot of hay in here.' Everybody laughed. That comment broke the ice," Bobby said.

With only 156 students, Milan was the smallest school in the Sweet Sixteen. But once again, it looked as if they'd gotten an easy draw. In their opening Indianapolis Semistate game, they'd play Attica, an unknown team from far across the state. But the Indians would have to wait for the tournament's opening game and biggest draw. The two powerhouses in the tournament — the Shelbyville Golden Bears and Indianapolis Crispus Attucks Tigers — would be playing each other in the first game of the day.

Shelbyville was no stranger to the Sweet Sixteen. Under renowned coach Frank Barnes, the Golden Bears had won the state championship just six years earlier behind future Indiana University great Bill Garrett, the first African-American player in the Big Ten Conference. That year, they'd upset undefeated Terre Haute Garfield, a team that featured Clyde Lovellette, who later starred at the University of Kansas and in the National Industrial Basketball League (NIBL). Later still, Lovellette had a great career in the NBA with the Minneapolis and Los Angeles Lakers.

On the other side, Attucks was building one of the most dominating programs in the history of Indiana high school basketball under coach Ray Crowe. Crowe's teams would win state championships in 1955 and 1956 with an almost unbelievable 62-1 record. In 1952, the Tigers were led by Hallie Bryant and Bailey "Flap" Robertson, Jr., whose little brother Oscar, just a freshman, was honing the skills that would make him one of the best college and professional players ever to compete in the game of basketball.

Attucks was the favorite. But Shelbyville prevailed on this day, 46-44, thanks to Frank Barnes's great game plan and a questionable foul call late in the game.

To meet the Golden Bears, Milan would have to get past the Attica

Ramblers. Easier said than done. Despite their size advantage, the Indians had trouble with Attica's determination and quickness. At the half, the game was tied at 29. The contest stayed close throughout the second half and was tied again, at 45, when Bobby Plump began holding the ball with just 3:10 on the clock. He held it.

And held it.

And held it. The clock kept ticking, winding down toward zero.

Still, Bobby held the ball.

And, with six seconds remaining, arched a shot toward the basket.

And missed.

"Hey, they don't always go in," Bobby said. "That was just a warm up for next year."

Attica missed a chance to win. For the second time in their run for the championship, the Indians found themselves in overtime.

The Indians played their trademark cat-and-mouse game. It was too much for Attica. Late in overtime, Gene White's two free throws sealed the victory, 49-48. Plump, White, and Bob Engel combined for all but nine of the Milan points.

The nearly 2,000 Milan fans in the stands were delirious. Their Indians had made it to the Indianapolis Semistate finals. But the press knew — and surely even some of the stoutest of Milan faithful suspected — that this would be the end of the line for the Indians. Surely the nightcap featuring Milan versus the powerful Shelbyville Golden Bears would hardly be a game — and might even be the biggest blowout of the century.

In fact, it was hardly a game. Milan clobbered the Bears, 43-21, in what might have been the biggest surprise of the century.

Big Jim Wendelman, never a big scoring threat, dominated the Bears on the boards. Early in the game, he pinned a Jim Plymate shot against the backboard. The crowd gasped. Wendelman showed the Bears who was boss inside, and they didn't test the lane much for the rest of the night.

Bobby led all scorers with 16 points. But the most shocking statistic of all belonged to the Golden Bears. They managed only two baskets from the field the entire game — still an IHSAA semistate tournament record for futility.

Here's how Bunny Shot (actually a pseudonym for sportswriter Leroy Hartford) told it in *The Cincinnati Enquirer:*

> What the Indians did to Shelbyville just shouldn't happen to a regional winner. They passed the Bears dizzy, opening up holes that from the press row looked big enough for a truck to go through. Led by Jim Wendelman, they swept both backboards. Generaled by Bob Plump, they had the Bears driving and stumbling in efforts to break up the passing game. And the fans at the fieldhouse love it. . .all except Shelbyville.

This time, with no snowstorm to slow them down, the people of Milan put on a celebration the likes of which Southern Indiana had rarely seen — a celebration without the Indians' players and coaches. "Coach Wood told us to put off the celebration until we lost or we won it all. He wanted to keep things low key. It was pretty smart," Bobby said.

Meanwhile, the Milan bandwagon was growing bigger and bigger. People from Osgood and Versailles and Batesville and all over Ripley County, who just weeks ago were the archest of Milan rivals, now claimed the Indians as their own. Newspapers across the county bragged about the Cinderella story and the upcoming "ball" in Indianapolis. Milan resident Will Haney, who owned the local movie theatre and the Dairy Moo and held a patent on a tap shoe called the "Haney Shoe," gave the rest of the state a taste of where the Indians were coming from in a letter to *The Indianapolis Star:*

> Milan is 39 miles west of Cincinnati on the main line of the B&O St. Louis-to-New York, with commuting trains daily to Cincinnati. . .Milan is on Highway 101 and 350, has a fine school and a heck of a good basketball team. It is a rich farming community. Most of the people work at the distilleries, Fisher Body in Hamilton, O., and the Jefferson Proving Grounds in Madison. The Milan Bank is so full that they will rebuild this spring. There is no poverty in Milan; everybody has plenty of money, new cars and fine homes.

The letter was a bit overzealous. But it was indicative of the sentiment this team inspired in its community. Daily McCoy, the man who introduced basketball in the Milan schools back in 1914, wrote a letter to *The Versailles Republican* to remind the Indians' players and coaching staff that they were carrying on a long winning tradition. His team had been the first Ripley County team to play in the state tournament, losing to eventual state champion Wingate and their star player, Homer Stonebraker. McCoy conjured up the names of past Milan greats: Tommy Thompson, Toner Overly, Arthur Allen, Wallace Rupp, Chris Volz. Would this new batch of Indians be able to add their names to this pantheon? Only time would tell. But in the meantime, "it's Milan for me and my house," McCoy wrote.

The Final Four teams were set for the 50th running of the Indiana high school basketball finals. Milan (24-4) would face South Bend Central (22-5). Terre Haute Gerstmeyer (30-3) would take on Richmond (24-4). All of the teams were loaded with talent. South Bend Central had Jack Quiggle, later a star at Michigan State. Gerstmeyer featured the twin attack of Arley and Harley Andrews and their uncle, Harold Andrews. Richmond built its team around a football player named Lamar Lundy. Lundy was later a star for the Purdue Boilermakers before beginning his NFL career as part of the Los Angeles Rams' Fearsome Foursome defensive line with Merlin Olson, Roosevelt Greer, and Deacon Jones.

The town of Milan staged a huge pep rally to send the boys off to Indianapolis. They didn't send them off alone, either. Thousands of Milan fans accompanied them, their cars decorated with signs and streamers. But Coach Wood was careful not to let the fans' overconfidence spill over onto the team. He checked his Indians into the Pennsylvania Hotel and kept the fans away while he attended the Coaches' Banquet. The boys ate at the Apex Grill at Pennsylvania and 16th Street — steaks for all of the boys. Gene White claimed it was perhaps the first steak dinner he'd ever had, and it was certainly the biggest.

As careful as Marvin Wood had been to keep the fans at bay, he certainly kicked himself later for not being a little more careful with the Indians themselves. His team was loose. Maybe too loose.

After dinner, one of the Indians broke out squirt guns. The squirt gun battle quickly degenerated into an all-out water fight, with glasses of water the heavy artillery of choice. The casualties: team manager Fred Busching chipped a tooth and had to be taken to an Indianapolis dentist. Another boy cut his foot on broken glass.

And the wounded kept piling up. The next morning, another Indian closed his hand in a trunk lid. In pre-game warm-ups, Bobby collided with a teammate, leaving both a bit woozy.

These events did nothing to instill confidence in Coach Wood. "And I thought I let the boys down. Here we were at the Final Four, and I let the boys get out of control. I should have stayed with them and made sure they were focused on the game."

But here they were. South Bend Central was a big school with an extremely talented team. The Indians were going to have to play the game of their lives to win this one.

It was not to be. After the Indians controlled the tip, Bobby was fouled and made a free throw to give Milan a 1-0 lead. It was to be their only lead of the game. The Indians were ice cold, hitting just five of 21 shots in the first half. The second half wasn't much better. Bobby had a game-high 19 points, but South Bend Central had balance, poise, and a great game plan. At the final buzzer, the scoreboard read South Bend Central 56, Milan 37.

Central would go on to win the state championship that night. While the boys from Milan watched, South Bend Central edged Terre Haute Gerstmeyer 42-41 in one of the hardest-fought, most memorable games in tournament history. Certainly, the Indians felt some disappointment as the winner and runner-up were awarded their rings. They were going home with nothing but memories.

Bobby Plump will never forget his first Final Four appearance. "I didn't feel like I had a very good game. They beat the heck out of us, and it was very difficult to take. I can still remember the names of their entire starting lineup: Harvey, Wiltrout, Schafer, Molnar, and Quiggle. It's one of the few starting fives I can remember."

Yet, the memories were pretty special in and of themselves. A Final Four team from a small town such as Milan was incredible, something that might happen only once in a lifetime, if that often. Going into the season, the fans' fondest hopes were to win the county tournament, and maybe the sectional. The rest had been unimaginable. Ralph Preble, who was a senior on the 1952-53 Indians, said that, in many ways, this team was even more remarkable than the one that followed. "It was the first time for all of us. It was all new to us. It paved the way for what followed."

What followed immediately was a huge banquet in the team's honor, with more than 2,000 fans and well-wishers. The featured speaker was Indiana University Coach Branch McCracken, who had just led his team to the 1953 NCAA championship. Even Bobby Plump had to smile.

"After it was all over, we felt great. Nobody from Milan had ever done anything like that before. It was excellent," he said.

Sportswriter Tiny Hunt agreed:
We know that all the citizens of Ripley County want to congratulate the Milan basketball team for putting Milan and Ripley County on the front pages of every newspaper in Indiana and bringing glory to their school and town that could not be bought at any price.

That was what followed immediately. But there were even greater things ahead.

"There isn't any question that, without that season and the experience we gained, we could never have come back in 1954. It gave us the background we needed. We'd been to the Big Barn. It was like the hardening of steel," Bobby said.

The boys Marc Combs and Snort Grinstead had shaped into basketball players were refined to a whole new level of brilliance by Marvin Wood. The good news was that most of them would be back for another season, another run for the roses. The big question was, would Coach Wood return at the helm, or would the school board give him the same sort of treatment they'd given Snort Grinstead?

CHAPTER NINE

THE MAKING
OF A CHAMPION

What's a town to do when its pride and joy, its boys, have exceeded all expectations and brought glory to the community? What's a kid to do after he's been to the mountain and nearly scaled its heights? If your town is Milan, Indiana, you take a couple of minutes to bask in the glory, then take care of business the same as you always have — with maybe just a touch of renewed pride in who you are and where you're from. And if you're a kid like Bobby Plump, you do what most of the other players on the Milan High School Final Four basketball team are doing: you go out for track and field.

Spring, 1953. Clarence Kelly built his track and his track team, whose star was not a basketball player but a local speedster named Jimmy Nickell. Bobby competed in the 100- and 440-yard dashes and the broad jump and was on the mile relay team. "A lot of those boys who played basketball were excellent track athletes, as well," said Kelly, who was dismayed to lose Bob Engel and Ronnie Truitt; they quit the team after sitting through a downpour in Lawrenceburg at the season's first meet.

Spring segued into summer. If Bobby Plump had been a star today, no doubt summer would have meant basketball camps and all kinds of off-season events to show off his skills. But those kinds of things simply didn't exist in 1953.

"I didn't know what a Nike camp was. Didn't know what a Nike shoe was, for that matter," Bobby laughed. "If you didn't have Converse All-Stars, you wouldn't play. I thought those cloth hightops were the greatest shoes in the world.

"Who knows? Maybe if we'd gone to some camps, we'd have been able to accomplish something our junior year," Bobby joked.

No camps. No gyms. No personal trainers or conditioning programs. Summer in Pierceville was an echo of summers past. During the day, the boys worked in the fields and played baseball. At night, they hung the lights outside Schroder's or Butte's and played basketball. Bobby's weightlifting program was pitching hay.

And there was time with Dad — precious time. Lester Plump was still working at A.D. Cook, still attending his Lutheran church at Stumpke's Corner, but still committed to family and community — so committed that, years later, when the little Methodist church in

Pierceville was about to be closed, it was Lester Plump who spearheaded the drive to save it.

That was another side of Lester Plump that everyone in the area knew. This man who had sacrificed so much for his family always had time for his community, as well. For many years, he served as the local precinct committeeman for the Republican party. "Even though he was a Republican, Dad used to send Bill and Les out to pick up everyone and get them in to vote. It didn't matter which party they voted. He just believed in the process and thought everyone should be involved. We often had ballot boxes lying around the house," Bobby said.

These days, there was more room for ballot boxes. Dot and Bill and Les still lived at home. But Bobby's other two sisters, Ginny and Esther, were married and moved away — Ginny to Bill Schwing, the Lawrenceburg boy she'd dated in high school, and Esther to Floyd Heidorn, a local farm boy. Fewer people in the house didn't mean that extra money was much easier to come by; even with Lester's good, steady job and help from Bill and Les, the Plumps were still far, far from financial security. "I remember once asking my dad for an allowance. I told him that some of the other guys in Pierceville had one and wanted to know if we could talk about it. Dad said, 'Sure, we can talk about it, but you're not going to get one. I just don't have any money, Bobby.'"

And Bobby needed a little money every now and then. After his long-time relationship with Jo Anne Steinmetz fell apart, Bobby started dating Nancy Sue Ratts, a cheerleader at Osgood High School. Drive-in movies were a popular and inexpensive date, paid for with money made delivering papers and working for the neighbors. Bobby and Nancy Sue also spent hours on the phone, which was an especially tough trick, since the Plumps still didn't have telephone service. "Schroders and Buttes did, though. I spent a lot of time at their houses," Bobby said.

Things were happening over in Milan, as well. Clarence Kelly, who had lived a bachelor life his first year in town with a rented room at Mr. Michaels' for $9 a week, was married to Jean Ferguson of Zionsville. The newlyweds moved to an apartment over the hardware store in Moores Hill. Kelly received a small pay raise, and assured the school board he'd be back to teach and coach in the fall.

Keeping Marvin Wood was going to be a little trickier. Although few around Milan knew it at the time, there were more than a few openings for a young, aggressive, successful basketball coach in Indiana.

"I had a lot of opportunities. But I had all those guys coming back. I thought it was going to be something worthwhile," Wood said.

Local people in the know were concerned about keeping their coach. Although Wood received a modest raise, others in the community offered to supplement his income with cash and gifts. He refused them all, although once when he and the family were away, they returned home to find that someone had installed a new washer and dryer. "All I knew was that the old ones were gone. I went down to the hardware store to find out what had happened, but they pretended they didn't know," Wood said.

But Coach Wood had already made up his mind. "I figured another year at Milan couldn't hurt anything."

Not that he was thinking about a state championship. "A coach has to be realistic in his thinking. I thought maybe we'd win another sectional and hopefully another regional and, if the ball bounced right, maybe we could go a little further. I couldn't fathom going all the way. Of course, everybody in the town knew we were going to win it all. Everybody but the coach."

In the fall of 1953, Marvin Wood coached many of his basketball stars as Milan High School baseball players. Their soft gloves and sharp bats, combined with the moundsmanship of Bobby Plump, Bill Jordan, Dale Smith, and others, made them virtually unbeatable.

But this was Indiana, and baseball was not basketball, especially not in a town that had tasted so much success on the hardwood and had so much talent returning. The Downtown Coaches kept Arkenburg's warm on cool autumn nights with hot speculation and high expectations for the season ahead.

And why wouldn't they? From the 1953 Final Four team, the Indians were losing only Jim Wendelman, Ralph Preble, and Jim Call. Nine varsity players were returning — led by Bobby Plump, who was back for his third season in the Milan backcourt.

"He was the best drag dribbler I ever saw. He could dribble with either hand and shoot with either hand," said Clarence Kelly. "He also had one of the fastest first steps I've ever seen. And he had huge hands."

"Great hands. Soft hands. And quick feet," Marc Combs agreed. "And he did whatever you wanted him to do. He never hogged the ball. Bobby always wanted to be the best, and he worked hard at it."

"Bobby Plump was a leader — the hub around which the wheel revolved. The greatest thing about Bobby Plump was that he made everyone else on the floor so much better. His leadership actually created problems sometimes. Everyone on both teams knew Bobby was the go-to guy. So our opponents would do everything they could to stop him. And in tough spots, our guys did everything they could to get him the ball, often when they should have been looking for the open man," said Marvin Wood.

Bob Engel had played the other guard position in the 1952-53 season. He was a fearless rebounder who knew how to cut and drive the lane. He also had a devastating two-hand set shot from outside. "He was an outstanding ballplayer, an excellent perimeter shooter and a great board man. He could open up the middle of the floor just by scoring from the outside," Wood said.

But Coach Wood had different plans for Bob Engel. Wood coveted the speed of Ray Craft at guard, but didn't want to lose Engel's basketball skills and on-floor leadership. So he asked Engel if he would move to forward.

It was no small sacrifice. The Indians' offense was guard-oriented. A move to forward most likely meant less shooting and scoring, less time in the spotlight. But Bob Engel was first and foremost a team player.

"Coach Wood said, 'I can't take the position away from you. You've earned it. But I'm asking you to play forward.' So I did it. I wanted to do whatever I could to benefit the team," Engel said.

"Bob Engel was especially dangerous because he could play two positions. And he always had a little smirk on his face — like he knew he was better than the guy he was playing against. He knew he could beat him," said Clarence Kelly.

Engel's move to forward left the other guard spot open for Ray Craft. "He was a brilliant passer and a great stutter-step dribbler," Kelly remembered.

"Ray's feet were so quick, he'd get traveling calls," said Marc Combs.

Marvin Wood saw something else in Ray Craft: smarts. "Ray knew that everyone was going to double up on Plump. He knew how to read it and take advantage of it. And he was a good shooter."

At the other forward spot, the Indians had a senior who'd started every game his junior year: Ronnie Truitt. "He was good from all over, but he was death from down in the corner," Clarence Kelly said. "That's the hardest shot in basketball."

Marc Combs was impressed with Truitt's floor sense. "Ronnie had great anticipation. He always knew where he needed to be on the floor."

"Ronnie couldn't get both feet off the floor at the same time," Marvin Wood laughed. "But he played big. He had long arms, and he was always in position."

That left only the center spot to be filled — no small task, with the loss of big Jim Wendelman. Coach Wood had no one of Jim's size to play inside. Fortunately, he did have Gene White's brains and heart. "Gene was four inches shorter than Jim, but he was brilliant. His basketball skills were only average. But he was a very good rebounder and a leader on the floor," said Clarence Kelly.

"Gene was like having a coach on the floor," Wood said. "He could tell you everything the other team was trying to do offensively and defensively. And he could make suggestions about what we could do. Gene was just an extremely intelligent ballplayer."

In addition to these five players, who would start most of the year for the Indians, Coach Wood had Bill Jordan, Roger Schroder, and Jim Wendelman's little brother Ken returning. "These kids played virtually mistake-free basketball," said Marc Combs. "They all could have started for most other teams in the state."

"Jordan was big and physical, and a good shooter. Roger Schroder was steady as a clock, and would have started if not for the fact that he played behind Plump and Craft. And we used Ken Wendelman a lot. He was a position player, quick and tough. He was a key performer in our zone traps," said Coach Wood.

Dale Smith, who played a reserve guard position on the Indians' Final Four team as a junior, failed to make the team his senior year. That left four spots open. When basketball practice began October 1,

Coach Wood had another 18 boys who thought they had the right stuff. The four who eventually made the team were two juniors, Bob Wichman, whose family had just moved to town from Flora, Missouri, that summer, and Ken Delap; and two sophomores, Rollin Cutter and Bobby Plump's Pierceville pal Glen Butte.

"Bob Wichman and Ken Delap were extremely valuable to us. They didn't get a lot of playing time, but they always gave us tough competition in practice that helped us prepare.

"Rollin Cutter was steady and dependable, a strong rebounder and a good defensive player. And Glen was very talented. He was a great shooter from anywhere on the floor, and an excellent passer," Coach Wood said.

This was not a team that needed a lot of coaching, said Clarence Kelly. "I think they could have coached themselves and won the championship. They were smart, skilled, unselfish players. They weren't greedy. They looked out for each other."

That they did, on the court and off. Bobby and the kids from Pierceville — Glen, Gene, and Roger — were always tight. They knew what it meant to play in Milan, a place they hadn't always felt welcome not so very long ago.

Ray Craft, Rollin Cutter, and Ken Wendelman were farm boys who lived north of town. They often made the long walk home together after basketball practice. "Ray walked to school in the morning, sometimes, too. He'd sometimes miss the bus if his chores took too long," said Milan resident Tootie Herbst.

Bill Jordan, Bob Engel, and Ronnie Truitt lived in Milan, and Bob and Ronnie were long-time best friends. They knew what it meant to look out for each other, because both shared one important trait with Bobby Plump: they were both from single-parent households.

Bob Engel and his older brother and sister grew up in an apartment in downtown Milan, over the beauty shop his mother owned. "She used to work six days a week, ten hours a day or more," Tootie Herbst said. "All the kids had chores to do to help out around the house."

Bob's father left the family just after Bob was born. He never even saw his father until he showed up at a game during the Indians' championship run in 1953.

But Bob's father came around now and again. "Once Bob's dad showed up for one of our games when Bob was a sophomore," said Marc Combs. "He and Snort Grinstead were friendly, and Engel's dad came and asked if it was okay for him to come and watch his son play ball. Said he didn't want to cause any problems. Snort told him that Bob was his boy, that he had a right to come and watch him play."

Bob, at least, had a mother to take care of him. Ronnie Truitt didn't. His father and mother were divorced, and, although both lived in town, Ronnie lived with his grandmother. His mother was remarried, and rarely saw her son.

Ronnie's father, Walter "Peck" Truitt, simply couldn't provide for him. Peck was one of the more colorful characters around Milan. He and his father-in-law were rumored to have done a little bootlegging in their time, and Peck's brother Rollie Truitt was something of a "medicine man." Peck was also an extremely talented musician. "He played the piano and sang beautifully, too. Peck used to sing for the silent movies and for area churches," said Tootie Herbst.

But his affection for alcohol made it nearly impossible for him to hold a job. "Everybody loved Peck. He wasn't a nasty drunk. He just had a problem.

"Ronnie's grandma did the best she could for him, but they were very poor," Herbst said. "He was kind of the town's kid. Such a sweet boy — everybody loved him. And everybody helped him when they could. He'd walk into Arkenburg's and someone would immediately buy him a meal."

Ronnie could count on financial help from local businessmen such as Don Voss and Bill Thompson and Doc Smaltz, a body man at Chris Volz auto dealership. He also got a helping hand from Tiny Hunt, the local sportswriter. Tiny knew what it was like to be poor and alone — he, too, was raised by his grandparents after his mother put him in an orphanage.

"Ronnie never asked for anything, and he was always grateful. He was always a gentleman — never had anything negative to say about his dad or his mom," said Marc Combs. "He was a quiet boy, but he liked to be around people. I could see he was a kid who needed a boost, so I used to take extra time with Ronnie. I told him he could be whatever he wanted to be — to just look around at all the people in

America who grew up poor and made something of themselves.

"Ronnie always listened, and he took those lessons to heart. He was the poorest of the poor. But even as a kid, he was a man. He decided he was going to be somebody."

Ronnie Truitt wasn't the only kid at Milan High School who wanted to be somebody. Early on, the faculty and staff at Milan realized that many of their players had chances to get college scholarships. So new principal Cale Hudson, with the help of English teacher Mrs. Kohlerman and others, set up a program to make sure their students were ready to take advantage of those opportunities. Many teachers worked in their spare time to make sure their student athletes — and the rest of the student body — had the best high school education possible. Hudson himself decided to teach a math class to show his personal interest in the students.

"They really helped us, and we responded," Bobby said. "I know the attention I got in high school was extremely important in my being able to get through college."

Clarence Kelly, who in addition to coaching taught five English classes, remembered Bobby Plump in class. "He was an A student, as were most of the kids on that team. They were all smart, and the cheerleaders were smart."

The extra effort from the faculty paid off. Ten of the 12 players on the 1953-54 team went to college, and nine finished. Others in the class benefited, as well. Of the 30 graduating seniors, 17 went to college — an extremely high percentage for a small town such as Milan in 1954.

But all that was nearly a year in the future. In the fall of 1953, the challenges were more immediate for the Milan Indians. They were a basketball team with a mission. The Indians had tasted success once before, and they liked it. But, in spite of the revved-up enthusiasm in town, not everyone thought Milan would get another chance.

CHAPTER TEN

DREAM SEASON

On Carr Street in Milan stands Nichols Barbershop, an old-fashioned place where the men of the community still sit and chat about the world which, even today, often revolves around Indians basketball. There is a photograph on one wall, hand-colored, of a basketball team, perhaps the most famous schoolboy basketball team in history. This is the place the boys received those burr haircuts they wear in the picture. Most of the boys are grinning. They have achieved something rare, nearly unprecedented, something that may never happen again. They are the underdogs, the small-town boys who conquered the world.

The picture didn't always seem so bright. In the fall of 1953, few outside the town of Milan gave the Indians much chance of repeating their spring success. Herb Schwomeyer, the most noted of Hoosier Hysteria historians, certainly didn't think it would happen. "I honestly feel that anybody who knew basketball and followed it the way I did was pleased with what they had done as juniors. Nobody thought they would come back to the Final Four, much less win it."

One big reason was right down the road at Aurora. Led by big Bob Fehrman, who would later star at Purdue, the Red Devils had a lineup that many thought could win the state. Aurora had beaten Milan in the regular season the year before, and had lost to Connersville in the regional. The team would spend the 1953-54 season ranked in the top ten.

"The local teams are always the major concern," said Bobby. "They know you so much better than other teams do. Teams from our county had played against us since grade school. Plus, the year before, they'd all had a great chance to scout us at the sectional, regional, semistate, and state. They knew everything we were going to do."

That didn't necessarily mean they could stop the Indians. Coach Wood and his boys worked hard in practice, the first five playing tough team ball and the second seven keeping them on their toes. "I may not have played a lot in games, but I ran as much in practice and took as many elbows to the head," said Roger Schroder.

"We were a much stronger team than the year before," Coach Wood said. "We had a lot more finesse, a lot more quickness, a lot better shooting. We were smaller, but quicker."

To go with his new team, Coach Wood also had a new, tougher schedule, featuring such big-school powers as Columbus, Frankfort, and Seymour. The Indians would face some powerful foes on the road. At home, they would play all but two of their games at Versailles' Tyson Auditorium. It was a bigger, newer fieldhouse than the Milan gym. But even though it held 3,000 fans, most Milan games that season had standing-room-only crowds.

The Milan Indians' season started November 3 with a game against Rising Sun. Tiny Hunt, newspaper man, fan, and promoter of basketball in the region, wrote:
Cage fans all over this great Hoosier State are going to be watching the results of Ripley County contests.

And not only cage fans, but referees. Elsewhere in Ripley County that weekend, an amazing 79 fouls were called in the game between Cross Plains and New Marion. But no one had to watch the Milan game too closely. The Indians opened their historic season with a 52-36 drilling of the Rising Sun Shiners. Bob Engel led the scoring with 15, while Bobby contributed 13 points.

Four days later, the story was much the same. Milan beat Vevay 65-41, with Bobby's 16 points leading all scorers.

But in the third game, Marvin Wood's private fears became an on-court reality. The Indians met Osgood at Tyson Auditorium, where the stands were packed with fans of both teams; in fact, Osgood High School pulled in $379.25 from the game, their biggest-ever take from a basketball game. The fans weren't disappointed. The Cowboys were indeed ready for everything in the Indians' arsenal. At the half, the score was tied. The Indians nursed a slim, four-point lead going into the fourth quarter, and finally pulled out a 36-31 victory, thanks largely to 12 points apiece from Bobby Plump and Ronnie Truitt.

Next, the Indians traveled more than an hour west to Seymour, a school many times the size of Milan. They didn't travel alone. More than 700 faithful Milan fans made the trip. Also in the stands that night were Indiana University Coach Branch McCracken and his assistant, Ernie Andress, who took this opportunity to scout the kids about whom they'd heard so much.

The Indians didn't disappoint. They proved that the size of the fieldhouse had no bearing on the quality of their game with a 61-43 victory. Ray Craft scored 18. Bobby added 15. Coach Wood was able to play his subs for most of the fourth quarter.

"Seymour wanted to embarrass us. They put a big kid on Plump with the intention of roughing him up, but Bobby left him in the dust," Wood said.

Obviously, the Indians could score. Someone had to try and slow them down. So Brookville, Milan's next opponent, put on the stall. Unfortunately for Brookville, the Indians had a pretty good stall game, as well. Milan came away with a narrow 24-20 victory. Again, Craft and Plump were the stars, combining for half of their team's points.

The next game was a blowout: Milan 67, Hanover 36, Craft and Plump with 12 and 10 points, respectively. The Indians were 6-0 and going to meet another tough local foe: the Lawrenceburg Tigers.

The Tigers were led by Bill Wullner, who started at one guard position. Sonny Edwards started at the other guard spot. The forwards were David Glenn and Wayne Wildridge, and the center was Bucky Dennis. They were big and they were fast. They respected what Milan had done the year before. But they had beaten them in '52. And they expected to beat them this night.

But Wullner had his hands full with Bobby Plump. "You didn't stop him. He would go right or left. He never took bad shots. The whole team was disciplined. Milan did things differently. They had a plan and they stuck to it and they got the job done," he said.

Wullner didn't fare too badly himself. On this night, Bobby outdueled him by only a 15-14 margin. But the Milan margin of victory was greater. After a good shooting battle, the Indians played cat and mouse in the final quarter to preserve a 50-41 win.

Back at Tyson, the Indians squared off against old rival Versailles. Bobby rippled the nets for 21 points. But so did the Lions' Jim Gabbard. Milan eked out a slim 39-35 victory.

The boys from Milan were now 8-0, ranked 18th in the state. And they were having a great time.

"We were having fun, just playing the games as they came along. I don't remember thinking ahead at all. Winning the state tournament never entered my mind. But neither did losing," Bobby said.

The people of Milan were having fun, too. The fan following was so huge, the town nearly shut down on game nights.

There was no fast food in 1953 — although this was the year Dick and Maurice McDonald moved from New Hampshire to California and discovered how much Americans loved their hamburgers. Sometimes when the Indians were on the road, the team ate at a restaurant along the way; Frisch's in Aurora was popular. But generally, the food at Arkenberg's was fast enough.

Rosie Arkenberg remembers the crowds. "We would close up to go to the ball game. We'd leave one girl in the kitchen. People would be standing in line by the time we got back."

The place would explode with applause when the Indians entered. Arkenberg's fed the team and usually sent the bill to Milan High School. The fans would stay until midnight reliving the game and talking hoops. "The milkshakes were flowing like wine," said Tootie Herbst.

And more than one Milan citizen was making sure they were flowing Ronnie Truitt's way. "We were never sure he got enough to eat. He used to get so tired in the games. So we tried to take care of him," said Herbst.

The Milan fans had plenty to be pleased about. Big schools, little schools, far away or close to home — it mattered little to the Indians. They were winning.

And they were working hard to keep up their winning ways. On Mondays and Tuesdays, Coach Wood drilled his team on defense. Wednesdays and Thursdays were offensive practice days. The subs kept pushing. The starting five kept proving they belonged.

Coach Wood did his share of pushing, too. "I was a very good defensive player at Butler, so I used to guard Plump in practice. I figured if he could get past me, he could get past anyone. I used to guard Ralph "Buckshot" O'Brien at Butler, and used to do just fine. But Plump used to take me to school on a regular basis."

Once, Woody stepped in front of the charging Bobby Plump, and neither gave way. They collided, and Bobby ended up with a broken nose. "He didn't miss any games, though," Wood said.

The broken nose notwithstanding, things on the basketball court were good for Bobby Plump. Off the court, things were good for Bobby, too. School was challenging but rewarding. His relationship with Nancy Sue Ratts had blossomed, as well. After the pain of his breakup with Jo Anne, Nancy Sue "may have saved my senior year. I felt like a pretty good person again," Bobby said.

But basketball wasn't all fun and games for Bobby. On game nights, the varsity sat in the stands to watch the reserves until the end of the third quarter, when they'd leave to dress for their game. Pepto-Bismal was a common element in Bobby's pre-game preparations. "He used to get so nervous. Sometimes, he'd drink a whole bottle of the stuff," said Clarence Kelly.

It never showed. It was becoming clear that Bobby Plump was one of the coolest ballplayers and best guards in the state. Bobby was a picture of confidence on the basketball floor. "I always had confidence on the basketball court," he said. "I never went into a game thinking we would lose."

With the final couple of minutes ticking away in the reserve game, Coach Wood would join his boys in the locker room. He would give the Indians a few final bits of advice. To get them loose, Clarence Kelly would come up with a joke, "usually a dirty one," he said.

"Then we'd usually have a moment of silence before we hit the floor," said manager Fred Busching.

Their next chance to do just that would be a big, high-profile affair. The Indians were set to travel to Frankfort for a holiday tournament featuring the host Hot Dogs and big school powers Columbus and Fort Wayne North. Unfortunately, that week in practice, Bob Engel reinjured his back.

It would never be the same. From this point forward, Engel would have to spend extended time on the bench. The rest of the team would have to step up to fill Engel's big shoes.

As enthusiasm for the holiday tournament was building, the rest of the state was beginning to take notice of the Milan Indians. Bob Collins, a future close friend of Bobby's who was to become sports editor of *The Indianapolis Star*, wrote:

...the mighty men of Milan refuse to be discarded. The Redskins have conked everyone in sight and reports from the Southeast say they are capable of handling one and all, large or small.

Those reports weren't quite accurate. At least, not yet.

The Frankfort Hot Dogs were widely regarded as one of the state's best teams. They were coached by Marvin Cave, another former Butler player who had actually been Marvin Wood's roommate at one time. Cave had been a star at French Lick High School, where his uncle was on the school board. The friendship between Cave and Wood was instrumental in Wood's landing the head basketball coaching job at French Lick after college.

On this day, the Milan backcourt played its typical stellar game, with Craft scoring 14 and Plump contributing 11. But Frankfort's Jim Ulm pumped in 19 to lead the Hot Dogs to a 49-47 victory and hand the Indians their first loss of the year. The turning point came late in the game when, for one of only two times in his high school career, Bobby Plump fouled out.

"I didn't think I fouled that fifth time. I drove to the bucket and the defender turned his back and bent over. I went over the top of him, and they call it on me," he said.

Coach Cave said his Hot Dogs matched up well against the Indians. "They were a small team. They played a pattern offense, and they weren't likely to beat you very badly. But they were likely to beat you. So you had to just hang close so you'd have a chance at the end."

Marvin Wood blamed himself for the loss. "I'd been sharing some of the things we'd been doing with my old roommate, and darned if they didn't use some of our own weapons to beat us," he said.

Ironically, Frankfort was the only team in the holiday tourney that would not make the Sweet Sixteen later in the season. But Cave's Hot Dogs would go on to beat Muncie Central later that year to become the only team to defeat both participants in the state final battle. "I suspect most of it came from playing both of them in historic Howard Hall. It's hard for visiting teams to win here," Cave said.

After suffering their first loss, the Milan Indians could easily have folded their teepees. Instead, they showed their fortitude by coming back later the same day to beat a strong Columbus team 52-49 in the consolation game. After a seesaw battle, the Indians took the lead in the fourth quarter and played cat and mouse to cement the victory. Columbus's Al Miller matched Bobby's 17 points in the losing cause. "I think that game gave Marvin a lot of confidence in us," Bobby said.

So 1953 ended with the Indians at 9-1. Even with the loss, Milan looked strong. The team's margin of victory wasn't as impressive as the previous season's, down from 18 points to 10. But, with the important county tournament fast approaching, the boys were doing what they needed to do to win.

New Year's Eve passed without curfew problems; all of the Indians players realized that Coach Wood's watch always told the right time. The Indians began the new year as they had begun the season, with a 74-60 victory over Rising Sun. Bobby scored 25 points in only three quarters of action, while Willis Holland scored 26 for the Shiners.

The Indians were primed and ready to take on the county. And this was a key tourney. Milan had won two Ripley County tournaments in a row. If they won their third, they'd take home the trophy known as "Old Vic." Three wins in a row, and the Vic would have a permanent home in Milan.

Milan drew the Versailles Lions in the opener, and Bobby Plump was on fire. He scored 28 points to lead Milan to a 53-46 victory.

Napoleon was up next, and gave the Indians an early scare, getting off to a 7-0 run to start the game. Bobby fouled out early and wasn't much of a factor. Luckily, Gene White stepped up to the mark, hitting 14 points to keep pace with 13 from Napoleon's Ray Rose. The Indians prevailed in the end, 36-30.

That left only Holton standing between Milan and the Vic. Holton Coach Mike Hafenbritle still wasn't convinced that the Indians were a team of destiny. "I watched them play most of their games — like us, they played most of their games at Tyson Auditorium in Versailles. At the time, I thought they had a nice team, but I didn't think they'd go very far in the tournament. I thought we could possibly beat them."

On this day, Hafenbritle was wrong. Bobby lit up the scoreboard with 20 points as Milan knocked off the Warhorses 40-30 and put the Vic on the bus for its victory ride. Today, the trophy has a permanent home as part of the Milan exhibit at the Indiana Basketball Hall of Fame.

(That same weekend in Dearborn County, the Moores Hill Bob Cats beat Guilford 61-46 to win their county tournament. The Bob Cats were coached by one Herman "Snort" Grinstead.)

After the tournament, the Indians had to face Napoleon again. This time, it was no contest. Milan destroyed Napoleon 61-29 to run its record to 13-1.

In rapid succession, the Indians disposed of their foes: Hanover fell 38-32 as Bobby scored 16. Sunman played a tough game but lost 42-36, as Bobby led the way with 20 points.

For the third time that year, Milan faced Versailles at Tyson. That night, a lot of fans showed up not only for the game, but to get a glimpse of the new scoreboard which, according to Tiny Hunt, "had the complete score and time...just like the scoreboards used at Butler Fieldhouse and other large gyms throughout the country."

Everybody got an eyeful of the big new board that night. The Indians took a 28-12 lead into the fourth quarter. But the Lions weren't ready to give up. Future Hall of Fame Coach Gus Morehead's boys poured in 30 points in the last quarter. Milan managed only 21, but hung on for the 49-42 victory. Bobby scored 23.

Next up was North Vernon. The Panthers were one of only five teams to have beaten the Indians the year before. This year's match went down to the wire. Panther Albert Jackson was the game's high scorer with 16 points. But Bobby's 14 were good enough to lead Milan to a razor-thin 38-37 win.

And the Indians had no time for rest. After the North Vernon game, Coach Wood and his Indians had to prepare for the biggest game of the season — the biggest game in the entire region that year. The Milan Indians were 17-1. But they had yet to play the Aurora Red Devils. Aurora had been turning heads all year and looked to be a major contender for the state title. Every basketball fan in the state had an eye on this game.

The packed house at Aurora High was ready for a showdown, figuring they could well be witnessing a preview of the regional tournament. They were right. But on this night, they wouldn't see Milan's best effort.

Coach Harry Ritter's Red Devils never trailed. In the fourth quarter, the Indians pulled to within one to bring the crowd to its feet. But Aurora pulled away again to nail down the victory, 54-45. Bob Fehrman had 23 points to nearly match Plump's and Engel's 12 apiece. "We always felt we could beat them," Fehrman said. "We thought we could go all the way to the Sweet Sixteen — maybe even win it all if we got a good draw."

Bobby didn't think he had a very good game at Aurora. "But we came back and won the next one, so we were back on the trail again."

The Indians closed out the regular season with an uninspired 38-30 win over Osgood. Bobby outdueled the Cowboys' Spike Wohlford 12-10.

In this era, no one used the word "burnout" to describe a team's state of mind. But Coach Wood sensed that his team needed a break. He gave them a few days off before beginning preparations for the sectional tournament — another smart call from a young coach who, in the words of Clarence Kelly, "was the world's best at knowing when to call time out. He could just sense it."

At 18-2, the Milan Indians had completed a fabulous season. But their greatest challenges lay ahead. To even be the best in the region, they'd eventually have to prove they could beat the Aurora Red Devils. They would get another shot.

CHAPTER ELEVEN

ANYTHING
CAN HAPPEN
(AND USUALLY DOES)

Did the Milan Indians have any chance in the state tournament in 1954? Perhaps. But even if they didn't, Bobby Plump figured he'd had a good run as a high school basketball player. Milan's success in 1953 was the highlight of his young life. In February of 1954, he wrote as part of a 12th grade English class assignment:

> Milan winning the Semi-finals was the greatest thing that has ever happened in Indiana High School basketball. Milan will be remembered by the smaller schools in every one of the 92 counties in Indiana for years to come. I think you will agree, after reading this theme, that anything can happen in high school basketball and usually does.

Down in Southeastern Indiana, Marvin Wood was preparing his Milan Indians for what he hoped was at least a small measure of success in the IHSAA Boy's Basketball Tournament — a sectional title, perhaps, with luck, a regional title to go with it. But up in Muncie, they were thinking state championship all the way.

They'd been there before. The Muncie Central Bearcats had won state titles in 1928 and 1931. More recently, they had amassed a three-season record of 74-12 and had won back-to-back state championships in 1951 and 1952. Their coach was Lawrence "Jay" McCreary, who endeared himself to Hoosier hoop fans as a star forward on Frankfort's 1936 championship team, and again in 1940 when he scored a game-high 12 points in Indiana University's 60-42 win over the University of Kansas in the NCAA championship game. McCreary had taken over at Muncie Central from Art Beckner after the 1950-51 championship season and inherited an awesome roster of talent: Tom Raisor, Jerry Lounsbury, Danny Thornburg, Carl Miller, Jim Sullivan, Charlie Hodson, Jack Hawley, James Burt, Calvin Grim, Marvin Dick, Gerald Wright, and Jesse Rhodes. After their 1951-52 championship, McCreary's Bearcats were ranked number one in the state going into the 1953 tournament. They lost a sudden-death double overtime heartbreaker to Richmond, 54-52, in the regional final. This year, they were out to prove that their dethroning was only temporary.

The 1953-54 Bearcats had lost enough talent to decimate most basketball programs. Guards Tom Raisor and Carl Miller had graduated. Both were starters for the Indiana Boys High School All-Star team. Raisor later played for the University of Michigan, while Miller started for Arizona University his freshman year. Still, Muncie Central had a squad that many fans thought could take it all. It was the tallest team most Hoosiers had ever seen, led by Jim Hinds and Gene Flowers. And they'd had a great season — although, for a Muncie Central team, a 15-5 record was considered a little shaky. During the season, the Bearcats had been upset by Shelbyville and torn apart 53-43 at home by Fort Wayne North. Then, after a nice winning streak, Muncie Central played poorly in a 49-45 loss at Frankfort. Still, the Bearcats won the North Central Conference, thought by most to be the toughest high school basketball conference in the state.

And they had tradition — and a lot of expert opinion — on their side. As the tournament tipped off, the United Press predicted that Muncie Central would be the only one of 753 entries left standing when the dust settled. One writer noted, "Surely, there won't be another Milan to steal the headlines."

He was right. It wasn't "another" Milan at all. It was basically the same team that had stolen the headlines around the state the year before.

With the Versailles Sectional at hand, Coach Wood had a difficult decision to make. Each team could dress only ten players for the tournament, rather than the 12 permitted during the regular season. The season before, Jim Call and Dale Smith had sat out the Indians' tournament run; this year, it would be Bob Wichman and Ken Delap. Both were always looked upon as integral parts of the team, however, and continued in their roles as practice players, helping the remaining ten Indians prepare for their opponents.

The first game of the Versailles Sectional was a cakewalk. The Indians clobbered Cross Plains 83-36. Coach Wood elected to play his subs for more than half the game. Bill Jordan led the scoring with 15 points.

"I went home and told my wife, 'The boys have been waiting for this all year. They're ready, right now,'" Wood said.

They were more than ready. In the second round, the Indians handled Osgood 44-30, setting up their fourth contest that year against the Versailles Lions.

The Milan Indians were in a dangerous position. They had already beaten Versailles three times, and six times in the past two seasons. But the victories hadn't been easy. The '53-'54 Indians had struggled to beat the Lions by four, six, and seven points. In the last victory, the Lions had poured on the points to outscore Milan in a wild and woolly fourth quarter shoot-out. Coach Gus Morehead and his boys were ready.

"We always played them close," Morehead said. "We had good teams those years, but they had an exceptional team. Our boys played them tough, but we weren't able to beat them."

Nor was the sectional finale any exception. The Indians posted a 57-43 victory to capture their second straight Versailles Sectional title. Once again, the Milan Indians were Ripley County's team, and basketball fans from all over the area jumped on the Milan bandwagon. Next stop: the Rushville Regional.

This year, the boys from Milan rode to Rushville in style. The Indians all showed up in new Pontiacs, courtesy of Chris Volz Motors. Would riding in those fancy cars spoil the kids who grew up playing alley ball next to a manure pile?

Not this day, anyway. The Indians faced the Rushville Lions on their home court in the first game of the day. This year, they didn't need any help from a stalled clock as they routed the Lions 58-34. Bobby scored 16, and the Indians appeared to be clicking on all cylinders. "It was a pretty easy game," Bobby remembered.

They needed an easy one. Because no matter who they played in the nightcap, it was going to be a tough game. In the other semifinal game, Aurora, the 20-2 Southeastern Indiana powerhouse and the last team to beat the Indians, was taking on 19-4 Connersville, who were definitely still stinging from Milan's slap in the face the previous year. As it turned out, Connersville couldn't keep up with Aurora's Bob Fehrman, who pumped in a regional record 35 points to lead the Red Devils to a 67-51 win.

Milan versus Aurora. The rematch was set. All of Southeastern Indiana had been waiting for this one.

And it seemed as though most of Southeastern Indiana made the trip to Rushville to watch the action. The fans arrived early and packed the stands. According to Milan cheerleader Patty Bohlke Marshall, the

Milan and Aurora faithful were chanting and screaming even before the players started dressing. At one point, the Milan fans all stood and yelled what had become their rallying cry: "Best team's in the black!"

"It just made you shiver. It was fantastic. I can still feel the excitement," Marshall said.

The fans exploded as the boys took the floor. They were ready for an all-out basketball war. They got their money's worth.

The Indians took the early lead, going up 6-1 in the first few minutes of play. But Aurora stormed back and tied the scored at 13 to end the first quarter.

They weren't through storming, either. By halftime, the Red Devils had built a seven-point lead, 27-20. The Mighty Men of Milan looked to be unraveling.

Bobby still remembers the halftime scene in the locker room. "It was the only time I can remember consciously thinking that we might lose a game. The game was half over, and they were up, and they'd beaten us before. Then Engel and Truitt came out and threw them in from everywhere."

There was no hotter shooter in the state than Ronnie Truitt when he was in the zone. There was no tougher, bigger-hearted player than Bob Engel. But even hot shooting and guts didn't seem to be enough to stop the Red Devils. The Indians hung tough through the third quarter, but closed the gap by only a point, to 34-28. Bob Engel was in foul trouble. It looked as though Aurora was going in for the kill.

But Coach Wood wasn't ready to concede the game just yet. "We used our zone trap beginning in the fourth quarter. They had a lot of trouble with our pressing defense, and we caught up. Usually when we caught up, we would play cat and mouse with the ball. But we didn't that night. We had a couple of guys with hot hands, and we just let them shoot. The next thing I knew, we had the lead."

Bob Fehrman said he and he teammates grew tired as the game wore on. "I thought after we beat Connersville, there would be no problem with Milan. But the thing I remember the most is that, from the third quarter on, we died on the vine. We were totally worn out after the afternoon game, and we just sort of ran out of gas. Milan played just a perfect game — and perfect games from then on."

It was a team effort. Down by six, Ray Craft hit a bucket, then Bobby and Gene White each hit a free throw before Ronnie Truitt hit a shot from the corner to tie the score at 34. The Red Devils canned a couple of free throws, but then Truitt hit another long shot and Craft drilled a free throw to give the Indians a one-point lead.

They never looked back. Bobby hit another free throw. Engel hit an outside set shot. The Indians now led 40-36.

Aurora started to get desperate. The Indians kept the pace slow and steady, running their slow down game. Whenever the Red Devils attacked the ball, the Indians attacked the bucket. Bobby, Gene White, and Bob Engel each contributed another field goal. The game ended with the score Milan 46, Aurora 38. The army of Milan fans breathed a collective sigh of relief. "They were one of the best teams in the state. We were very fortunate in that one," Coach Wood said.

Despite his back problems, Bob Engel had 17 points to go with Bobby's 12. But it was Gene White who was the real star. After Aurora's Bob Fehrman had scored 35 points earlier in the day, White, playing in the middle of Milan's zone, held him to only 12.

"Whitey always did a masterful job in the post," Coach Wood said. "He wasn't big, but he was intelligent, and he always played a smart game against a bigger guy. We knew that if the guy he was guarding was going to take a shot, he'd better hit it, because Gene was going to have him boxed off and he wasn't going to get a second chance."

Today, a lot of people in Aurora still think they came close to bringing the state championship trophy home in 1954. Many think Aurora's starting five of Fehrman, Mel Johnson, Jerry Drew, Hugh Gabbard, and Ronnie Klingelhoffer were as good as any the State of Indiana had to offer. Fehrman would later play at Purdue, Klingelhoffer at Michigan State, Gabbard at Eastern Kentucky, and Drew at Hanover.

Bobby agreed. "I think they had the best talent of anybody we played that year."

Bob Fehrman remembered following the Indians for the next two weeks. "I was up there rooting for them. I was thrilled somebody from down here was doing what they were doing. We didn't get any recognition down in our part of the state before that," he said.

Aurora's season was over. The Red Devils' fans celebrated their success; in Indiana high school basketball, a sectional title and a trip to the regional final have always been fine accomplishments.

But even with a second straight Rushville Regional trophy in hand, Coach Wood wasn't having anything of celebrations for his Milan Indians. Not just yet. Milan was a team on a mission. The Indians were back where they wanted to be — back at the Big Barn, Butler Fieldhouse in Indianapolis. The Indians were just four games away from Hoosier Hysteria immortality, and Coach Wood didn't want any distractions. The team had only a modest pep session on the Friday before the semistate. Then it was off to Indianapolis.

This year, it was a more business-like Milan squad that arrived at Butler University. Perhaps one reason was that they arrived for the Indianapolis Semistate in stylish Buicks from Chris Volz. Or perhaps it was because they had been there before, and had a better idea of the task ahead.

For the second year in a row, it looked as if Milan got a favorable draw. The 24-2 Indians were slated to take on the 23-5 Montezuma Aztecs, from Parke County in Western Indiana, in the first game. In the second, the 21-5 Columbus Bulldogs, a team the Indians had beaten in the Frankfort holiday tournament, were to play the 23-4 Indianapolis powerhouse Crispus Attucks Flying Tigers.

For once, Milan was the big school in a game. Milan picked its basketball team from only 75 boys in the school, but Montezuma had only 36.

And, for a while, the game seemed a huge mismatch. The Indians jumped out to a 20-10 first quarter lead and took a 29-19 lead into the locker room at the half. Everything was going according to plan.

The plan started to fall apart in the third quarter. With the lead, Coach Wood elected to play cat and mouse. It was the Indians' favorite offensive weapon. But the stall strategy that had taken the Indians so far in the past was not so effective against the boys from Montezuma. The Indians hit just one bucket in the third period, and the Aztecs took advantage. After three, Milan had a slim two-point lead.

The game was being carried on television across the state. Early in the fourth quarter, Coach Wood received some help from a fan out in TV land — a telegram that read:

WATCH YOUR OUT OF BOUNDS AT FAR END ONLY ONE RECEIVER BACK AND HIM NOT ALERT FOR PRESSING YOU MUST EXPECT FOULS INEVITABLE AGGRESSIVE PLAYS BUT TOO MANY OF TYPE WHEN ODDS ON BENEFIT ARE LOW AND ODDS ON FOUL HIGH

Coach Wood wasn't quite sure of the writer's point. And he didn't have time to pay much attention to the wire. He decided it wasn't yet time to abandon the cat-and-mouse offense.

And, finally, it started to work. The Indians built a 38-31 lead that evolved into a 44-34 victory. Bobby finished with 17 points to lead all scorers. The Indians were one step closer to their dream.

This next step was going to be a big one. The Indians sat in the stands to watch the second game, hoping for an upset victory by Columbus, a team they were confident they could beat. The Bulldogs were up by 14 in the second half. But Attucks charged back. With just 25 seconds left in the game, an Attucks sophomore named Oscar Robertson hit a free throw that gave his Tigers a 68-67 come-from-behind victory.

The stage was set for another great game, and for a story with many interesting twists. This would be the Big City team against the Little Town team. An all-black team against an all-white team. The veteran Bobby Plump against the young-but-talented Oscar Robertson.

Ray Crowe was coach of the Crispus Attucks Flying Tigers. In his younger days, he had been a great athlete at Whiteland High School and Indiana Central College (now the University of Indianapolis). Ray's brother George Crowe was one of the first African-Americans to play in major league baseball.

The next two years would prove to be Coach Crowe's time in the spotlight. He led Crispus Attucks to back-to-back Indiana state championships in 1955 and 1956 behind the greatest basketball player Indiana ever produced, young Oscar Robertson. The 1955 championship was notable for at least two reasons: it would be both the first all-black championship team and the first Indianapolis city school to win the title. The 1956 Tigers would also become the first undefeated team to win the state title.

Many years later, Ray Crowe would land a role in the movie *Hoosiers* as the coach of South Bend Central, Hickory's opponent in the final game. (His former star Bailey Robertson, Jr. played his assistant coach in the film.)

But on this night in March, 1954, the coaching challenge was very real.

Bobby Plump remembered hearing about Attucks earlier that year. "We were familiar with them. Remember, they were an Indianapolis team, so we read about them in the *Indianapolis Star* and the Cincinnati papers. We'd all heard about how good they were."

Marvin Wood knew how good the Tigers were, as well. He knew his boys weren't easily rattled, but this was a huge game, and the Indians might start out being just a bit intimidated — something Wood knew could be deadly to their title chances.

But Coach Wood saw something just before game time that gave him confidence. As the Indians sat in their dressing room, Coach Wood watch the Attucks team pass in the hall. Each and every one of the Tigers peered into the dressing room to have a look at the Indians. "I thought if they were looking at us, I knew they were worried about us," he said.

Race was never an issue in Coach Wood's pregame talk. "Woody told us they could shoot real well, that they were real quick, and that a couple of their kids could jump up and take a dime off the top of the backboard," Bobby said.

That's when Bob Engel offered the remark that rings in the memories of everyone in that locker room to this day: "That may be true, Woody, but they're going to have to prove it to us."

Even the warm-up proved a study in contrasts. Milan came out in their basic black; Attucks wore bright green and gold uniforms and socks with fleecy warm-up shorts. Not that the Indians saw them.

"Woody made it a rule that we never looked at the opposition during warm-ups. We never did. We just did our thing," Bobby said.

It was a good thing they didn't look. They saw plenty of young Oscar Robertson after the game started. Oscar scored 11 early points, and Milan led by just one, 17-16, after the first quarter. But the Indians turned it up a notch and took a 39-32 lead into the locker room at halftime. Unfortunately, their star guard was nursing a sore leg.

"I had terrible leg cramps," Bobby said. "Fred Busching spent the whole halftime rubbing my legs."

Fred must have done a great job, because the leg cramps didn't bother Bobby again. With his leadership on the floor, the Indians pulled away from the Tigers and never looked back. Attucks cut the lead to seven one more time in the second half, but that was as close as they got. Engel, Plump, and Truitt hit back-to-back-to-back buckets to put the game on ice. Milan 65, Attucks 52. Bobby scored 28 big points for the victors.

Future star Oscar Robertson remembered that "Milan was a very talented team. They had good athletes on the floor and great depth on the bench.

"Bobby Plump was their leader, a winner. He brought everyone's game up a notch or two. Ronnie Truitt guarded me and did a heck of a job. But you have to remember, he was a senior and had been there the previous year. I was just a sophomore, and I'd never been there.

"It was a big game for me. After losing to Milan in 1954, I made it my goal to never lose another game — sectional, regional, semistate, or state — in the tournament," Oscar said. A quick check of the record book reveals that Oscar was true to his word.

Bobby Plump remembered Oscar Robertson, as well. "He was a fantastic talent. He was the guy we had to shut down. We did — but only enough to beat them. The Attucks game may have been the best game we had as a team. It was definitely the best game I had along the tournament trail."

Ray Crowe said the Indians were lucky to catch Oscar as a sophomore. "He was 6'5" and he was a toughie. He was a good one, but he was much better the next year. Oscar was the hardest worker on the team. You had to turn off the lights to get him out of the gym."

Coach Crowe also had nothing but praise for Milan. "They had a terrific team and a game plan that wasn't conducive to us playing well."

Marvin Wood agreed. "It was the best tournament game we ever played. We were at our peak."

After the game, Coach Crowe visited the Milan locker room and personally congratulated each player. It was a gesture not lost on young Bobby Plump. He and Ray Crowe maintain a close friendship to this day. "I think he's a great person," said Crowe.

And history has shown Ray Crowe to have been a great coach. In his seven-year career, Crowe compiled a remarkable 179-20 record. This 13-point loss to Milan in the Indianapolis Semistate was the worst defeat any Ray Crowe team would ever suffer.

That points up a little-recognized fact about the 1954 Milan Indians: not only could they play cat and mouse, they could put up a lot of points in a hurry against an athletic opponent.

"People think we were just a slow-down club, and we were definitely not. We liked to run and score," Bobby said.

That they did. The Indians' 65 points was the fourth highest total for any team in the final 16. Earlier, Attucks had beaten Columbus 68-67. And Mississinewa had scored 66 in a win over Kokomo.

The Indians may have favored a slow-down game sometimes. But the Milan bandwagon was picking up steam. They left Indianapolis knowing they'd be back the next weekend. And this time, they weren't leaving without a championship.

CHAPTER TWELVE

ANOTHER
FINAL FOUR

It was the week before the Indians' second Final Four appearance in two years, and basketball fever was running rampant in the town of Milan. The Milan Board of Trustees issued the following resolution:

WHEREAS, the great basketball team representing Milan Public School did participate in the Semi-Final Elimination Championship held at Butler Fieldhouse on the 13th Day of March, 1954; and

WHEREAS, on said date, they did win the Semi-Final game and once again became one of the final four basketball teams in the State of Indiana remaining in the contest for the Indiana State High School Basketball Championship; and

WHEREAS, this will be the second consecutive appearance of the Milan Public School in the championship contest; and

WHEREAS, once again, Milan Public School will be the smallest school entered in the final contest of four schools; and

WHEREAS, being a winner in the Semi-Finals for the second consecutive year, the basketball team and coaches have added further achievement and honor to the Milan Public School and the Town of Milan and surrounding community which is served by the Milan Public School.

NOW THEREFORE, BE IT RESOLVED by the Board of Trustees of the Town of Milan, that Saturday, March 20, 1954 be and the same is hereby proclaimed a legal holiday for the Town of Milan, and respectfully asks the citizens of all the business places in the Town and surrounding community to comply with this resolution in order that all business places and citizens of the Town of Milan and surrounding communities might give their active support to the team and coaches.

Passed this 15th day of March, 1954.

Students couldn't pay attention in class. Grown-ups couldn't pay attention to anything but basketball, either. The Downtown Coaches Club, once so leery of Marvin Wood and his new system, were his biggest fans. The town was loaded with signs from well-wishing merchants, many declaring "Best Team's In The Black." Cars that had been decorated to accompany the boys to the regional and semistate tournaments stayed decorated. Chris Volz lined up Cadillacs to drive the boys to their date with destiny. The Milan Fire Department was lining up volunteers from other communities to cover for them on Saturday. Milan was going to become a virtual ghost town. Everybody was going to the finals.

Everybody who could get tickets, anyway. Tickets were at a premium. People went to extraordinary lengths to get them. The name of many a deceased relative was placed in the Milan ticket lottery. Even some of the local dogs had their names entered, according to Rosie Arkenberg. "You'd do almost anything to get a ticket," she said.

Apparently, someone even tried to steal tickets. One night that week, the school safe was broken into by thieves. Legend has it that they were looking for tickets (which they didn't find), because the teachers' payroll checks were untouched.

Milan fan Tom Kohlmeier said there was no doubt that basketball was top priority in Milan that week. "My grandmother, Mary Thompson, was in her 80s, and she was an avid basketball fan. On the Friday morning before the game, we bought a television set so she could watch the game in her home. She died Friday afternoon — a day before the state finals.

"We didn't know what to do. But as it turned out, Mom and Dad stayed home and the rest of us went to the game."

Grandma Thompson would most likely have wanted it that way. Her only son Tommy played for the 1915 Milan Indians — a team some basketball historians say might have gone all the way had its star guard not quit school just a couple of days before the tournament.

No such tragedy would befall this year's model of Milan Indians. Coach Wood kept the boys focused — not an easy task with the hoopla surrounding them. Wood and Marc Combs reviewed Clarence Kelly's scouting reports, while Kelly himself worked with center Gene White, just as he had worked the year before with Jim Wendelman.

The Indians had caught the fancy of much of the State of Indiana with their giant-killing heroics. But no one expected them to get much further. Milan was already a pleasant surprise and the second installment in a nice and memorable story. Bob Collins wrote in *The Indianapolis Star:*

> . . . any way you look at it, win or lose, the Milan story is a happy one. Hoosiers will cherish it, resurrect it, and tell it through many more basketball seasons.

But as much as Hoosiers' hearts were with Milan, their heads were elsewhere. The experts were pointing toward Muncie Central, the school that had won four state titles in its eleven Final Four appearances to go with its 16 regional and 28 sectional crowns. The Bearcats had knocked off top-ranked Fort Wayne North 62-48 and undefeated Mississinewa 63-48 in their semistate tournament. They'd also beaten their first-game semifinal opponent — 25-3 Elkhart — earlier in the season.

But the Indians couldn't look past their own first-game opponent: the dangerous Terre Haute Gerstmeyer Black Cats, the team that had lost by a single point, 42-41, in the state finals the year before to South Bend Central. Coached by the legendary Howard Sharpe, Gerstmeyer was 31-2 this season. They played a schedule that ranged from the top of the state (Gary Wallace) to the bottom (Evansville Reitz) and even a little way across the border (Lexington, Kentucky and Chrisman, Illinois). In their semistate, they'd beaten a couple of Southern Indiana powerhouses: Jeffersonville (49-46) and Evansville Central (55-44).

Gerstmeyer was a heavy favorite. Although they'd lost Harley Andrews to graduation the year before, they still had Arley and his uncle, Harold. The Black Cats were big, and they were strong, and most pundits didn't give the courageous little Indians much of a chance.

But no one could tell that to the Indians. Friday morning, March 19, the boys rode to Indianapolis in their Chris Volz Cadillacs for practice at Butler Fieldhouse, after which they checked into their rooms at the Pennsylvania Hotel. Bobby and his teammates ate at the Apex Grill — "great, big steaks," according to team manager Oliver Jones.

This year, there was no horseplay, no injuries to teeth or cut feet. "This year, it's all business," Gene White reminded his teammates. The Indians had been here before. They were composed.

On Saturday, March 20, the team was met by Indianapolis motorcycle policeman Pat Stark, the officer who had escorted the boys to Butler Fieldhouse on all of their trips to the city. Stark had adopted the Indians as his team, and he made them an unusual promise: if they won the state championship, Stark would escort them backward around Monument Circle in the very heart of Downtown Indianapolis.

But it wasn't yet time for any Milan heroics. This year, the Indians found themselves in an unaccustomed position: watching the first game of the tournament instead of playing in it. They watched Muncie Central and Elkhart battle into the third quarter before heading for their dressing room in cavernous Butler Fieldhouse. While Coach Wood gave the boys his usual brief, to-the-point talk before the game, Muncie Central polished off Elkhart 59-50. Bearcat stars Jim Hinds and Gene Flowers had 17 and 16 points, respectively.

By the time the Indians took the floor, the fieldhouse was awash with Milan fans and well-wishers. Win or lose, the boys from Southeastern Indiana were going to be loudly cheered.

From the opening tip, the game was hardly in doubt.

The Indians started strong, compiling a 21-12 first quarter lead before slipping to 29-23 at the half. Gene White played like a demon, completely dominating Gerstmeyer's center, the 6'5" Jerry Sturm. Young Rollin Cutter played most of the game in relief of Bob Engel. After nearly two years of constant back problems, the pain had finally caught up with Engel. (Before the game, Coach Wood and Marc Combs had huddled to discuss Engel's situation. They decided that Bob Engel had been a starter ever since he was a sophomore, and that in this, his last hurrah as a high school basketball player, he deserved to start and go for as long as he could before the pain made playing unbearable.)

The Indians and Black Cats played nearly even in the third quarter, which ended 39-34. But the fourth quarter was all Milan. In spite of a combined 21 points from the high-flying Andrews family, the Indians prevailed, 60-48.

And Bobby? Bobby Plump far outpaced all scorers with a sizzling 26 points. He had now scored 54 points in a two-game explosion, and would eventually lead all scorers in the tournament.

Gerstmeyer Coach Howard Sharpe remembered Bobby's performance that afternoon. "Plump is the one who caused us all the trouble. He's the one who did the job. I should never have lost to them. They just put that dang ball in the basket more than we did. And I had a weakness. I had a center, 6'5" and 225 pounds, and he couldn't guard his mother."

Coach Sharpe and all three of his Andrews family players would eventually be elected to the Indiana Basketball Hall of Fame. But this afternoon belonged to the Milan Indians. The boys rode back to the Pennsylvania Hotel and found a legion of fans gathered outside, calling their names, shouting congratulations and good luck. As Bobby made his way through the crowd, he knew the Milan Indians had already cheated the odds. They had done something unusual, perhaps remarkable. That night, they'd be back at Butler to do something historic.

CHAPTER THIRTEEN

THE GAME

March 20, 1954. The first day of spring. It would be a day that would loom large in the history of Indiana high school basketball — a day that would live forever in the minds of sportswriters and fans, that would bring honor to a tiny high school in a small Southeastern Indiana town, nationwide attention to the Hoosier State, and fame to Bobby Plump and the Milan Indians.

It was time for the match that many had secretly wished for and few thought would happen: little Milan, the giant-killer, versus Muncie Central, one of the state's all-time leading basketball powerhouses. Muncie had tradition, size, and quickness on its side — not to mention an experienced coach who'd been here before and won. Milan had on-the-floor experience, starting five seniors as compared with Muncie's three juniors and two sophomores. Each had disposed of its first Final Four opponent rather handily. Both were charged and ready for their historic showdown.

And if they hadn't been charged before they arrived at Butler Fieldhouse, they couldn't have stayed flat after entering the building. The air was absolutely electric. The Big Barn was filled beyond capacity with more than 15,000 screaming, cheering basketball fans from all across the State of Indiana. Most of them were betting that the showdown between Milan and Muncie Central had the makings of a great game — maybe even one of the greatest in IHSAA tournament history.

Nearly the entire town of Milan was there — Bill Thompson and Chris Volz and Rosie and Arky Arkenberg and Tootie Herbst and all the moms and dads and students and well-wishers. The Downtown Coaches Club was out in force.

Milan High School Principal Cale Hudson was there, wearing the scowl he'd worn on his face throughout the tournament. Hudson told reporters that when he smiled, the Indians lost.

Lester Plump was there, as usual, in his plaid jacket and striped shirt. ("Old Lester didn't always match when he went out," said Tootie Herbst.) The rest of the Plump clan was there for the game, too, all ready to cheer for their baby brother — all except sister Ginny, who was pregnant with her third child, Ronnie, and was listening to the game back in Lawrenceburg.

Tiny Hunt was there, of course, sitting with the press, more excited than anyone else in the building because there was so much more of him to excite. Tiny had been singing the praises of the Milan Indians for two years. He was about to see his faith rewarded.

Journalists and sportscasters from around the state remember the game as the highlight of their careers — more spellbinding than any World Series, more exciting than any Super Bowl, more chilling than the Indy 500 or a Muhammad Ali title fight. Tom Carnegie, the long-time Indianapolis 500 announcer and sportscaster, said you could feel the excitement rising as the tip-off approached. Hilliard Gates was announcing the game on television. "The energy kept building and building," he said.

Bob Williams, who covered basketball for *The Indianapolis Star*, agreed. "It was very exciting. I don't think anyone thought Milan would really win, though."

But that didn't stop the fans. *The Indianapolis Star's* Bob Collins said the game was like a huge, noisy Milan home game. "Oh, lord, you couldn't hear yourself. Other than one little section of purple, the whole place was for Milan."

Including Collins. "Everybody knew I wanted Milan to win. I had been on their bandwagon for two years."

None of which bothered Muncie Central Coach Jay McCreary and his Bearcats. "There were 15,000 people there, and 14,000 of them were for Milan. But the Bearcats liked it that way. Everywhere we went, people booed us. It made us go."

As the teams took the floor for warm-ups, the crowd rose to its feet. As was their tradition, Bobby and his teammates took care of their own business. The Indians didn't so much as glance down at the other basket. They didn't have to. Clarence Kelly's scouting reports had prepared them so well, they knew everybody on the floor: Gene Flowers and Jim Hinds, the soon-to-be All-Star forwards and major scoring threats; John Casterlow, the imposing, 6'6" center; and the quick guards, Jim Barnes and Phil Raisor. Behind them was an impressive group of subs: Bob Crawford, Leon Agullana, Max Abrell, Benny Fellerhoff, and Eddie Collins. The Bearcats were deep and dangerous.

But the Indians were ready. They had the slicing, driving Ray Craft at one guard spot. They had the dead-eye shooting of Ronnie Truitt at forward. They had the smartest player on the floor in Gene White. They had five backups — Rollin Cutter, Roger Schroder, Bill Jordan, Ken Wendelman, and Glen Butte — who would have started on nearly any other team in the state.

And they had Bobby Plump — who was looking more and more like a solid candidate for Mr. Basketball, the state's award for the year's top high school basketball player. Thousands in the stands — and countless thousands more watching on television in their homes and at storefronts across Indiana — were focused on the tough little guard in black. Bobby was carrying the dreams of fans across the Hoosier State on his shoulders. In a way, he was playing for all the small-town kids who never had the good fortune to make it to a state final.

Only Bob Engel was ailing. He was ready to start the game. But his painful back meant that Milan's versatile, tough-as-nails forward would see little action in the crowning game of his high school career.

With game time just minutes away, the excitement was at fever pitch. The crowd stayed on its feet as the team captains — Bobby Plump and Gene White for the Indians — met with referees Marvin Todd and Cyril Birge at center court. Jack Buckner, a student at Indianapolis Tech High School, played "The Star Spangled Banner" on his trumpet. The starting lineups were introduced. The Milan cheerleaders, Jinky Voss, Marjorie Ent, and Pat Bohlke, began to coax 14,000 Milan fans — many of whom who had no idea were Milan actually was — in supportive cheers. (Of course, if few knew where Milan was, barely anyone knew that Pierceville even existed.) It was tip-off time at the biggest, most anticipated high school basketball game anyone could ever remember.

And it didn't go Milan's way, not right away, anyway. The Muncie Central Bearcats jumped out to a 3-0 lead.

What was worse, Milan's star guard, Bobby Plump, was rolling on the floor in pain.

To this day, Bobby barely remembers his collision with Muncie's Jim Hinds. Marvin Wood remembered, though. "Plump got run over early in the game. He was playing defense against the fast break. They weren't worried about scoring a basket, they just wanted to run over him. They flattened him, and he played in pain the rest of the way."

If, indeed, it was the Bearcats' strategy to take Bobby out of his game, it appeared to work. Bobby's shots went everywhere but in. "It was the worst game I played in two years of tournament play. Absolutely the worst. I couldn't do anything against Muncie," Bobby said.

Fortunately for the Indians, Ray Craft would step up to the mark. The little guard had the magic touch this evening and took his game to a whole new level, hitting short jumpers and slicing down the lane for lay-ups. Bob Collins wrote, "Ray Craft took over Plump's driving chores, since every move Robert made was watched by ten Muncie eyes."

Perhaps the Bearcats were a bit too focused on Plump and not focused enough on the bucket. They shot poorly after their initial run, hitting only 19 percent from the floor in the first quarter. The Indians tied the game at seven and led 14-11 at the break, thanks in large part to Craft's six points. The Indians had a slim lead. But Coach Marvin Wood knew the game was far from over.

"We knew what would happen if we played them the conventional way. We had to find an equalizer," he said.

The Indians found their equalizer in Gene White. "Gene came into the huddle and told Woody he could handle Casterlow. 'Where do you want him, Coach? I can move him anywhere on the court,' I remember him saying. He had Casterlow completely tied up," Bobby said.

All the long hours of hard work Whitey had put in with Coach Clarence Kelly were paying off. Gene White, often one of the shortest men on the floor, was playing like a giant. Bearcat Coach Jay McCreary could see his much bigger center was outmatched, and went to reserve center Bob Crawford to try to get even in the middle. It didn't work. Neither Casterlow nor Crawford scored a point in the first half. In the eyes of thousands of basketball fans, Gene White was gaining the respect he'd deserved all season long.

But the Indians had other worries. Early in the second quarter, Milan's star forward, Bob Engel, was hurting so badly that Coach Wood sent in Rollin Cutter to replace him. Engel made only one bucket that night, a shot that many believe to be the last two-handed set shot in an Indiana high school final.

Rollin Cutter had his hands full. On this night, the sophomore was celebrating his 16th birthday. The state title would be a great birthday gift — but having to guard an all-state forward in Jim Hinds was a heck of a way to go about getting it. Cutter didn't score a point in 20 enormously stressful minutes. But his tough defense, strong rebounding, and skillful passing were big contributions to the Milan cause.

Cutter didn't have to score. Craft and Truitt saw to that. The pair combined for five early in the quarter, and suddenly the Bearcats found themselves in a hole. Gene Flowers led a furious charge at the end of the half, contributing all six of Muncie's points for the quarter. The Bearcats closed the gap. But the upstart Indians doubled their lead, taking a 23-17 lead into the locker room at the half.

Coach Wood was cautiously optimistic, even though his star player couldn't find the bottom of the basket. Bobby would end the game only three of 11 from the field. In spite of this, he would lead the tournament with 81 points and a 51 percent shooting average.

Meanwhile, Bob Engel was trying to get back in the game. "At halftime, I begged Jim Morris, the Butler trainer, to give me a shot so I could play," he said. Morris refused. Bob Engel's high school basketball career was over. Coach Wood and his Indians knew they'd have to go the rest of the way without him.

And they were going to have to do it against a revitalized, motivated Muncie Central team. "They made great adjustments at the half," Marvin Wood said. To counter, the Indians went to the cat and mouse. They knew how to be patient.

Perhaps a little too patient. What few shots the Indians took missed the mark. And, in reality, the Bearcats weren't much better. They had another relatively dismal quarter, hitting only 33 percent from the floor. But that was plenty to put the game in doubt. At the beginning of the half, the Bearcats' Bob Crawford sank a pair of free throws. Jim Hinds hit a bucket. Just like that, the Bearcats had closed to within two, 23-21, just two minutes into the quarter.

And the Bearcats kept up the pressure. Substitute guard Leon Agullana hit a shot to tie the game at 26 as the third quarter ended. Suddenly, the momentum had shifted. Suddenly, the Milan faithful began to wonder: Had the afternoon game taken too much out of their heroes? Could they beat the best in the state with Engel on the bench?

And where in the heck was Bobby Plump?

"It was the only time the cat and mouse didn't work," Bobby said.

With Bobby shooting poorly, the run-and-gun game wasn't going to work, either. What was left?

Only what Tom Carnegie has called, "the greatest quarter of basketball I have ever seen."

CHAPTER FOURTEEN

THE SHOT

The fourth quarter of the 1954 Indiana high school basketball championship game is the most famous eight minutes of schoolboy basketball in history. It has been described in hundreds of gallons of ink, on film, on videotape, replayed in restaurants and barrooms and living rooms and, of course, on basketball courts across America and around the world. The people who saw it will never forget it. People who didn't see it — including legions of basketball fans of younger generations — will never forget it, either. They've heard it discussed in such detail that they may as well have been there.

What happened? Almost nothing. But it was the way that almost nothing happened that was so thrilling.

Muncie Central had taken the wind out of Milan's sails in the third quarter, outscoring them 9-3 to tie the score at 26. The Indians had played the second game of the afternoon. The Bearcats were better rested. They had the momentum.

And suddenly, they had the lead. Jim Hinds hit a pair of free throws with 7:41 on the clock, and the Bearcats were ahead for the first time since the first quarter, 28-26.

Bobby brought the ball down the floor and across the half court line. He stopped his dribble, pulled the basketball onto his hip, and held it.

And held it.

And held it.

For the next four minutes and 15 seconds, Bobby Plump held the basketball, in spite of the fact that his team was behind and Milan's chances for victory were literally ticking away. "That was a smart thing to do," Bobby said. "I remember getting across the half court line and looking over at Woody. He was sitting there with his legs crossed and his palms out, telling me, 'Everything's fine.'"

"Actually, I was trying to think of something to do," Wood said facetiously.

Even though Muncie had beaten the cat and mouse in the third quarter, the Indians were a patient team. There was no sense in going for the tie yet. "If we miss and they get a bucket, we're down four. We needed to stay within a bucket of them to stay in the ballgame. There really was no reason to do anything until it got toward the end of the game," Bobby said.

That was okay with the Bearcats. They didn't attempt to put any pressure on the ball. They didn't chase the other four Indians around the floor. They were content to keep the lead. They watched and waited. It seemed that everything else in the world had come to a stop and that everyone on the planet was watching Bobby Plump.

And screaming.

"It was the loudest four minutes in the history of sports when nothing was going on," said Bob Collins.

Bob Williams, who has seen nearly every Indiana high school championship game since 1943, said there was never anything like this. "It was really exciting, even though Plump was just holding the ball. It was a heck of a game."

Milan fan Tom Kohlmeier remembered the incredible response in the stands. "It was a roar like I've never heard before or since. It got progressively louder as Bobby held the ball. It just kept going; people were crying, praying, laughing, yelling."

And the fans weren't the only ones yelling. Coach Wood had some things he needed to tell his team. So he gave team manager Fred Busching instructions to run down the sideline and yell as loud as he could to try to get the attention of the players on the floor.

"While Bobby was standing with the ball, the other guys were just standing, too. Coach Wood wanted the other guys to move around so they wouldn't get stiff. So he sent me down the floor to tell them to start moving. But they were all zeroed in on what was going on. They didn't hear me," Busching said.

Meanwhile, Tom Carnegie was trying to broadcast all the non-action over the radio with Butler University Basketball Head Coach Tony Hinkle at his side. "I would say, 'Plump is still standing there holding the ball.' Then a little later, Tony would say, 'Yeah, that's still Plump.' It was the dullest play-by-play I've ever done in my life."

And still Bobby Plump didn't move. Still, he held the ball. Bearcat Coach Jay McCreary sat on the bench, wondering what Bobby was going to do. But he was doing everything he was going to do, just standing on the floor holding the basketball.

Then Marvin Wood made his move. With 3:38 left on the clock, he called time out.

To get a pair of fresh legs on the floor and put on the trap press, Coach Wood substituted Ken Wendelman for Rollin Cutter. He instructed the boys to go back into their regular offense when they got back on the floor.

The crowd cheered in relief and anticipation when Bobby began to move the ball. With less than three minutes remaining, he took a pass, squared up to the basket, and shot.

And missed.

The Bearcats grabbed the rebound and started up the floor, looking to put the game away. But the Indians' trap press forced an errant pass that gave them the ball right back. Ray Craft picked his way through the Bearcat defense and tied the score at 28 with just 2:12 remaining.

Again, the Bearcats started up the floor. And again, the brutal press forced a turnover. A Milan steal put the ball back in the Indians' hands. This time, the Bearcats weren't going to be patient. Muncie's Jimmy Barnes fouled Bobby and put him on the free throw line.

Bobby hit both shots. Milan 30, Muncie Central 28.

And again the Bearcats brought the ball up the floor. And again, the Indians stole it. With a little over a minute left in the game, Ray Craft, the sure-shot hero of the game thus far, saw an opening down the lane — a chance to seal the Milan victory with a layup. He drove. He shot.

The ball rolled around the rim and out.

"If Ray Craft makes that shot," said Bob Collins, "Bobby Plump is just another guy pumping gas back in Pierceville today,"

"I've thanked Ray ever since," Bobby laughed. "If he'd have made that shot, we'd never have had all that excitement."

Bearcat ball. This time, no mistakes. Muncie got the ball into the dependable hands of Gene Flowers, who buried a short jumper to tie the game at 30 with only 48 ticks left on the clock.

Bobby brought the ball up the court. What would he do?

Put it on his hip, of course.

Bobby held the ball until just 18 seconds remained. The crowd was on its feet and screaming.

Now Marvin Wood knew what to do. With almost no time left and a chance to win, Coach Wood called time out.

This was it. Only 18 seconds stood between the thrill of victory and the uncertainty of overtime. So what did Marvin Wood, the master strategist, the cool-headed leader of this upstart band of Indians, do?

He let one of his players call the play.

"We were designing a play for Plump to shoot," Wood said. "He had always been good under pressure, and he was bigger and more experienced than the guy they had guarding him (Jimmy Barnes).

"So we had the play all diagrammed, and Whitey said, 'Why don't we get everybody else out of the way and get them over to the side of the floor?' I told him I thought it was a great idea. These were good boys, and we all thought alike. I was willing to ask them what they thought, and willing to listen to what they had to say. If I thought it was good, I used it."

This was certainly one of those times. Coach Wood broke the Indians' huddle confident that Gene White's suggestion was a good one, especially if the Bearcats stayed with their man-to-man defense. "Jimmy Barnes was a little shorter than Bobby. I thought Bobby would read him and read him right," Wood said.

Marc Combs was a little less confident. "Bobby was the one who always stayed cool. He didn't let his nerves get to him. He had faith in himself, and we had a lot of faith in him. So it was a well-designed play. But I figured they'd put two men on him to keep him from going in."

The play was designed for Ray Craft to throw the ball in bounds to Bobby. Then the rest of the Indians on the floor — Craft, White, Truitt, and Wendelman — were to take their men to the left side of the floor, isolating Bobby with Jimmy Barnes. Bobby would dribble until the clock showed five or six seconds. The shot was his all the way. "Woody told me, 'If you miss, we'll go into overtime. If you hit, we'll win the game,'" Bobby said.

The horn sounded and the teams took the floor. Bobby was so excited, he forgot that Ray Craft was supposed to throw the ball in. Bobby threw it in to Craft, and Craft quickly returned it to Bobby.

There would be no holding the ball now. Bobby put the ball on the floor, trying to maneuver into position for a shot. The other four Indians did as they had planned, taking their men to the left side of the court.

Dribbling. . .dribbling. Hundreds of thousands — perhaps millions — of fans watching and listening. More than 15,000 people inside

Butler Fieldhouse, all on their feet, unable to sit for this classic conclusion to the greatest basketball game they had ever seen.

And Bobby Plump, the boy with the ball, was thinking, "He's not going to get the ball from me. No way is he going to get the ball from me. And I'm going to get off a good shot and make darn sure they don't get a shot after me."

Bobby glanced at the clock. Six. Time to make his move.

"I faked left, then went right. He dropped back a pretty good distance. At the edge of the free throw line, I found myself open."

He was open. He stopped. He squared. He jumped.

He shot.

It was a shot he'd hit thousands of time — a shot he'd practiced over and over with the Pierceville Alleycats at Buttes' and Schroders' and in his own backyard, in gyms in Milan and Versailles and across the State of Indiana. It was the shot Snort Grinstead had told him to practice, with the promise that, if he could learn to hit it, he'd be able to play ball for the Milan Indians. It was the jump shot he'd copied from Bill Gorman, the varsity player whose technique he'd scrutinized years earlier.

All of a sudden, it was no longer a shot. It was The Shot.

Fred Busching remembers praying on the bench. "Please hit it. Please hit it."

High up in the stands, Milan fan Tom Kohlmeier watched the ball sail toward the hoop. "I can still see him trying to get around Barnes. When he let it out of his hands, I was on a dead run down the steps. I knew Bob was almost perfect from that spot. It was mania. It was wild."

It was beautiful, a single orange drop arching up and falling out of the Butler Fieldhouse ceiling. The fans who saw it say it was as if time stood still.

Bobby followed the shot all the way. "They don't all go in. But when I released it, I knew it was going in."

He was right.

Here's how Bob Collins described it:

After Milan threw the ball in, Plump took it in midcourt and started that slow drag dribble, his face an inscrutable mask. With eight seconds remaining, he cut to his right and headed for home. Three steps down, lean forward, fake, pull back, jump and shoot. With a great deliberation, Plump jumped, cocked his right arm and watched the ball sail through.

The radio announcers screamed, "Plump hit it! Milan wins!"

Back in Lawrenceburg, Bobby's sister Ginny was on the edge of her seat. "I was probably shaking more than the ones who were there," she said.

Older sister Dot would dispute that. Although she was in the stands at Butler Fieldhouse, Dot never saw the world-famous shot fall through. "We were all standing up and I felt like I was going to faint, so I sat down. I didn't see it. Everybody was so excited, standing up and hollering and going on. I heard the screaming and everybody rushed the floor. I knew we'd won, but somebody had to tell me that Bobby'd hit the shot."

"It was in from the moment it left his hands," said Bob Collins. "It was the perfect shot."

The fans in the stands went crazy. A roar rose in Butler Fieldhouse and echoed across the state.

Roger Schroder remembers looking at the clock to see how much time was left. "I saw there were only three seconds when it went through the net. That's when I realized we were going to be all right."

After the shot, the Indians immediately fell back on defense. The Bearcats managed a prayer — a desperation toss from well beyond half court. But the horn had already sounded. And the shot wasn't close, anyway. The big Butler Fieldhouse scoreboard told the tale: Milan 32, Muncie Central 30.

"Pandemonium broke loose," said Bobby. "It was hard to describe. I don't think a person could have a greater, more instantaneous thrill than that. We were ecstatic."

"It was nothing but bedlam," said veteran *Indianapolis News* sportswriter Jimmie Angelopolous.

The fans mobbed the floor. Everyone was screaming. Cameras were flashing everywhere. "I was running around hugging everybody and thinking it was the greatest thrill of my life. It was such a blur. Everybody was happy and hugging. It was just fantastic," Bobby said.

Hoosier Hysteria specialist Herb Schwomeyer had one of the best seats in the house that day. "My wife and I sat right behind Marvin Wood's wife. I remember they were all so excited."

Schwomeyer also remembered seeing Tiny Hunt jump up and over the scorer's bench and literally roll onto the court, more than 300 pounds of small-town sports reporter as happy as a man could be. For two years, he'd told the world about the Milan Indians. The boys had proved that Tiny was right.

Amid the crowd, Marvin Wood saw his old high school coach, Gerl Furr, standing under the basket at one end of the floor. "I remember thinking that it wasn't quite fair, that he'd coached for so many years, and I'd won the championship," Wood said.

Wood also saw his parents in the stands. "They were so proud, and the game meant so much to my mother. She's had a very tough time. My younger brother had gotten two girls pregnant, and Mother had been stricken with Bell's palsy, which had left half her face paralyzed. Mary Lou always told me the good Lord let us win the championship to help my mother."

Up in the stands, Peck Truitt was crying. Someone seated nearby asked if everything was okay. Peck nodded. "That's my boy," he said, pointing to Ronnie, as Ronnie made his way through the crowd to hug his dad.

Butler Fieldhouse wasn't big enough to contain all the emotions. The cries of joy rang across the state, from thousands and thousands of radios and TV sets. At his home in Indianapolis, Ripley County native Richard Hill was giddy. He'd have cause to be even happier later that night. His wife Frances was three weeks overdue with the couple's fourth child. Frances was having labor pains throughout the game — but never told Richard because she knew how much the game meant to him. As soon as the game was over, they dashed to St. Francis Hospital in Beech Grove. Elizabeth Hill was born less than an hour after the shot heard 'round the world.

Back in the fieldhouse, Bobby was mobbed by the press. Asked after the game if he wanted to say hello on statewide radio to anyone back home, he said bashfully, "No, everybody I know is here," (forgetting sister Ginny, who was listening on the radio, and has given Bobby good-natured grief about the comment ever since). He was awestruck. "It's wonderful. It's wonderful," he repeated.

But for every victory, there is defeat. The Muncie Central Bearcats were devastated.

"When the shot goes through and the game is over, there's not much you can do except go home," said Muncie Central alternate Terre Broadwater.

Bearcat Coach Jay McCreary said he never cast any blame on any of his players for the loss. "A lot of people asked me if I got on Jimmy Barnes. You don't get on a player when he makes only one mistake in a ball game."

Although they were terribly disappointed, the Muncie Central players were gracious in defeat. The players and coaches all came by the Milan locker room to congratulate the victors. "I really thought that team had class," Coach Wood said.

Leave it to Bob Collins, though, to sum up the relationship between the two rivals. In the next day's *Indianapolis Star*, he wrote:

Cinderella marched proudly off the floor, her slippers intact and her coach — a shiny Cadillac — in no danger of turning into a pumpkin shell. It was a disappointing defeat for Jay McCreary and the Muncie lads seeking to make their school the first ever to win five state titles. It was just their misfortune to run head on into destiny's grandchildren at the wrong time.

"I felt like I had seen one of the great moments in Indiana basketball history. I was just happy I was there to see it," Collins said.

Tom Carnegie agreed. "No one ever scored a more dramatic basket."

Jimmie Angelopolous has seen more than his share of great Indiana high school basketball games. He also broadcast NBA games for the Ft. Wayne Pistons (before they moved to Detroit) and the Minneapolis Lakers (before they moved to Los Angeles), for whom George Mikan, the game's first outstanding big man, played. But for Angelopolous, the Milan win was still an unbelievable story.

"Muncie was probably the better team, but Milan was better that day," he said. "The pieces just fit right. You can easily have a better team in Indiana and still not win the tournament. A few of the great ones never made it past the regional. But that's Indiana basketball. That's what Milan stands for."

It was a great victory for the Milan Indians — if not a great game.

"We played a terrible game against Muncie, but we still won," said Clarence Kelly. "Were we the best? We beat the best, so we were the best."

The facts support Kelly's opinion. As Bob Hammel, sports editor for the Bloomington *Herald-Times,* pointed out, "Everybody thinks of the 32-30 game as a fluke, as if they were a team that had no business winning. But at the time they did it, they beat Crispus Attucks, Terre Haute Gerstmeyer, and Muncie Central. They were probably the three biggest basketball schools in the state at that time, and Milan beat all three in a row."

Jay McCreary agreed with Angelopolous and others that the Bearcats had the better team, but gave credit where credit was due. "They won, and they deserved to win," he said.

Marvin Wood, who led the Indians to their dramatic victory, has seen Milan as "a team of destiny."

And life for Bobby Plump, the boy from Pierceville who held the ball, who hit the shot heard 'round the world, would never be the same.

CHAPTER FIFTEEN

CELEBRATION TIME

"One question I've been asked many times over the years," said Muncie Central Coach Jay McCreary, "is 'When did you begin going gray and losing your hair?' That's easy: March 20, 1954, about 9:30 p.m.when I looked up at the scoreboard and it read 32-30."

After the game, Coach McCreary slipped quietly away from Butler Fieldhouse. "I walked down the street and saw this little restaurant. It was rather dismal looking. I sat down at the counter and the waiter asked me if I'd seen the game. I nodded. He said, 'I tell you one thing, if I was that Jay McCreary and had those powerful Muncie Bearcats and let a little town like Milan beat me in the state tournament final game, I would go out and cut my throat!'"

McCreary wasn't quite that depressed. But the whole town of Muncie felt the sting of defeat. The Muncie *Evening Star*'s Herb Silverberg quoted Adlai Stevenson after he'd been beaten in the 1952 presidential race: "It hurts too much to laugh, and I'm too old to cry."

Meanwhile, the rest of the state was celebrating. The "holy pandemonium," as Milan school secretary Betty Dobson described the hugging and kissing and laughing and crying at Butler Fieldhouse, was just the beginning.

"You just can't explain," said Milan native Kenneth Bockhurst. "It was such a shock."

Soon after his fateful shot, Bobby Plump received what was to be the first of many official honors in his storied athletic career. As the hysteria at the fieldhouse died down to a mere uproar, Bobby was awarded the Arthur L. Trester Award for Mental Attitude, given each year to the Final Four player who best exemplifies the Indiana High School Athletic Association's standards for scholarship, attitude, and sportsmanship. It was a special and perhaps unexpected honor: Bobby made Indiana sports history by becoming the first player on a state championship team to be given the Arthur L. Trester Award.

The Trester Award presentation was made by Connor Salm, principal at Madison High School and an IHSAA board member. As Salm approached the microphone, Butler Fieldhouse was still ringing with cheers and laughter. Salm tried to quiet the happy crowd. Finally, he achieved something like order — or as close to order as he was going to get that evening.

Then, when the crowd was relatively quiet, someone in the stands yelled, "Give it to Plump!"

"That's exactly what I'm going to do," said Salm.

"I honestly didn't know what the award was for. I knew it was something special, because everybody was cheering again after they gave it to me," Bobby said.

More interviews and congratulations followed. The game had been over for nearly two hours before Bobby and his teammates and coaches finally made it into the locker room. "I'll bet I've had fifty thousand people tell me they were there and that I signed an autograph for them. I guess the place seated more than I thought," Bobby said.

After showering and dressing, the Mighty Men of Milan met Pat Stark, the Indianapolis motorcycle policeman who had escorted them on all those trips from the Pennsylvania Hotel to Butler Fieldhouse. Stark intended to fulfill the promise he had made to the boys earlier in the day: to close off Monument Circle and take them backward around the downtown landmark.

Stark led the victorious Indians down Meridian Street in their three Chris Volz Cadillacs. When they got to the Circle, Stark shut down traffic. Everyone stopped to watch the newly crowned state champions drive in reverse around Indiana's best-known monument. (The next year, the Crispus Attucks Flying Tigers, the first team from Marion County to win the title, would repeat the backward trip around the Circle.)

The stunt was not without consequences. Indianapolis Mayor Alex Clark was initially unhappy with his police officer for taking liberties with traffic without clearing it with anyone.

"He got kind of upset about it," said Stark. "I told him it was good public relations for the city to show we cared about a small town. I let him know that it had been my decision, and I was prepared for the consequences.

"He did nothing. He just laughed about it."

After their backward drive, Bobby and his teammates went back to the Pennsylvania Hotel to spend what was left of the night drinking pop and watching TV and talking about all that had happened to them. Not many Indians got much sleep that night.   Nor was there much of anyone sleeping that night back in Milan — although fans' post-game activities were a bit louder than the players'. Bonfires blazed. The Milan streets were jammed with fans celebrating the Indians' historic victory. Arkenberg's was a madhouse. "It was a once-in-a-lifetime experience," said Rosie Arkenberg. "There will never be anything else like it again."

There had been very little like it ever before. Dave Pert, well-known in Indiana basketball circles for his pocket-sized list of all the state's high school and college schedules known as the "Little Book," could find only one precedent: Charles Secrist's last-second shot in 1928 that, ironically, gave Muncie Central a 13-12 win over Martinsville. Martinsville's star that year was a senior by the name of John Wooden.

"Plump's shot was out of this world — the ultimate," said Pert.

And the ultimate victory demanded the ultimate celebration.

Sunday, March 21. The Miracle Men began Sunday morning in Indianapolis as most of them would have at home: they went to church. As a team, the boys and their coaches attended the 9 o'clock mass as St. Peter and Paul Cathedral in downtown Indianapolis. After church, they ate brunch at the Apex Grill, the site of all of their team meals in the big city. Bobby and the rest of the squad downed heaping helpings of chicken, mashed potatoes, peas, and peach cobbler.

Just before noon, their bags packed, the conquering heroes bade good-bye to Indianapolis and Butler Fieldhouse. Marvin Wood, the Indians' mentor and friend, drove one of the Cadillacs. Coach Clarence Kelly drove another. Bringing up the rear was a Cadillac driven by the guy who'd made The Shot, Bobby Plump.

There was no Interstate 74 linking Indianapolis and Cincinnati in 1954. The Indians traveled south on U.S. 421, led by the blaring siren of Pat Stark's motorcycle. Along the road, other police cars joined the front of the pack to make way for the Indians from Milan, Indiana.

In Shelbyville, the first sizable town they encountered outside Indianapolis, the Milan caravan took some unscheduled victory laps around the town square, escorted by police cars and fire engines, their sirens blaring. Bobby smiled as two little boys, one holding a basketball, waved from the side of the road.

As the caravan got closer to Milan, the boys began to notice signs: "Congratulations Milan," and "The Mighty Men of Milan." In Greensburg, a little boy and girl who were shooting baskets stopped and saluted. Firetrucks got into the act. The sirens wailed in Greensburg; Batesville's fire truck met the boys at the Ripley County line.

Cars joined the parade. It took the Indians 35 minutes to travel the 18 miles between Batesville and Sunman, where they were greeted by the Sunman High School band. Now just 11 miles from Milan, both sides of State Road 101 were crowded with people and cars waiting for the champs.

And 11 miles weren't enough to contain the procession. *The Indianapolis News* reported that the six-car motorcade that had left Indianapolis was 13 miles long by the time it hit the Milan city limits. Some say it was even longer.

Tom and Duke Kohlmeier, whose family operated the Milan Furniture Factory with Bill Thompson, were there for all the action. Tom and his family were part of the traffic jam. He claims the caravan grew to 18 miles long — that when the first car was coming into Milan, the last car was just leaving Batesville — and that it took longer for the parade to get through Milan than to drive the distance between Milan and Indianapolis.

"I got out of my car in Sunman and told my wife I was going to start walking. I walked eleven miles between Sunman and Milan and beat her to town," said Kohlmeier, who also said he saw license plates from all over Indiana, Ohio, Kentucky, Michigan, and Illinois along his trek.

As the caravan entered Milan, Coach Wood's car stopped. Ray Craft and Ken Wendelman got out and rode the rest of the way on the Cadillac's hood, holding the state championship trophy between them for all to see.

Near the school, a mammoth crowd had gathered to honor the state champs. Reporters estimated the crowd at more than 40,000 people — quite an impressive turnout in a town of only 1,150.

Steve Hoffman, now a reporter for the *Cincinnati Enquirer* and once publicity director for the Cincinnati Royals, was one of the out-of-town fans who decided to travel to Milan for the celebration that day. "The town was so little, and it was mobbed. There were fire trucks everywhere. I couldn't get anywhere near the players."

And the players themselves could barely make it through the crowd. When they finally did, they assembled on the stage — a flatbed truck — in front of the school.

Everybody got to take a turn at the microphone. The players thanked their parents and their coaches and their teammates and their fans. Coach Wood remarked, "Boys like these make my life a dream." Mary Lou Wood, the coach's wife, reminded everyone that "it's nice to be important, but it's more important to be nice."

Bob Collins, the Indianapolis sportswriter who had covered and rooted for the Indians all season long, was named an honorary mayor, as was *The Cincinnati Post*'s Robert Terry. Motorcycle patrolman Pat Stark had tears in his eyes as he spoke about the team he'd adopted as his own. "I wish we had more like them in Indianapolis," he said. The Indians' players and coaches adopted Stark, as well. He can be seen in numerous team photos taken at the post-game celebrations.

"It kind of got to you. Dealing with thieves and burglars all the time, and then to be with kids like that — it was a little different from routine police work," Stark said years later.

In next day's *Indianapolis News*, Jimmy Angelopolous wrote: It was the greatest day in 44 years of Indiana high school basketball. Nothing has surpassed Hoosier Dome's show of admiration for this clean little town. . . .Modest Bobby Plump exclaimed, "Gosh, I didn't think Milan could ever hold that many cars."

Things didn't slow down much that evening. After the initial celebration, it was off to the Milan Country Club for dinner. Bobby and the Pierceville Alleycats had never been to the country club before, thinking such a place was off-limits to poor kids from Pierceville. But all of a sudden, nothing seemed to be off-limits.

Nor did the celebration end after dinner. That evening, a bonfire was held at Milan High School. Everyone in town was asked to bring a little wood to keep the fire blazing late into the night.

And still it wasn't over. The warm glow from the Milan victory spread across the Hoosier state and lingered for months to come. Bloomington *Herald-Times* sports editor Bob Hammel said, "There are very few events I can remember that left everybody feeling so upbeat. There was just an 'isn't the world nice?' feeling that hung on and hung on. It was an extremely popular triumph in the sport that meant the most to people. It renewed their faith in the one-tournament system. It's hard to estimate how many of the four or five million people in the state would have loved to have been there that Sunday when the Indians came back to town.

"It sounds odd, but the only thing I can compare it to is the opposite extreme — the general mood after the Kennedy assassination. There was such a pall over things for so long. But in that period after the Milan victory, it seemed to me that everything took on such a positive glow."

Bob Williams put it this way: "The whole state adopted the team. There are teams that had that kind of following in their own county, but the whole state got involved in this thing. I don't think it will ever happen again."

In the days and weeks that followed the game, the Milan players became high school students again. Clarence Kelly had a track team to run. But it was difficult to concentrate on school or other sports. The Milan Indians were the toast of the state, the Midwest, even the nation. The coaches and players received a seemingly never-ending stream of invitations to banquets and speaking engagements. Most of the boys visited the Indiana State Reformatory at Pendleton, where the inmates put on a boxing and wrestling exhibition. Bobby couldn't attend: he was busy appearing on a television show clear across the state in Evansville to help raise money for crippled children.

School secretary Betty Dobson said the truth about what had happened never really hit her until years later, even though, "we received all kinds of mail at the school. One letter was addressed to 'Plump, Indiana.' One youngster made a birdhouse and sent it to Bobby. I still pinch myself when I think about it."

And the Milan victory had international implications, as well. A week after the Indians' victory, Bobby's Pierceville buddy Lloyd Freeman, who was in the U.S. Army stationed in France, was still waiting for word of the outcome of the tournament from his parents in Pierceville. Freeman had spent most of the year telling his platoon about Milan basketball — and had been particularly vocal about the Indians with a guy from Muncie just a few bunks down. The Ripley County papers got to France about a week late. So Freeman knew his boys were in the Final Four. He just didn't know how the tournament had played out. Half a world away, Lloyd Freeman waited and wondered.

He probably wouldn't have had to wonder had the celebration been a little smaller. Edwin and Geneva Freeman had intended to send Lloyd a telegram with the good news. But the night of March 21, the streets of Milan were so thick with partiers that the Freemans couldn't get anywhere near the Western Union office. They decided he'd just have to wait for his paper.

Finally, it arrived. The young soldier walked nervously to the stack of mail. "I was almost afraid to open the thing. It didn't say anything on the outside. I was praying, and I was getting cold feet.

"Finally, I opened it. The headline said, 'Milan Wins!' I went crazy. I ran around laughing and telling everybody, 'I told you so!'" Freeman said.

Lloyd Freeman never saw the 1954 championship game until forty years later, when he bought a copy of the game on video cassette. Even forty years after the final buzzer, he found himself a nervous wreck while he watched the game. "It came down to the shot and I was still wondering if it was going to go in. I was up on the edge of the chair. It would be the same if I watched it another hundred times. Bobby hit the shot, and I was happy all over again."

The Milan victory still affects Hoosiers, said Bob Williams. "It's the game that's remembered the most and written about the most. Every time the tournament rolls around, we read about Milan. That's never been done with any other team. There have been some other thrillers, and some great teams — Attucks, Gary, Kokomo — but nobody gets the attention that Milan does. It's the one people talk about more than any other."

"What else is there?" Milan fan Janet Purdom once challenged a reporter from the *Boston Globe*.

Plenty. There would be big changes ahead for the town of Milan and for Bobby Gene Plump. The honors were only beginning — as was Bobby's illustrious basketball career.

CHAPTER SIXTEEN

BIG HONORS, BIG DECISIONS

Along the staircase at Plump's Last Shot, the restaurant and Hoosier Hysteria shrine in the Broad Ripple district of Indianapolis, hangs a poem. It was written by Kyle Wright, a nine-year-old boy from Greenfork, Indiana. Bobby received the poem in 1987 — many years after the historic events of March 20, 1954.

But the story still stirred young Kyle Wright. Here is the poem in its entirety:

The Shot of Bobby Plump

10 . . . Oh boy!
I am not filled with joy,
With this team's fate behind me,
The shot I take had better be.

9. . .What am I doing dribbling this ball?
If I fail, we'll probably fall.
If we lose
Our fans will give us boos.

8. . .Why is this guy guarding me?
To get a win for thee?
I got to start moving soon
Or the game will end at the next full moon.

7. . .It's a 30 tie!
Well Bearcat, I'll have to say goodbye.
I'm going to dribble now.
I could win it for us. Wow!

6. . .There, I just got past my man.
Our fans are giving me a great big hand.
I can win this game, I can do it yet.
I'll hit the shot, I'll do it, I bet.

5. . .What am I doing?
The fans are booing.
Now I see.
But it can't be.

4. . .What happened was, I picked up the ball.
Now the bunch of players are like a wall.
I feel my arms rearing up.
I feel like I'm going to jump.

3. . .There, I just got rid of the ball.
The thing had better start to fall.

2. . .The ball just went through the net.
Now we're going to win, I bet.

1. . .They just took their desperation shot.
But, apparently, they're not too hot.
The shot of theirs, just didn't go,
Because we were a bit too slow.

0. . .WE WON!

Kyle Wright was dreaming the dream of more than four decades of Hoosier schoolboys: he was wondering what it must have been like to be Bobby Plump. At no time was that question more pervasive or more important than in the summer of 1954. It seemed that everyone in the state was wondering what was going through the mind of Bobby Plump. Everyone wanted to know where Bobby was going to go to college.

But before he went off to college, Bobby had another award to win — and another "first" to accomplish.

One day that spring, Bobby was home in Pierceville when he got word of a call waiting for him at Schroder's store. Little did he know that the call was his notification that he'd been chosen the 1954 Mr. Basketball of Indiana and earned the right to wear the Number One jersey for the annual Indiana-Kentucky All Star Game. The title honored Bobby as the state's best player that year. And it completed a rare triple crown: a state championship, the Arthur L. Trester Mental Attitude Award and Mr. Basketball. No one had ever done it before, and only two players have since: Marion's Dave Colescott in 1976 and Bedford North Lawrence's Damon Bailey in 1990.

Bobby's backcourt mate Ray Craft made the Indiana All-Star Team, too, and wore Number Five. Actually, all five Milan starters led the state in balloting for all-star nominations. It's believed that this was the first and last time this ever happened.

So, in addition to finishing their senior year in high school and handling all the publicity and requests for appearances they were receiving from across the state, the Milan guard duo had another foe to prepare for, another chance to bring glory to their high school and their state.

Coach Wood was in great demand as a speaker, too. "I was still so young, and there was so much happening to me," Wood said. "I was being asked to participate in clinics for other coaches in the state. Here I was, speaking in front of guys like Marion Crawley, one of the most respected coaches in the business. What was I going to tell them that they didn't already know?

"I also regret not having championship rings made for Bob Wichman and Ken Delap. Technically, they weren't on the championship roster, but they were as much a part of the team as anyone. Ordering another two rings wouldn't have been a problem. I can see that it would have been a good thing for them. But it just never occurred to me at the time that it would be important. There was just so much going on for me."

Including coaching offers. Wood interviewed at Elkhart, "but I told them I wasn't ready for such a big school yet. They thanked me for my honesty," he said.

His old college coach Tony Hinkle had a little advice. "He told me that some of the new consolidations that were happening at the time looked to have better talent than some of the older big schools. And he told me, 'Kid, go to the school that's going to pay you the most money. If it doesn't work out, you can always take the money and run.'"

One day in April, Coach Wood approached Bobby and asked him if he'd like to go to a speaking engagement with him up near New Castle. Bobby agreed; it was fun to go out with Woody, and he usually got a good meal out of it.

The coach and his star drove north, and Woody spoke to an appreciative and attentive crowd. It was just like all the other events where they'd spoken, as far as Bobby was concerned.

After the banquet, Coach Wood pulled Bobby aside and said, "Bobby, I have to go talk with someone in New Castle. You might as well come along."

So Bobby found himself at the New Castle school superintendent's office. He sat there for several minutes before he realized that there was something funny about this meeting.

"I guess I must have still been thinking about dinner or something. Because it took me a few minutes to realize, 'Hey — Woody's talking about *leaving*,'" Bobby said.

So he was. Marvin Wood had caught the fancy of schools across the state — and New Castle was one of the most respected. It was a hotbed of Hoosier basketball.

Bobby couldn't understand why Coach Wood would want to leave Milan. "I thought, why would he want to do that? Milan has everything anybody could want. Remember, my perspective was that Milan was a big place. And he had all those guys coming back next year."

Bobby was shocked. "I don't even remember what they talked about. I just couldn't believe it."

Neither could the folks around Milan. Everyone wanted to keep him. "After the 1953 season, Milan gave me a $1,000 raise. They told me after the 1954 season that they couldn't do that again, that maybe they could go another five or six hundred. Chris Volz let me know I could sell cars for him all year long. I'd never have to worry about money if I stayed in Milan. But it wasn't about money," Wood said.

On April 22, just a month after Marvin Wood led his Milan Indians to the state championship, the Ripley County newspaper reported:
Milan is stunned. Wood is going to New Castle. Word spread quickly around Milan and expressions of regret were heard everywhere... down to the last rooter, they were hoping for a miracle. . . .

But it seemed that one Milan Miracle was all the fans would get. And everyone knew the New Castle job was a great opportunity for the young coach. In the end, the people of Milan wished Marvin Wood and his family well. Little did anyone suspect that a second state championship would elude him for the rest of his Indiana high school coaching career, first at New Castle, then at North Central High School in Indianapolis, and finally at Mishawaka.

"He once told me that the biggest mistake he ever made was leaving Milan," said assistant coach Marc Combs.

Wood's resignation was a blow to the Milan Indians of the future. But the town was still basking in the glow of all the attention the Miracle Men of Milan continued to receive. And two of them — Bobby and Ray Craft — had another big game to play.

Today, the Indiana and Kentucky All-Stars play a home-and-home series each summer. But in 1954, there was just one game, held at Butler Fieldhouse in Indianapolis on June 19. Once again, the house was packed. Once again, the game was close and the finish was in doubt. Once again, Bobby Gene Plump made the difference.

Both teams were loaded with genuine stars. The Hoosier squad included future Michigan State All-American Jack Quiggle of South Bend Central. Rounding out the team were Arley Andrews from Terre Haute Gerstmeyer; Ray Ball of Elkhart; Evansville Central's Jerry Clayton; Larry Headen of Mississinewa; Joe Hobbs of Sheridan; Bill Mason of Indianapolis Crispus Attucks; and Jeffersonville's Pete Obremsky. The Kentucky All-Stars featured Vern Hatton, who would go on to lead Adolph Rupp's Kentucky Wildcats to an NCAA championship in 1958. Another Kentuckian who went on to play for the University of Kentucky was Abraham Lincoln Collinsworth of Salyerville. Collinsworth's son Cris later starred as a wide receiver at the University of Florida and as an All-Pro player for the NFL's Cincinnati Bengals before becoming a respected broadcaster for NBC, HBO, and WLW radio in Cincinnati.

But that night, as in that fateful night just three months earlier, the magic belonged to Bobby Plump. With only a minute to play, Kentucky led 74-71. Indiana's Ray Ball from Elkhart hit a pair of free throws to pull the Indiana All-Stars within one. Kentucky had only to kill the clock to claim victory.

But Jeffersonville's Pete Obremsky stole the ball. He put up a shot that glanced off the rim — and right into Bobby's hands. Bobby's jumper from the left side hit nothing but net. Indiana 75, Kentucky 74.

With hardly any time left on the clock, Collinsworth was fouled. The Kentucky All-Star went to the line with a chance to win it all — or at least secure a tie and send the contest into overtime. But he was no Bobby Plump. With a capacity crowd of partisan Indiana fans screaming, he missed both shots. The Indiana All-Stars won, and Bobby Gene Plump, Indiana All-Star, Milan Indian, and Pierceville Alleycat, was again the hero.

Jack Quiggle was the game's leading scorer. Bobby had ten, including an eight-for-eight performance from the free throw line. His backcourt mate Ray Craft had seven points.

Most Hoosiers think the Indiana-Kentucky game is the only IHSAA-sanctioned high school all-star game in the state. But since 1954, there's been another game that's sanctioned by the IHSAA. That summer, the Ripley County Voiture No. 1047 Forty and Eight American Legion post at Versailles saw an opportunity to raise some money for their nurses training program. So they began what has become an annual tradition: an all-star game between the Versailles Sectional Senior Stars and the Lawrenceburg Sectional Senior Stars.

In 1954, the Versailles All-Stars included Herman Streuwing of Batesville, Jim Gabbard of Versailles, Dale Linkmeyer of Cross Plains, John Wolford of Osgood, Kenneth Dunbar of Napoleon, Roger Ertel of Sunman, Ethan Jackson of Holton, and Irvin Meierle of New Marion. But the big story was that all five Milan Indians starters — Bobby Plump, Ray Craft, Gene White, Bob Engel, and Ronnie Truitt — would start for the Versailles team.

The team was coached by R.F. "Dutch" Struck, athletic director and head football coach at Hanover College. On the first day of practice, Struck instructed his eight reserves to go to one end of the floor and sent the Milan five to the other. "I don't want to coach you guys. You already know what you're doing, and I might ruin something," Struck said.

That night in June, the Versailles All-Stars made quick work of the

Lawrenceburg All-Stars. But the tradition has lived on. Bobby coached the Versailles team one year, and was asked to referee another. "I always respected refs," he said, "but I had even greater respect for them after I did it myself that game. It was a tough job. I was always two or three seconds behind the call. By the time I blew the whistle, the ball was at the other end."

The summer of 1954 wore on, as did the speculation about where Bobby would go to college. Many of his teammates had already decided. Gene White and Roger Schroder and Ken Wendelman were going to Franklin College. Ronnie Truitt wasn't sure he'd be able to afford college. But he had a sister in Houston. And Ronnie had attracted the interest of University of Houston Coach Guy Lewis. So he was off to Texas.

Bob Engel couldn't be talked into going to college, in spite of great interest from many programs. "Cincinnati wanted him," said Marc Combs. "In fact, an alumnus from Cincinnati approached me and offered me money to get Engel into their program. He said they'd take care of him. I told the guy that I didn't do that kind of thing, and that Bob could make up his own mind about college."

But Bob thought his Mom needed his support more than he needed college. He went to work at the atomic energy plant in Hamilton, Ohio, after graduation.

Bobby wasn't certain just what he was going to do. "Woody advised me to go to the biggest school that would give me a scholarship. Dad just wanted me to go to college," he said.

Lester Plump was proud of his youngest son's accomplishments on the floor. But Lester knew that there was more to life than basketball. "We never really talked about basketball at home, even though Dad was at every game. I can remember talking about basketball only two times. Once, Dad told me that Mr. Grinstead had told him I was the best player he'd ever coached. And another time, after we'd won the championship, Dad told me that he wished my mom had been alive to see what we'd done."

Basketball was definitively going to be a part of Bobby's future. But where? The kid from Pierceville received letters from more than 50 major universities, each offering a scholarship in exchange for his basketball skills.

Bobby narrowed the list to Indiana, Purdue, Michigan State, and Butler. But zeroing in on a decision was tough. Sure, he was a champion. But he still lived in a house with no telephone and no indoor plumbing, in a place where going to town still meant walking around the corner and going to the city meant a three-and-a-half mile drive to the teeming metropolis of Milan. How was this kid going to make a decision that big?

If a lot of local supporters had their way, Bobby would be going off to Indiana University. Most Milan High School graduates who went to college went to IU, and local businessmen and IU grads such as Bill Thompson and Duke, Tom, and Jon Kohlmeier would have loved to have sent their favorite son to Coach Branch McCracken's program.

And McCracken wanted Bobby. The Hoosiers had won the national championship in 1953 and were looking to build for the future. One of their stars, Bobby "Slick" Leonard, the future NBA player and coach of the Indiana Pacers, remembers recruiting Bobby. "We had him down to IU. He was a heck of a player. He could shoot and he had a lot of heart. He could have played anywhere."

The late Don Schlundt was another star of IU's championship team and is still one of the Big Ten's all-time leading scorers. He wrote Bobby a note:

> Before you make up your mind on any one college, would you please visit Indiana University and see what IU can offer you?

Bobby visited IU a number of times that summer, usually staying at the Acacia fraternity house with Milan friend Jon Kohlmeier, who was a member. He learned that the coaches wanted to groom him as Leonard's replacement. To do so, he'd have to change his shot — from the jumper he'd worked so hard to develop to a two-handed set shot.

That wasn't something he wanted to do. And Bobby just wasn't comfortable on the sprawling IU campus. "Branch McCracken was a nice man. But when it came down to it, IU was just too big. I was uneasy with the atmosphere there, and I didn't really care for the fraternities," Bobby said. So, in spite of a full ride scholarship offer, IU was out.

What about Purdue, Indiana's other Big Ten school? Joe Sexson, another famous name in Indiana high school basketball who later was to become head basketball coach at Butler University, was playing for the Boilermakers at the time. "I tried to get him to come," Sexson said. But after a couple of visits to the West Lafayette campus — and in spite of another full scholarship offer — Bobby knew Purdue wasn't for him, either. Although he was impressed with the late Ray Eddy, Purdue's head basketball coach, Purdue, like IU, was just too big for the kid from Pierceville.

Bobby also had lots of out-of-state interest. "I received some letters from Art Beckner, who was the coach of Muncie Central's 1951 state championship team. He thought I might be interested in going to Michigan State."

So Bobby took a trip to Michigan State along with Ron Klingelhoffer from Aurora to meet with Michigan State's coach Fordy Anderson. Anderson's Spartans played a guard-oriented offense similar to the Hinkle system. And a local auto industry executive promised Bobby a job in the off season.

"It was just too far away from home for me, though," said Bobby. Klingelhoffer became a Spartan. Plump was still undecided.

But he was leaning.

"I kept going back to Butler," Bobby said. "I stayed at the Phi Delta Theta house a couple of times, and at the Sigma Chi house a couple of times."

He felt comfortable at Butler. It was a good size for him. He knew the campus and the fieldhouse. "That floor had been nice to me," he said.

Butler Fieldhouse was one of the premier basketball venues in the nation. Because it was an Indianapolis school, more Butler games were televised back in the '50s than IU or Purdue games. Butler played as tough a schedule as any school in the country. And, unlike at the Big Ten schools, where freshmen couldn't play for the varsity, Bobby thought he might be able to be a starter all four years at Butler.

Also unlike the Big Ten, Butler couldn't offer scholarships. But they could help their athletes in other ways. That summer, Bobby got a handwritten letter from Butler Coach Tony Hinkle:

Dear Bob:

First may I congratulate you and your teammates on winning the IHSAA championship. I probably got as big a kick out of it as you boys did. Bob, I want you to come to Butler. We have a swell school and I know you will be satisfied here. We have a bunch of good boys. Also, I have a man who has taken an interest in you and wants to help you through school financially. Some time when you get some free time, I want you to come up. I want to introduce you to the man and get your application for admission filled out. Many schools will probably be after you, but just make up your mind to be with us. You can't go wrong. When can you come up?

P.S. If any of the other boys want to come with you, bring them up also.

About the same time, Marvin Wood received a telegram that he shared with Bobby:

Dear Coach:

There has been a rumor mentioned to me by Samuel Bloome that Mr. Ray Howard, president of Howard Enterprises, Distributors of Deering Air Conditioners, wants to sponsor the boy by the name of Plump that won the state tournament with the assistance of Paul D. Hinkle, one of the greatest coaches in the world. I will send you by Western Union money order or certified check for his four year tuition at Butler. It is a rumor that Paul D. Hinkle told Mr. Plump to stall if my check or money order is no good. If my money order is no good I can borrow the money from William Allison, president of Allison real estate Company at Tenth and Tibbs. This politician will back me to the tune of one hundred thousand dollars with no interest. His credit is good in above mentioned amount. I know my credit is good because everybody has some of it including Paul D. Hinkle. I borrowed one hundred and eighty dollars to get through college and am still paying Paul interest.

Col. Raymond Archie Howard

Versailles, KY

It seemed clear that Butler was going to find a way to attract Bobby Plump. Bobby decided to visit. He convinced Ray Craft and Bob Engel to go with him. While there, he was introduced to Frank Reisner, the man Coach Hinkle had mentioned in his letter.

Reisner was an alumnus, a member of the Sigma Chi fraternity. "He offered to pay for my room and board and all my books," Bobby said. "I asked him if I had to join Sigma Chi to get the deal."

That wasn't part of the deal, Reisner told him. Nor was tuition. But instead of getting the money from another Butler backer, Coach Hinkle proposed to give Bobby a tuition job to pay for his school. Bobby was to take care of the floor at Butler Fieldhouse.

So the finances were all arranged. But the kicker was the people Bobby met at Butler. He knew he didn't have to join Sigma Chi. But he got along very well with the guys he met there. "On one trip there, I met Mark Peterman and Scott Chandler and Dave Gentry. I thought they were great guys," said Bobby.

Soon, Mark and Scott and Dave were visiting Bobby in Pierceville. "I really felt wanted there. And I felt like I belonged."

And so the decision was made, late in August of 1954. Bobby Plump, the kid from Pierceville, was going to college: Butler University, Indianapolis, Indiana. He'd met some new friends. He'd be playing basketball for a coach he respected. There was just one problem: a mysterious, powerful headache he just couldn't seem to shake.

Butler Fieldhouse was one of the premier basketball venues in the nation. Because it was an Indianapolis school, more Butler games were televised back in the '50s than IU or Purdue games. Butler played as tough a schedule as any school in the country. And, unlike at the Big Ten schools, where freshmen couldn't play for the varsity, Bobby thought he might be able to be a starter all four years at Butler.

Also unlike the Big Ten, Butler couldn't offer scholarships. But they could help their athletes in other ways. That summer, Bobby got a handwritten letter from Butler Coach Tony Hinkle:

> Dear Bob:
>
> First may I congratulate you and your teammates on winning the IHSAA championship. I probably got as big a kick out of it as you boys did. Bob, I want you to come to Butler. We have a swell school and I know you will be satisfied here. We have a bunch of good boys. Also, I have a man who has taken an interest in you and wants to help you through school financially. Some time when you get some free time, I want you to come up. I want to introduce you to the man and get your application for admission filled out. Many schools will probably be after you, but just make up your mind to be with us. You can't go wrong. When can you come up?
>
> P.S. If any of the other boys want to come with you, bring them up also.

About the same time, Marvin Wood received a telegram that he shared with Bobby:

> Dear Coach:
>
> There has been a rumor mentioned to me by Samuel Bloome that Mr. Ray Howard, president of Howard Enterprises, Distributors of Deering Air Conditioners, wants to sponsor the boy by the name of Plump that won the state tournament with the assistance of Paul D. Hinkle, one of the greatest coaches in the world. I will send you by Western Union money order or certified check for his four year tuition at Butler. It is a rumor that Paul D. Hinkle told Mr. Plump to stall if my check or money order is no good. If my money order is no good I can borrow the money from William Allison, president of Allison real estate Company at Tenth and Tibbs. This politician will back me to the tune of one hundred thousand dollars with no interest. His credit is good in above mentioned amount. I know my credit is good because everybody has some of it including Paul D. Hinkle. I

borrowed one hundred and eighty dollars to get through college and am still paying Paul interest.

Col. Raymond Archie Howard
Versailles, KY

It seemed clear that Butler was going to find a way to attract Bobby Plump. Bobby decided to visit. He convinced Ray Craft and Bob Engel to go with him. While there, he was introduced to Frank Reisner, the man Coach Hinkle had mentioned in his letter.

Reisner was an alumnus, a member of the Sigma Chi fraternity. "He offered to pay for my room and board and all my books," Bobby said. "I asked him if I had to join Sigma Chi to get the deal."

That wasn't part of the deal, Reisner told him. Nor was tuition. But instead of getting the money from another Butler backer, Coach Hinkle proposed to give Bobby a tuition job to pay for his school. Bobby was to take care of the floor at Butler Fieldhouse.

So the finances were all arranged. But the kicker was the people Bobby met at Butler. He knew he didn't have to join Sigma Chi. But he got along very well with the guys he met there. "On one trip there, I met Mark Peterman and Scott Chandler and Dave Gentry. I thought they were great guys," said Bobby.

Soon, Mark and Scott and Dave were visiting Bobby in Pierceville. "I really felt wanted there. And I felt like I belonged."

And so the decision was made, late in August of 1954. Bobby Plump, the kid from Pierceville, was going to college: Butler University, Indianapolis, Indiana. He'd met some new friends. He'd be playing basketball for a coach he respected. There was just one problem: a mysterious, powerful headache he just couldn't seem to shake.

CHAPTER SEVENTEEN

BUTLER BOUND

1954-55 was to be a big year at Butler University. The school celebrated its centennial in 1955, and festivities commemorating Butler's founding and its 100-year history were planned all across the campus. This was also the year Butler dedicated Holcomb Observatory, featuring one of the Midwest's largest telescopes. Budding astronomers could look forward to up-close views of the planets and stars.

1954 was a big year for Bobby Plump, too. When Bobby moved into the Sigma Chi house on Butler's campus, it was the first time he'd ever lived in a house with indoor plumbing and a telephone. Bobby was shooting for the stars, too: it was the beginning of a storied four-year college basketball career in which Bobby Plump rewrote the Butler University basketball record books.

Bobby arrived on campus in the fall of 1954 with his clothes packed in a little tin box, Milan teammate and pal Ray Craft by his side, and promises from Mark Peterman and Scott Chandler that there'd be places for both of them at Sigma Chi. This was particularly reassuring to Bobby; as the youngest child in the Plump family, he'd always had older brothers and sisters around the house. Although being away at school was scary, having the fraternity was "like coming home after a hard day of classes or practice. I felt like I belonged there."

Friends like Mark and Scott made it easy to belong. They knew basketball. Scott's father had played for Tony Hinkle's 1928 national champion Butler Bulldogs, and Mark's dad was the basketball coach at Indianapolis Shortridge High School. Mark himself was a basketball player who looked to be a starter for the Bulldogs as a sophomore that year.

But school came before basketball. Bobby found the transition from high school to college classes to be difficult, but not as tough as he'd expected. The extra attention he and his classmates had received at Milan High School helped him to adjust quickly to college-level academics. The fraternity helped in this area, too. Bobby could find men in just about every field of study living at Sigma Chi to help him with his coursework. And five nights a week, freshman pledges were required to spend several hours studying. "This discipline was really important to me. I'd always found it tough to study on my own," Bobby said. "Having Ray Craft as my fellow pledge and roommate was an immense help, too. We studied together and always supported each other."

Bobby had decided to major in Education at Butler. He wanted to teach and coach after graduation. Before taking many education classes, though, he had to complete Butler's basic liberal arts requirements — English, history, math, philosophy, and more. "English was difficult for me," he said. Yet, Bobby credits Butler English Professor Alegra Stewart with inspiring his life-long love of reading. In history, "I was always impressed with Dr. Silver's knowledge of history. He'd stand at the front of the room and talk for the whole hour, maybe glance at his note cards every once in a while to keep his place."

College life wasn't all studying, of course. There were all kinds of social events — something big every weekend, it seemed. Bobby stayed for some of the festivities, but didn't have too much to do with the coeds at Butler. His on-again/off-again relationship with high school sweetheart Jo Anne Steinmetz was on again. Jo Anne was in nursing school at Good Samaritan Hospital in Cincinnati, and sometimes Bobby hitchhiked home on weekends to see her. Jo Anne came to Butler for weekend visits whenever she could, too.

Fraternity life kept Bobby busy, too. Bobby's pledge class at Sigma Chi was big — 21 freshmen — and there were fraternity activities every week. Most were fun. To Bobby, being a pledge was like being on a team: you stuck together and played together and, together, you achieved your goal. For those aspects of pledgeship that weren't so much fun — line-ups at which the active brothers made pledges perform calisthenics and endure a lot of yelling — Bobby had Mark Peterman to guide him. "Those line-ups would have scared the heck out of me if not for Mark. He took me under his wing. I remember once when something was about to happen, Mark took me to a movie so I didn't have to go through it," Bobby said.

Mark could protect Bobby at the Sigma Chi house. But he couldn't protect him on the basketball floor. Here, the competition was going to be tougher than ever. "I was surrounded by guys who had been the very best players at the high school level," Bobby said.

But his first impression was that he could play. "I knew the Hinkle system just about as well as anybody," said Bobby.

Paul D. "Tony" Hinkle was already a coaching legend in 1954. He'd coached at Butler since 1921, not just basketball, but football and baseball, as well. He was also Butler's athletic director. Mr. Hinkle had played football at the University of Chicago for Amos Alonzo Stagg, who pioneered such innovations as the huddle and the T-formation. And, as a coach, Mr. Hinkle himself was an innovator. It was Tony Hinkle who first suggested the use of an orange basketball. His more than 30 years of coaching made Tony Hinkle one of the most successful three-sport coaches in collegiate history, and a man respected and revered by coaches, players, and sports fans across the nation. John Wooden referred to Tony Hinkle as "the great one" and said, "I have said for years that I think Tony Hinkle is one of the best coaches the game has ever had. I enjoyed knowing him and learning from him. I had the utmost respect for Mr. Hinkle."

"If they ever had a hall of fame for gentlemen in athletics, the first two inductees in my mind would be Everett Dean and Tony Hinkle," IU Coach Bob Knight once said.

The first time Bobby Plump met Tony Hinkle was on the baseball diamond, where Mr. Hinkle was manicuring the field, pulling up dandelions and putting them in his pocket. The second time, Mr. Hinkle traveled to Milan to see him. Butler tennis and basketball player Dave Gentry went along for the ride and remembered Bobby as "very modest. I guess I expected him to be off the wall." The third meeting was the one at which Mr. Hinkle introduced Bobby to Frank Reisner, the man who took care of Bobby's room and board at Butler.

But the fourth meeting didn't take place until later in the fall of 1954. When basketball practice began, Coach Hinkle was still in the middle of football season. "Pop Heddon had us over in the little gym. He and Coach Bob Dietz were drilling us on the Hinkle system. I wasn't too excited about that. I remember wanting to get out on the big floor," Bobby said.

Pop Heddon was a football coach, as well. He had a reputation for telling tall tales. Danny Lehane, who played football for the Bulldogs and was president of the Butler B-Men's Club, said, "Pop would tell us stories that just didn't make sense. We used to challenge him on them, and we got him to admit he was lying about half the time.

"Pop said, 'I can see you guys are onto me. So whenever I'm going to tell a true story, I'll hold my fist up in the air. If I don't have my fist up, you'll know it's just something I'm making up.'

"One afternoon, Pop was talking with a group of us out on the football field, telling us a true story. He was standing there with his fist in the air and his back to the field. Meanwhile, Leroy Thompson, this big strong fullback, came running from about a mile away on a real long pass play, not looking where he was going. We could see the impending collision, and we started to say something to Pop.

"But it was too late. Leroy hit Pop and knocked him clear over us, about ten yards. Pop landed in a mud puddle. He got up and rubbed some mud off his arms and rubbed that bald head of his and said, 'Kid, get up and do that again. I love it!'"

Bobby finally made his way back to the big floor when Tony Hinkle arrived. He walked onto the floor and called to trainer Jim Morris, "Get ready, Jim. There are going to be some blisters."

He was right. "Practices were long and hard. But Mr. Hinkle made them fun. We did things over and over. He wanted you to learn his system, and he wanted you to get it right every time. And you wanted to get it right, because you knew you weren't going to play unless you did."

Coach Hinkle never yelled. But sometimes he had a way of emphasizing his points through caricature. "You didn't want to mess up, because Mr. Hinkle would do an imitation of you, overemphasizing what you were doing wrong."

Practices often ended with shooting contests. "Mr. Hinkle had an old-fashioned shot. He brought the ball down real low and shot it from his side. He banked everything, no matter where he was on the court, except for free throws. And he could make them."

Bobby and Ray Craft weren't the only freshmen on the Butler squad that year. Ted Guzek was a big forward, a good shooter and rebounder. Wally Cox, who had been the top high school scorer in Indianapolis at Broad Ripple High School the year before, and was first alternate on the Indiana High School All-Star Team, looked to compete for a starting backcourt job.

But Bobby received the lion's share of attention from the Bulldog returnees — a couple of whom were determined to make life rough for Mr. Basketball. Not all of Bobby's Butler teammates were happy to see him. A couple of them decided to cut Bobby down to size.

"A few guys challenged me, taking sort of an 'I'm going to show you just how good you really are' attitude. But I never let it bother me much. I just went out there and played. You can't let things like that get to you. You have to let your skills on the floor do the talking for you."

That Bobby did with a vengeance. "Bobby was made to order for Butler basketball," said Chris Theofanis, former Butler player and sports information director whose older brother George took over the reins of the basketball team when Mr. Hinkle retired in 1970. "Bobby wasn't big, but he was smart. He was a natural for the Hinkle system. He had the vision, like Larry Bird, Buckshot O'Brien, Billy Keller, and Damon Bailey, to see plays developing. Not many have that kind of talent."

But Bobby had another challenge that was potentially much more serious: a headache that wouldn't go away. "Every time I took a step, it felt like somebody was driving a hot poker through the back of my head," he said.

His trainers and doctors whispered their worst fears: polio. The dreaded killer of more than 50,000 and crippler of another 150,000 in the United States was on its way out in the mid-50's, thanks to the vaccine developed by Dr. Jonas Salk. But doctors still found cases of polio, and suspected Bobby's headaches to be the result of a slight case.

"I knew something was wrong. I hadn't felt well all summer," Bobby said.

Bobby received injections of penicillin and reticulose, sometimes twice a day. He missed practice. He missed classes. The Bulldog basketball season began without him. Bobby would miss the first nine games of the 1954-55 season. But he never considered leaving school. "I just wanted those headaches to go away," he said.

Slowly, they did begin to go away. The pain lessened. Bobby started to get more flexibility. He was on his way back.

And throughout his ordeal, Bobby knew he was part of the team. A few games into the season, Coach Hinkle asked Bobby if he wanted to accompany the team to Michigan. That would mean a plane ride, and Bobby had never been on a plane. He jumped at the chance.

"I remember seeing all those lights from the air. If a farmer had a porch light on, it lit up the whole area. It made me think of World War II, when we had the blackouts. They never made sense to me then, but now I understood how even a little light had a big effect."

As a player, Bobby missed most of Butler's pre-conference schedule — Illinois, Ohio State, Michigan, Purdue, Northwestern, Notre Dame, and Wabash. The Bulldogs were 3-6 without Bobby in the line-up.

The tenth game of the season was a rematch against Wabash, and Bobby was ready for action. He didn't start, but did get in the game. He was ready to show the world that a Pierceville Alleycat was good enough to play college ball.

One of the first times Bobby touched the ball, he tried to shoot a two-handed set shot — a shot he was being taught by Butler great and recent graduate Ralph "Buckshot" O'Brien.

The set shot fell short. By about two feet.

"I never shot another one," Bobby laughed. "And I knew I made the right decision not to go to IU."

Butler had already beaten Wabash for one of its three wins. That night, though, Wabash spanked the Bulldogs 83-62. It was time for Coach Hinkle to make a line-up change.

The next game at home at the fieldhouse. Bobby Plump was among the starting five. The result? Butler 72, Indiana State 59.

Bobby would be a starter for the rest of the year, the Bulldogs going 7-7 after their 3-7 start. The Bulldogs were 8-4 in Indiana Collegiate Conference play and split the season series with conference champion Evansville.

Bobby led the Bulldogs that year with a 12.6 point per game scoring average. Even after missing nine games, he was fourth on the team in scoring with 189 points. His 28-point performance in a conference game against DePauw was the Bulldogs' one-game individual scoring record for the season.

And Bobby wasn't the only underclassman to stand out for the Bulldogs that year. Bobby's freshman backcourt mate, Wally Cox, led all scorers with 254 total points, setting a Butler freshman scoring record along the way. Bobby's buddy Mark Peterman was a frequent starter, a strong rebounder with a 6.6 points per game scoring average. It looked as though the Bulldogs would have a strong team for several years to come.

The season was memorable for other reasons, as well. Once in the winter, as the Bulldogs were boarding the team bus for a road trip, Trainer Jim Morris approached Bobby and asked, "Where's your topcoat?"

"What's that?" Bobby asked innocently.

Morris laughed and gave him his own topcoat. He told Assistant Coach Bob Dietz about the situation, and Dietz went to the alumni for some money to outfit the kid from Pierceville. One afternoon, he called Bobby and said, "Let's go downtown. We're going to do some shopping." Bobby made his first visit to a department store that day, and Dietz bought him a handsome gray wool suit, along with shirts, ties, and shoes.

In spite of this, Bobby never received any money while playing for Butler. "I heard that it happened. In fact, I know one player who said he got a handshake with money in the palm to play at Butler. But it never happened to me. No one ever approached me," he said.

Next year, as a sophomore, Bobby would be among the first Butler athletes to receive a scholarship. But money never seemed to be a problem. With basketball and the fraternity and schoolwork, there was always plenty to do. Bobby's diligence in the classroom paid off: he made the Dean's List his freshman year.

There was also baseball to consider. The Bulldogs weren't very good this spring, finishing the season 5-11-1. Bobby started every game at shortstop in 1955 and 1956, but didn't earn a varsity letter in baseball until his junior year.

"I guess Mr. Hinkle was kind of stingy with the letters, at least when it came to baseball," Bobby laughed.

But, all in all, Bobby Plump's freshman year had been a success. His prospects were bright. But he never expected the life-changing development that was to occur near the end of his sophomore year. It was then that true love came to Bobby Plump.

CHAPTER EIGHTEEN

LOVE
AND FIREWORKS

Bobby Plump may have known the Hinkle system when he arrived at Butler University, but he had plenty to learn about other things. One was gin rummy; although the Plump family loved to play cards, gin was a new game for Bobby.

Bobby got a few lessons in the culinary arts, too. Once during a gin rummy game at the fraternity house, roommate Tom Rohrabaugh suggested going out for pizza.

"Pizza? What's that?" Bobby asked. He'd never heard of the stuff. "I remember my first one, though. Sausage, mushrooms, green peppers. Pretty good, I'd say."

Of course, there were more serious things to learn. It was in Bobby's sophomore year that Tom Rohrabaugh really taught him to study.

"I've got a big test tomorrow, and I'm going to study by osmosis," Rohrabaugh said. He proceeded to put his textbook under his pillow and go to sleep.

"He got an 'A' on the test. I tried it, but it didn't work too well for me," Bobby said.

Rohrabaugh did help Bobby out of a potential jam that year. C.B. Dyer, the jewelry company that made the rings for the Indiana state tournament, asked Bobby to be their representative on campus. Bobby had his own sample case and sold jewelry, rings, party favors, beer mugs, fraternity pins, and other merchandise.

After selling his wares for a while, Bobby received a letter from a competitor whose founder was a Sigma Chi. "The letter told me they had the exclusive rights to sell these things at Butler, and that if I didn't cease and desist, they'd revoke my fraternity pin," Bobby said.

Bobby didn't know what to do. So he turned to Tom Rohrabaugh. "Tom said, 'Let's write a letter back to them.' So that's what we did. I told them I wasn't going to cease and desist, and they could kick me out of the fraternity if they wanted to. I never heard from them again."

Overall, college life was going well for Bobby Plump. His classes were difficult but interesting. His long-distance relationship with Jo Anne Steinmetz wasn't always easy to manage, but they were getting along. And a new basketball season was just around the corner. This time, there'd be no illness to keep Bobby Plump out of the starting line-up.

This year, it was a powerful, unexpected explosion that very nearly did the trick.

One weekend evening in the fall of 1955, most of the men of Sigma Chi were out of the house at the first annual Cross and Shield Dance, an affair they sponsored with the Phi Delta Theta fraternity next door. They'd received special permission from the university to allow their dates to stay out later than usual so they could enjoy each others' company for a couple of extra hours. Coach Hinkle's basketball team had no such special privileges: they were in training, and he expected them to be in bed early. But Jo Anne had come up to Indianapolis especially for the dance, and Bobby decided Mr. Hinkle would probably be none the wiser if the two of them stayed out just a little late.

How wrong he was. And how lucky.

Late that evening, a gas leak developed in the water heater in the basement of the Sigma Chi house. When the gas hit the pilot light on the furnace, the furnace exploded, leveling an entire side of the house.

The eardrum-shattering blow rocked the entire campus. Three entire storeys — and anyone and everything in between — fell into the basement.

Wally Cox couldn't believe the wreckage. "The roof was at ground level. We formed lines to dig out bricks. Everybody thought Plump was inside."

They had good reason to think so. Bobby had been seen in the house just minutes before the explosion. Now he was nowhere to be found. And Bobby's bunk in the fraternity dorm was right above the boiler. Meaning that Bobby's bed was now in a pile of rubble in the basement.

"We couldn't locate him," said Assistant Coach Bob Dietz. "We thought he was dead."

Crews searched frantically through the rubble, fearing the worst, hoping they were wrong. It didn't seem as if anyone could walk away from a blast like that.

Fortunately, Bobby and Jo Anne had walked away before the Sigma Chi house came crashing down. Unbeknownst to the frantic rescuers, they'd left the house shortly before the explosion. The entire school breathed a collective sigh of relief when they were found.

Incredibly, no one was killed in the blast that rocked Sigma Chi, and only a couple of brothers sustained minor injuries. Only seven people were in the house at the time of the explosion. Most were still out with their dates. Even Hoagie Elliot, who fell three floors into the basement, was relatively uninjured: a mattress fell on top of him and protected him from falling bricks and concrete.

"I have to be the luckiest guy in the world," said Bobby. "Right where my bed was, there was nothing but a big hole."

The local newspapers thought he was lucky, too. "They reported that I'd lost 12 beer mugs. They never said it was my sample case from C.B. Dyer," Bobby laughed.

He didn't think he was so lucky when Coach Hinkle got ahold of him in practice. "Mr. Hinkle really let me have it for a while for being out so late," Bobby said. But Tony Hinkle couldn't be too angry. Coach Hinkle knew he probably wouldn't have had his talented sophomore guard at all if he'd been in bed at a decent hour.

The Bulldogs were shaping up to be a pretty good ballclub in the fall of 1955. Bobby was putting his knowledge of the Hinkle system to good use. "Mr. Hinkle had no use for what he called 'bouncers.' He said a bouncer was someone who put the ball on the floor to help himself. A dribbler, on the other hand, put the ball on the floor to help someone else. There was a big difference. Mr. Hinkle wanted dribblers, and he wanted you to pass and cut, pass and cut."

That Bobby Plump did beautifully, to the benefit of the Butler Bulldogs. The team posted an impressive 14-9 record for the 1955-56 season, besting the likes of Wisconsin, Michigan, Notre Dame, and Princeton. Their 8-4 Indiana Collegiate Conference record was good enough to share second place with Valparaiso. Evansville again finished on top, beating the Bulldogs twice, once in a tough overtime battle.

Once again, underclassmen held the keys to the Bulldogs' success. Guard Dave Scheetz was the only starting senior. Bobby started at the other guard spot. Junior Henry Foster started at center and was the team's leading rebounder. At the forwards, the starters were Mark Peterman and sophomore Ted Guzek, who finished the season as Butler's leading scorer with 370 points and 16.8 point per game average. Against Notre Dame, Guzek shattered the Bulldogs' individual Butler Fieldhouse scoring record with 37 points, four more than the previous record Ralph "Buckshot" O'Brien had set in 1950. His stellar performance made Guzek a unanimous selection for the ICC All-Conference team that year.

Bobby received an honorable mention on the ICC team. He was proving to be a steady, dependable performer, finishing third on the team in scoring with 270 points and a 12.3 point per game average — nearly identical to his 12.6 point average his freshman year. His unselfish play helped others mount impressive point totals, as well. The young Bulldogs were looking to be one of the most well-rounded, best-shooting teams Coach Tony Hinkle ever had.

Especially at the free throw line. Senior guard Dave Scheetz finished first in the Midwest and fourth in the nation with an .848 shooting percentage from the stripe. Bobby's .825 percentage was good enough for fourth in the Midwest and fourteenth in America.

Baseball season, 1956, went a little better for the Bulldogs than their shaky 1955 season. They finished 7-9, with Bobby starting every game and earning a service award in his second year.

But with all of Bobby's athletic success, and all the notoriety he'd already received for sinking the shot that had brought the state championship to Milan, and all the leadership he showed on the basketball floor and the baseball diamond, he was still a bit backward in the social department. Many of his fellow students considered him to be stuck-up. The truth was, he was terribly shy.

And his relationship with Jo Anne Steinmetz didn't seem to be going anywhere. The high school sweethearts still saw each other, still dated. But the spark that had fired their relationship for so long had just about fizzled.

That spring, Bobby hooked up with his buddy Elmer Pollard for a double date for a popular dance in Versailles. The dance was held at Tyson Auditorium, the site of so many significant events in Bobby's past. Bobby brought Jo Anne. Elmer brought a high school senior from Holton, Jenine Ford. Bobby didn't really know Jenine, although he'd played basketball against her brother Jon many times.

Jenine was 18 years old, and had already made plans to join her brother at Hanover College, where she would study English, in the fall. She was born in Syracuse, New York, and moved with her family to Chicago shortly thereafter. But the cosmopolitan life didn't suit her parents, Jack and Marie Ford. Marie had grown up in Holton. And, although Jack was from St. Louis, he wanted to try his hand at farming.

So the couple bought Marie's family's place in Holton and moved there to raise their family.

"I had a wonderful life growing up in the country," said Jenine. "I was very fortunate. Nobody had anything, but we didn't know the difference. It makes you more appreciative of the things you have — and more realistic about what's important."

Thanks to the Milan Miracle, everybody in Ripley County knew about Bobby Plump. In fact, Jenine had seen Bobby play at the Indianapolis Semistate in 1954, when Milan beat Crispus Attucks at Butler Fieldhouse. But for Jenine, that evening was more memorable because of something that happened off the basketball floor: Jenine, her brother, and their friends were attacked on their way out of the fieldhouse.

"We left a little early to beat the crowd. Right when we got outside, we were jumped by guys with brass knuckles.

"One guy had my arms pinned. I remembered my Mom telling me that, if anything like that every happened, I should kick the guy in the groin. So I did. I don't think he got very far," she said.

The attackers fled. "We ran to our car and drove home — never even thought of calling the police," said Jenine.

So Jenine knew about Bobby Plump. But she had never thought twice about him. She'd seen him play basketball many times. "But he didn't stand out. He wasn't really cute, like Ronnie Truitt and Bob Engel. And anyway, he already had a girlfriend, so all the girls thought he was unavailable."

So it seemed. The night of the dance, Bobby and Elmer picked up their dates. It was the first time Bobby had ever consciously laid eyes on the beautiful young woman from Holton.

The four arrived at Tyson Auditorium. The gym was packed with young people. Once inside, it seemed that both Elmer and Jo Anne were more interested in socializing with others than dancing with their dates.

"Bobby had to keep asking me to dance," said Jenine. "I thought he was really nice, and I could tell he was really shy."

After one dance, Jenine did something that was to stay in Bobby's mind long after the dance was over.

"She squeezed my hand," Bobby said. "I thought she kind of liked me."

That small squeeze gave Bobby the idea that maybe Jenine would go out with him. The next chance was the alumni dance at Milan High School. Bobby called Jenine to ask her to the dance, and she accepted. But, as usual, Bobby forgot to make arrangement to get home that weekend. So he called his old buddy Lloyd Freeman. Bobby caught up with Lloyd at the Dairy Moo in Milan.

"He told me he wanted to go to the alumni dance, and he needed a way home from Butler. I had a new car, so I went to get him. And he told me he was taking Jenine Ford to the dance," Freeman said.

"I asked him, 'What's Jo Anne going to say?'"

"She's going to be pretty surprised," said Bobby.

And so she was. But maybe not as surprised as Jenine Ford's father.

"Dad hated all of my boyfriends. He thought all of my dates came crawling out of holes on all fours. But when I told him I had a date with Bobby Plump, he said, 'Thank God!'"

Jenine's mother had a different reaction. "Bobby Plump? He's not very cute," said Marie Ford — a remark that's been a source of amusement in the Plump household for decades.

That night, Bobby picked up Jenine at her home in Holton "an hour and a half late. It gave her a taste of what life with me was going to be like," he said.

Apparently, it was okay with Jenine. That night, Bobby gave Jenine a six-foot cardboard cane — so big she had to hold it out the window of the car on the way home. Not that the cane was necessary: Jenine was already hooked on Bobby Plump.

And Bobby was smitten with Jenine. She was so friendly, so kind, so much fun, so outgoing — just the kind of girl to bring this shy country boy out of his shell. Bobby and Jenine dated all that summer, spending more and more time together as the weeks passed. By the time school started again in the fall, the two were very much in love.

But both already had made plans that were to keep them 90 miles apart for much of the next nine months. Bobby was going back to Butler for his junior year. Jenine was taking advantage of a scholarship at Hanover. Bobby's long-distance relationship with Jo Anne hadn't worked out. Could young love survive this long separation this time?

Young love, if it's true love, can survive practically anything. The shy young man from Pierceville, who had written only a handful of letters in his life, wrote to Jenine Ford practically every day. "I still have all of those letters," said Jenine.

And Jenine returned every letter Bobby sent. "It seemed I was always writing to him," she said.

Getting together in person was more difficult. That summer, Bobby had been able to borrow brother Bill's new Pontiac to take Jenine on dates. "I think she thought we were rich. Boy, did she get a surprise," Bobby said.

But during the school year, Bill's Pontiac stayed in Pierceville. So, to make things easier, Bobby bought his first car — a '51 Dodge convertible — from fraternity brother Bob Stanzak for the princely sum of $75. It was worth every penny: the engine had thrown a rod, but Mark Peterman knew a guy who had a truck engine they could buy for $100. Bobby was in business. "It was the kind of car you filled up with oil and added a quart of gas," Bobby laughed.

Even with the car, it wasn't always easy for Bobby to get to Hanover to see Jenine. During basketball season, Coach Hinkle made the boys practice on Sunday if they lost Saturday night (something that happened with regularity during the 1956-57 season). Often, that meant Bobby would make the two-hour drive to spend half an hour with Jenine on Sunday afternoons. Sometimes when he had more time, Bobby would stay at the Beta Theta Pi fraternity house with Jenine's brother Jon.

"That caused a bit of controversy," Jon said. "Since Bobby was a Sigma Chi, the Sigs on campus always thought they'd be able to use Bobby for recruiting pledges. But he always stayed at the Beta house, so, if anything, we used him to our advantage."

One weekend that winter, when Bobby had a little bit more time with Jenine, he took her on a date to the Milan Country Club. He was getting to be a local big shot. The country club was becoming a familiar place.

But the date didn't go so well. Bobby and Jenine argued and left the country club barely speaking to each other. Bobby was so flustered that he forgot to fasten the top of the convertible on the way home. "We were driving down the road at about seventy miles and hour when the top flew off," said Bobby.

Did that stop him from using the car that winter? Absolutely not. "We'd just roll up the windows and turn on the defroster," he said. Once Bobby and Jenine even double dated with Jenine's brother Jon and Judy Miller, his bride-to-be. Their destination? The drive-in.

"We put blankets over the top to keep the snow out," said Bobby.

"He used to wrap every blanket he could scrounge up around him. It's a good thing he never had to get out of the car quickly, because he'd never have been able to," said Jon Ford.

Jenine got to Butler to see Bobby as often as possible, too, although girls were allowed off the Hanover campus only one weekend a month, and only with special permission. So most weekends, Jenine studied and wrote letters. Because she was wearing Bobby's fraternity pin, she also went to Sigma Chi dances at Hanover with boys who didn't have dates.

Perhaps it was a good thing that dating was so difficult that year: It prepared Bobby for an equally tough basketball season. They opened at Ohio State, the Buckeyes' first game in the brand-new, $4 million St. John's arena. While the Bulldogs played tough, the Buckeyes proved to be too much. Ohio State christened their new home with a win, 98-82.

The Bulldogs won their own home opener, 54-50 against Wisconsin. It was a hard-fought game, with Bobby and Ted Guzek leading the way for Butler. But the victory was costly. Bobby's best friend and team captain Mark Peterman tore a ligament in his right knee at the end of the first half. The injury would keep him sidelined for the next thirteen games — including games against Illinois, Indiana, Purdue, Michigan, Michigan State, Notre Dame, the University of Denver, and John Wooden's UCLA Bruins.

Actually, the Bulldogs acquitted themselves rather well. Over the course of this tough schedule, they posted victories over Wisconsin, Denver, and Notre Dame, and won a big overtime battle against Michigan State. They played reasonable well even in defeat; UCLA shot .686 at the fieldhouse and still managed to beat the Bulldogs by only 11, 82-71. But the Bulldogs finished the year with a disappointing 11-14 record, and were only 6-6 in conference play. Even so, they were in the hunt to win a share of the ICC title right up to the last game, a 78-67 loss to Ball State that eliminated the Bulldogs.

The disappointment could barely mask other on-court successes, though. Both Bobby and Ted Guzek broke Keith Greve's single-season Bulldog scoring record of 427 points. Bobby scored 470. Guzek set the new school record with 531. The 1,826 points scored by the Bulldogs that year were also a team record. (Unfortunately, they also gave up 1,866 to their opponents — another Butler record.)

Ted Guzek led the Bulldogs with a 21.2 points per game scoring average. He was named to the third team of the 38th annual Helms Athletic Foundation All-American squad and received an honorable mention from the Associated Press.

Bobby's individual performance was nearly as strong. He averaged 18.8 points a game. His .860 free throw percentage was fifth in the nation among major college basketball players.

That year's basketball banquet was special. Bobby shared center stage with his pal Mark Peterman. The Indianapolis sportswriters named Bobby the Bulldogs' Most Valuable Player. Mark received the coveted Hilton U. Brown Award for sportsmanship, scholarship, and school spirit.

And the 1957 baseball season was a great one for the Bulldogs. They opened with a doubleheader sweep of Earlham College and finished 11-5-1. Bobby had a great year as the starting shortstop, hitting .301 and winning all-conference honors along with teammate and catcher Ken Seamon.

All the while, Bobby's relationship with Jenine flourished. By the end of her freshman year at Hanover, Jenine had a pretty good idea about where her future was heading. Suddenly, school didn't seem as important as being with Bobby. The big question was, did Bobby feel the same way about being with Jenine?

CHAPTER NINETEEN

REWRITING
THE RECORD BOOK

Bobby passed the summer of 1957 as he'd passed the summer of 1956: working on a highway road crew with Jon Ford. The job took the boys far from Ripley County. They spent their weekdays hacking through brush in some pretty wild Southern Indiana county, clearing the way for new roads. "It was a bunch of college kids getting an education in real-life living," said Jon Ford.

It was hard work, but the boys were up to it. The pay was decent, and the boys got a per diem for food and lodging expenses. "We used to do whatever we could to save money. Once down by Vincennes, we found a motel that had a separate little cabin unit with two double beds. It also had a little hotplate, so we could buy groceries and cook meals. Four of us rented the place, and we were saving a bundle. Unfortunately, one night we decided to do some exercises on the bed and broke both of them. We weren't welcome back the next week.," said Jon Ford.

One time, the boys had hacked through a particularly nasty gully only to find a 50-acre field full of ripe watermelons on the other side. They thought they'd died and gone to heaven.

"All day, we did our best work as professional thieves," Jon Ford said. "We hid a huge pile of watermelons in the woods by the side of the road with the idea of going back for them that night. But when we went back, we ran into the farmer. 'By the way, boys, if you want any melons, take them. They've all got the blight, and I can't sell them.' I expect our pile is still sitting there in the woods."

The boys worked hard all day and played hard at night. But toward the end of the summer, they always knew it was time to get back into basketball shape. They found a little YMCA gym in Speed, Indiana, where the likes of Bobby Plump attracted a pretty good crowd for pick-up basketball games. "We used to get off work then play basketball from six to midnight," Jon Ford said.

In the fall of 1957, Jenine Ford decided not to go back to Hanover. Instead, she moved to Indianapolis to be closer to Bobby while he finished his senior year at Butler. Although her parents were a little disappointed in her decision, they didn't protest too much. And Jenine's moving to Indianapolis made at least two other people very happy. One was Bobby Plump. The other was Tony Hinkle.

"Bobby used to call me three or four times a week when I was at Hanover, and Mr. Hinkle picked up his phone bills. I guess they amounted to several hundred dollars that year. So when I decided to move to Indianapolis, Mr. Hinkle told Bobby, 'I sure am glad Hanover moved to Butler,'" said Jenine.

It was Mark Peterman who found Jenine a place to live. He knew a widow named Thelma Morgan who was a home economics teacher at Indianapolis Manual High School. Mrs. Morgan lived in a little house not far from campus and had a room she wanted to rent. Jenine moved in with Mrs. Morgan, who promptly set about trying to make a homemaker out of the young lady from Holton.

"I'm afraid I wasn't too good a Home Ec student," Jenine said. "Mrs. Morgan tried to teach me to cook, but I didn't want to learn. I couldn't even boil an egg."

Soon after arriving, Jenine found a job working on the switchboard at Indiana Bell. The job enabled Jenine and Bobby to replace the Dodge convertible with something a little newer: a pink-and-white '56 Ford with green interior. They bought the car from Charlie Thompson, a friend of Jenine's family from Holton. Bobby and Jenine were sold on the car after they were told it had been driven only to church on Sundays by a little old lady — a story they believed.

Perhaps it was true. But that didn't mean the car always ran well. One evening after a date, the Ford's transmission decided it didn't want to go forward anymore. So Bobby dropped off Jenine at a friend's house on the south side of town and backed all the way to Butler on the north side — meaning that Indiana's Mr. Basketball and Butler's star guard set another record, one for driving in reverse through Indianapolis. It's believed that this record still stands.

Such was the price of love. And Bobby and Jenine were very much in love, so much so that their engagement was merely a formality. It didn't surprise much of anyone when, that fall, the question was popped — by Jenine.

"That's true. I told Bobby I thought we should be married when he was done with school. He said that sounded fine with him. If I'd have waited for him to ask, we'd never have gotten married," said Jenine.

Jenine's engagement made her quite a celebrity around the

engineering department at Indiana Bell. Most of her co-workers were men, and, "they all wanted to talk basketball with me on Monday mornings," Jenine said.

This season, they had plenty to discuss. Bobby led the Bulldogs to their best season in nearly a decade and National Invitational Tournament (NIT) post-season play, while having a career year, claiming several Butler records along the way.

The season began with a tough loss to Michigan State — the previous year's Big Ten co-champions and a team the Bulldogs had beaten the year before. After drubbing the Fort Knox Tankers at home 90-64, the 'dogs hit the toughest part of their schedule: a pre-conference stretch that saw them play Ohio State, Illinois, Wabash, Wisconsin, and Michigan prior to the Hoosier Classic tournament that featured IU, Purdue, and Notre Dame. Butler acquitted itself well, knocking off Ohio State, Wabash, and Michigan, and losing to Wisconsin by only a point.

The Hoosier Classic was played at Butler Fieldhouse in December. In the Friday games, the Bulldogs met IU and Purdue played Notre Dame. The 'dogs were more than ready. They whipped the Hoosiers 84-78 — a feat that became even more significant later that year, when IU finished as champion of the Big Ten. Wally Cox had 19 points for the Bulldogs. Butler wouldn't defeat IU again until November, 1993, in a huge upset victory at Hinkle Fieldhouse.

The next night, Purdue turned the tables on Butler. After losing a tough game to eventual NCAA tournament semi-finalist Notre Dame on Friday, the Boilermakers bested the Bulldogs 83-78 on Saturday, in spite of Bobby's stellar performance — 25 points in the first half and a total of 33 for the game. In the late game, Notre Dame's junior sensation Tom Hawkins scored 28 points. IU All-American Archie Dees scored 32 which, added to his 30 against Butler, set a new Hoosier Classic scoring record. But Notre Dame prevailed 89-74, finishing 2-0 in the tournament and claiming the "championship of Indiana."

The Bulldogs marched on. After disappointing losses to Fresno State and Notre Dame, the Bulldogs were ready to take on the rest of the ICC. They were just 5-6. But it was clear that Coach Hinkle's team could light up the scoreboard.

"We used to joke that we argued about taking it out of bounds," said Wally Cox, Bobby's four-year mate in the Bulldog backcourt. "Because once you took it out, you would never get it back. That team of ours had such good shooters. Everybody had to have the ball. Mr. Hinkle used to laugh that nobody wanted to play defense."

The Bulldogs dropped their first conference game, losing 64-62 to St. Joseph. But the next game, Bobby and his teammates mounted the biggest scoring attack in Butler history with a 101-76 defeat of arch rival Evansville. Keith Greve, the former Butler scoring champ who'd returned to finish his eligibility after two years in the service, pumped in 17, as did Ken Pennington, the big sophomore center from Warren Central High School.

But their combination of 34 points didn't hold a candle to Bobby Plump's output that night. Bobby hit nearly everything he shot, scoring 41 points — a new Butler single-game record. Twenty-four of those points came on a 12-for-18 performance from the field. The other 17 came on 17 free throw attempts — another Butler record, and one that still stands today.

"He was unstoppable that night — just unbelievable," said Wally Cox.

That year, Butler closed its season with 11 wins in 14 games, going 10-2 in the ICC to win the conference championship with relative ease. Their impressive 16-10 record was good enough to earn a spot in the NIT — their first NIT invitation ever. The 'dogs would fly to Madison Square Garden in Manhattan to take on St. John's of Brooklyn. Spirits were high; the Bulldogs were big, quick, and on a roll.

Unfortunately, so was St. John's. Butler had uncharacteristic trouble at the free throw line, and trailed St. John's 35-33 at the half. A surge at the beginning of the second half gave the Bulldogs a 41-38 lead. But the next five minutes were all St. John's. They outscored Butler 19-11 on skilled outside shooting. The Bulldogs never caught up. Final score: St. John's 76, Butler 69. Ted Guzek tied with St. John's Al Seiden for scoring honors with 23 points. Wally Cox had 19, and Bobby added 14 in the loss.

It was a disappointing finish to a great season. But the Bulldogs had played a good game against a tough opponent. St. John's would go on to win the NIT that year.

And it was difficult to be dissatisfied with their overall performance. That year's Butler squad set school records for most points in a game (101) and most points in a season (2055). They led the ICC in field goal accuracy (.448) and free throw percentage (.740). Those figures were good enough for sixth and fourth in the nation, respectively, and the Bulldogs' average of 79 points a game was eleventh in the nation. Had the three-point shot existed during the 1957-58 season, the Bulldogs could have been serious contenders for a national championship.

Individually, the Bulldogs shone, as well. Forwards Ted Guzek and Keith Greve both broke the previous four-year scoring record of 1,248 points. All five starters averaged in double figures: Plump (19.6), Greve (14.0), Cox (12.7), Guzek (11.9), and Pennington (11.4).

Bobby Plump not only eclipsed the old Butler scoring record: he set the new record. His four-year total of 1,439 points was the most in Butler history. Late in the season, he ranked 22nd in the nation in scoring and 13th in field goal percentage. His career total of 475 free throws is still a Bulldog record. He finished sixth in the nation with an .832 free throw percentage and, for the second year in a row, was named Butler's Most Valuable Player.

The honors kept coming. Bobby was named an All-Indiana Collegiate Conference selection. For the second year in a row, he was also honored by being named to Sigma Chi's All-Sig basketball team, along with Pitt All-American Don Hennon, Dick Haga of Stanford, John Nacincik of Maryland, and John Powell of Miami of Ohio. Here's what *The Magazine of Sigma Chi* had to say:

Recognized by many as "the best all-around small man in college basketball," Bobby Plump of Butler joins the All-Sig team leaving a trail of adoring and impressed followers in his wake.

It was a great finish to a great career. According to former Butler teammate George Theofanis, "Pound for pound, Bobby was the best ballplayer Butler ever had. He was fundamentally sound. He was a very team-oriented player — a good shooter, passer, and defensive player."

Mert Prophet, who was Butler's trainer in the mid '50s, agreed. "They were super, super years. They were all good. Plump had a great shot and fit in well with the Hinkle system."

Bill Davis, 1935 Butler grad and a college track star, followed

Bobby's career at Butler. "He was an excellent player, a great floor general. He had an excellent career here."

And Tony Hinkle, who was never one to play favorites, agreed. In 1989, while sitting at an Indianapolis Indians baseball game, Indiana basketball historian and 1942 Butler grad Herb Schwomeyer persuaded the great coach to list his greatest ballplayers.

"Schwo, you have been after me for more than 30 years to tell you who my best players were in each sport I coached. Well, I'm going to tell you. But please don't share this with anyone until after I'm gone. I don't want anyone to be mad at me if I forgot to include them. I've given this a lot of thought, but I may still forget somebody," the great coach said.

Schwomeyer agreed. Here, according to his records, were Hinkle's lists, each in alphabetical order:

Basketball: Frank Baird (1934), John Barrowcliff (1949), Jeff Blue (1964), Tom Bowman (1963), Archie Chadd (1929), Bob Dietz (1941), Dick Haslam (1962), Ralph "Buckshot" O'Brien (1950), Ken Pennington (1960), Bobby Plump (1958), Bill Shepherd (1949), Jerry Steiner (1940), and Gerry Williams (1962).

Baseball: Immon Blackraby (1938), Norm Ellenberger (1955), Tom Harding (1940), Oral Hildebrand (1929), and Paul O'Connor (1951).

Football: Don Benbow (1963), Paul Furnish (1959), Lee Grimm (1964), Tom Harding (1940), Vic Lanahan (1940), John Schnesler (1952), Al Sporer (1939), and Leroy Thompson (1956).

Schwomeyer pressed Hinkle to name his all-time greatest basketball player. But the coach declined. "We never had any great players, only great teams. The kids did what I told them, and we played as a team. That was why we could win so often," Hinkle said.

Certainly, the 1957-58 Bulldogs were among Hinkle's greatest teams. Bobby was proud to have been a member — and fortunate to have shared the season with his dad, Lester Plump. For four years, Lester had made it to nearly every Butler home game to watch his son light up the scoreboard. "We didn't talk about basketball much, but I knew he was proud of me," Bobby said.

Even though he'd graduated the year before, Mark Peterman kept up with the Bulldogs, too. After graduation, Mark married Myrna Hickman. The young couple soon had twin boys, Ken and Mike.

Mark's fatherly duties precluded him from seeing Butler games on the road. But he was always among the first in town to get the news of victory or defeat. "We had a system all worked out," Bobby said. "After the game, I'd call Mark collect. If we won, I'd ask for Mike. If we lost, I'd ask for Ken." Mark would then refuse the charge, content to know who'd won and catch up on the details later.

Jenine got to see most of Bobby's games that year, too. And she was beginning to realize that she was engaged to a basketball star. One evening, after the Bulldogs had lost at home to Notre Dame, Jenine met Bobby down by the locker room. She was hoping to catch a glimpse of Fighting Irish star Tom Hawkins. But what she noticed was that it was Bobby who most of the fans were waiting to see.

"People were asking him for his autograph, and I didn't understand why anybody would want it. I started to see that a lot of people thought he was somebody special," Jenine said.

Along with her work schedule and keeping up with basketball, there were wedding plans to make. Sometimes, Jenine and Bobby would sit in their car in the alley behind Mrs. Morgan's house to discuss their plans.

Mrs. Morgan didn't always trust the young couple. Once when she was hosting a tea for some of her fellow teachers, she found the two out in back — then read Jenine the riot act when she came inside.

"I yelled right back at her. I told her we were just talking, and she had a dirty mind," said Jenine.

The plans came together. The Fords were devout Catholics, and Bobby and Jenine planned to be married at St. John's Catholic Church in Osgood. This came as news to Lester Plump, who had been a devout Lutheran since he was a boy.

"He was such a sweetie," said Jenine. "I always admired Lester. He asked us how many people we were going to have to the wedding, and I said, 'Oh, about two hundred.' Lester said, 'I don't think the church will hold that many.'

"So I said, 'The church in Osgood is pretty big.' Lester never said a word. He'd never considered that we'd be getting married in Osgood. He always figured we were going to get married at his little church. But he never said a thing about it."

Among the preparations Jenine made was sending the announcement of her engagement to *The Indianapolis Star.* "In those days, six or eight announcements made the front page of the section in the Sunday paper. I was hoping ours would be one of the ones that made it."

Her announcement made the front page, all right. Of the sports section.

Which may have been appropriate. Even as baseball season was beginning, Bobby had more basketball to play. He was invited to play with local Amateur Athletic Union (AAU) team Marion Kay, the Indiana state champion. The team was going to Denver for the national tournament. At the same time, Bobby was named one of the top seniors in the nation and invited to play for the East squad in the annual East-West All-Star Game at Madison Square Garden in New York City.

The problem was, the schedules were in conflict. Bobby could play in the AAU tournament or the East-West All-Star Game — not both.

Bobby turned to Coach Hinkle to help him decide.

"Do you want to play ball after college?" Hinkle asked.

Bobby said he did. He'd already piqued the interest of several NBA scouts.

"Then go to New York," Hinkle advised.

The trip also conflicted with Butler's annual awards banquet. Jenine agreed to pick up Bobby's Most Valuable Player Award — along with the Andy Williams Award, a sportsmanship award similar to the Trester Award he'd won in high school — and Bobby was off to New York.

The All-Star game was a great talent showcase. While there, Bobby roomed with Archie Dees, the IU star who was to become the first-round pick of the NBA's Cincinnati Royals. One afternoon, both players received telegrams from Abe Saperstein, founder and impresario of the Harlem Globetrotters. Saperstein approached Bobby and Archie with an offer that was almost too good to refuse: $100 a game for an 18-game series against the Globetrotters. "That was a small fortune in those days," said Bobby.

Once again, Bobby turned to Coach Hinkle for advice. "Take the money if you want," said Hinkle. "But you should know that I've arranged an interview for you with the Phillips 66ers. And if you play in the Globetrotter series, you'll be considered a professional, and you won't be able to play for Phillips."

The 66ers, sponsored by Phillips Petroleum, played in the National Industrial Basketball League (NIBL). NIBL players were considered amateurs. It was a great chance for good players to continue playing basketball at a high level of competition after college — and offered the security of a full time job. That sounded pretty good to a young man about to become a husband.

While Bobby was calling Coach Hinkle, Archie Dees was calling his own mentor, IU Coach Branch McCracken. McCracken gave Dees exactly the same advice. Both passed on the Globetrotter series and $1,800. (Dees was eventually the first-round draft pick of the Cincinnati Royals. His first NBA offer was for $8,000.)

Bobby finished his athletic career at Butler as the Bulldog baseball team's regular shortstop. The 'dogs finished 9-9, fourth in the ICC.

And Coach Hinkle made good on his promise of an NIBL interview. Before he'd graduated from college, Bobby was on his way to Oklahoma to show the 66ers what he could do with a basketball. Was he good enough to make the team? He was about to find out.

CHAPTER TWENTY

OFF TO OKLAHOMA

The National Industrial Basketball League isn't exactly a household name outside of serious basketball circles today. But in the late 1950s, the NIBL was a legitimate, albeit weaker, alternative to the NBA. In fact, the NIBL was a forerunner of the late, lamented American Basketball Association (ABA), the league that gave the world the red, white, and blue basketball and some of the biggest hairdos ever seen on an athlete, male or female.

The haircuts were still pretty short in 1958, though — just what you'd expect from players who played basketball all winter and held down regular jobs in the off season. That was the primary attraction to the NIBL. Its players were given jobs with major corporations who sponsored the teams. The teams were spread across the nation: NIBL teams included the New York Tuck Tapers, Cleveland Pipers (owned by the not-yet-so-infamous George Steinbrenner), Seattle Buchan Bakers, San Francisco Investors, Denver D.C. Truckers, Peoria Caterpillars, Wichita Vickers, and Akron Goodyears. (In the early 1960s, the American Basketball League picked up some of these teams. Several years later, the ABL became the ABA. And, several years after that, a handful of ABA teams, including the Indiana Pacers, joined the NBA.) This gave the players the opportunity to travel, occasionally even on world tours.

The play in the NIBL wasn't up to NBA standards. But it wasn't far off, either, according to George Durham, who was publicity director for the Phillips 66ers. "I doubt we could have competed with the Celtics and the Knicks. But we had some very strong teams," he said.

NIBL players made about half the money they could have made in the NBA, and sometimes the stronger players in the industrial league were lured away to the pros with big contracts. But most were interested in the long-term job security the NIBL offered. The league also offered another big advantage: the NIBL was part of the AAU, and players were considered amateurs, which meant they were eligible to compete for spots on the U.S. Olympic Team (in those dark days before the birth of the Dream Team).

Bobby Plump had a shot at the NBA if he wanted it: an offer to try out with the St. Louis (now Atlanta) Hawks. He figured his shot was a pretty long one. At less than six feet tall, he was small by NBA standards even then. Still, he was considered one of the top guards in the nation, and he'd played for one of the most respected coaches in the history of the game. And he'd buried plenty of long shots in the past to make up for his lack of height.

But even a tryout with the Hawks would strip Bobby of his amateur status, making the possibility of playing in the NIBL null and void. So Bobby told the Hawks the same thing he'd told the Globetrotters: thanks, but no thanks.

Phillips' headquarters were in Bartlesville, Oklahoma, about 40 miles north of Tulsa. "At the time, I didn't know Phillips existed other than as a gas station. I told Jenine I was going to Bartlettsville, not Bartlesville."

Fortunately, he didn't have to find it on a map. On the day of his interview, Bobby flew into Tulsa and was met at the airport by Assistant Coach Gib Ford. They drove to Phillips headquarters to meet the head coach, Bud Browning.

Bobby had heard of Browning. Collegiate All-American at the University of Oklahoma. . .three time AAU All-American. . .coach of the gold-medal-winning 1948 U.S. Olympic team at the games in London. . .not to mention an incredible .903 winning percentage in six seasons as coach of the 66ers. Browning was a legendary figure to generations of basketball fans.

Bobby and Browning talked for a few minutes. Bobby then suited up and met Browning and Ford on the gym floor for a shoot-around.

"I shot for maybe ten minutes. Then they sent me to the showers. I was devastated. All I could see was $1,800 flying right out the window," Bobby said, remembering his offer from the Globetrotters.

Instead, Bobby got the shock of his life when he finished showering and met Bud Browning in his office.

"I'd like to offer you a position with the 66ers," Browning said.

Years later, Bobby found out how he won the job. One night at dinner with Browning, he asked the coach why he'd been hired. "You never saw me play, never saw any film of me, and you'd only watched me shoot for ten minutes," Bobby said.

But while Bobby had been showering, Browning called Lou Wilke, the AAU representative who Coach Tony Hinkle had contacted to arrange the Phillips interview for Bobby. "I guess he can shoot," said Browning, "but he's awfully small."

"If Mr. Hinkle says he can play, hire him," Wilke advised. And the decision was made, just like that.

So there *was* to be basketball after college for Bobby Plump. But he had a major responsibility to handle before he could leave. There was the small matter of the official sanction of marriage.

One week after graduation, on June 14, 1958, Bobby Plump and Jenine Ford were married at St. John's Catholic Church in Osgood. It was a big, joyous affair, with hundreds of friends and relatives from both families — Lester Plump and all of Bobby's brothers and sisters, and Jack and Marie Ford and aunts and uncles and cousins. Jenine's brother Jon was Bobby's best man. His groomsmen were Pierceville buddy Glen Butte, Ray Craft, Mark Peterman, and Elmer Pollard, whose sociable nature at the Versailles dance had left Bobby and Jenine alone together for the first time. Jenine's bridesmaids were all high school friends: Ruth Miller, Margaret Flick, and Gloria Furlow (who later married Jack Bradshaw, star of the 1954 Osgood Cowboys), and her Maid of Honor, Pat Ryan.

After the wedding, Bobby and Jenine drove to Lake of the Ozarks in Missouri for their honeymoon. The day after they arrived, a Monday, was to be spent fishing, one of Bobby's favorite pastimes.

"We spent all day on the boat and, before we left, Bobby told me to be careful of the sun. I told him I wasn't worried. I never got sunburned," said Jenine. So they were both a little surprised when Jenine came up with a sunburn so bad, she could hardly touch a sheet, let alone clothing, to her skin.

"For two days of our honeymoon, I lay there like a smoked salmon," she laughed.

Otherwise, it was a wonderful week. Bobby and Jenine relaxed and talked about their lives together, and their upcoming move to Bartlesville. Jenine had hardly been out of Indiana since she was a little girl. And all Bobby had seen of the outside world amounted to little more than the insides of a few dozen gymnasiums.

But when the honeymoon was over, the Plumps packed their new car — a '56 Pontiac station wagon purchased from Chris Volz — and set out for the west. Lester Plump made sure Bobby put new tires on the car before they left. After all, it was to hold everything they owned, including their entire fortune: a hundred-dollar bill they'd received from Volz as a wedding present. "There was a time not too long after that when we had a single quarter between us. Twenty-five cents. That was it," said Jenine.

When the station wagon crossed the state line from Missouri into Oklahoma, Bobby caught Jenine looking around nervously. "What are you doing?" he asked.

"Looking for Indians," she replied earnestly. She'd expected to find almost no one else in Oklahoma. "Indians and scorpions and tornadoes," she said. "That was my idea of Oklahoma."

She would find all three — and a lot more. "We had a wonderful life in Oklahoma. We made a lot of good friends there. It was a wonderful experience."

But the Plumps didn't know much of anyone when they arrived. And they didn't have anyplace to stay. Bobby called Gib Ford, who arranged to put them up in a little apartment at the Phillips Apartment Hotel, where "the bed pulled out of one wall, and the kitchen pulled out of the other."

Jenine set about trying to put the kitchen to good use. But, despite Thelma Morgan's attempts to teach her to cook, Jenine hadn't yet mastered the skills that made her an excellent cook in later years. "Bobby loved liver and onions, and I remember trying to make them one of the first days we were in Oklahoma. I threw everything into a pan of hot grease. I figured something was wrong when the apartment filled up with smoke. It was pretty ugly when I put the meal on the table. In fact, my liver and onions weren't too good for years. But Bobby never complained," Jenine said.

Such is the nature of true love. Bobby settled into his new job working in the Phillips recreation department — a men's club, swimming and diving pools, bowling alleys, and other sports facilities. Jenine got a job with Phillips, too, working in the engineering department, just as she had at Indiana Bell.

Jenine's job didn't last long. Soon after the Plumps arrived in Oklahoma (and Jenine's sunburn wore off), Jenine announced that she was pregnant. The choice to go with Phillips rather than the uncertainty of a career in the NBA was already looking like a pretty wise decision.

After a couple of weeks at the Phillips Apartment Hotel, Bobby and Jenine found a small, furnished one-bedroom apartment near work. They quickly made friends with an older couple, Mosina and Harold Malone, who became the Plumps' adopted parents. But that first summer in Bartlesville, Bobby and Jenine had real relatives visit, too. Bobby's dad made the drive with Dot and Bill to make sure the parents-to-be were getting along in the wild west.

There wasn't much place to spread out in the little apartment. Dot and Jenine slept on the double bed in the bedroom. The sofa pulled out into a double bed, which was where Lester and Bill slept. Bobby pulled a cot into the living room and slept next to his father and brother.

That first night, Jenine awoke suddenly in the middle of the night. "Dot was snoring so loudly, she woke me up. So I snuck into the living room and got on the cot with Bobby," Jenine said.

Bobby was horrified. "You can't stay here! My dad's here!" he whispered urgently.

"Bobby! We're married!" Jenine insisted.

"It doesn't matter. You can't sleep in here when my dad's here," Bobby said. So Jenine snuck back into the bedroom. She spent most of each night awake that week, listening to Dot snore.

Which was, in many ways, preferable to her days, which she spent in the bathroom, sick from Lester's cigar smoke. "Bobby's dad was such as sweet man, but I just couldn't handle the cigar smoke. And I would never have asked him to go outside. You wouldn't think twice about asking someone to smoke outside today. But back then, it never would have occurred to me," she said.

But the snoring and the cigar smoke and the cramped quarters were worth the sacrifice to see family. Lester and Dot and Bill hadn't been gone an hour when Bobby and Jenine started to miss them and wish they, too, were going back to Indiana.

But there wasn't much time to be sentimental. Basketball season was fast approaching. And, although he was considered to be an amateur, Bobby knew better. There was nothing amateur about the NIBL. This was professional basketball!

CHAPTER TWENTY ONE

LIFE IN THE PROS

The Phillips 66ers had a long history of basketball success. The team was the pet project of K.S. "Boots" Adams, who, as a young warehouse employee, formed the team with six of his cohorts in 1920. When Bobby started playing for Phillips in the 1958 season, Adams just happened to be Phillips' chairman of the board and chief executive officer. The 66ers hadn't had a losing record in their entire history. The team had captured nine national AAU titles and ten consecutive NIBL crowns. All that hardware required a trophy case nearly 50 feet long at Phillips headquarters in Bartlesville. It was a great source of pride for the town, the company, and its customers and employees.

In addition to the team honors, 12 Phillips players had been members of American Olympic basketball teams. In 1948, they'd defeated Adolph Rupp's "Fabulous Five" two-time NCAA champions from the University of Kentucky — All-American center Alex Groza, Ralph Beard, Wah-Wah Jones, Cliff Barker, and Joe Holland — to earn the right to represent their country in the Olympics. Groza, Beard, and Jones later made career moves to the NBA. Groza regularly battled big man George Mikan of the old Minneapolis Lakers for top scoring honors.

So Bobby was joining a proud tradition — and a team of tough veterans. That year, his 66er teammates included Burdie Haldorson, the 6'10" center from the University of Colorado who owned most of the team's scoring records and not a few of the NIBL's. In four seasons with the 66ers, Haldorson had been all-NIBL three times and led the league in scoring twice. He was coming off a season in which he'd been named the league's Most Valuable Player. He'd also won a gold medal as a '56 Olympian, as had Billy Evans, another Phillips rookie who came to Phillips and the NIBL from the Armed Forces All-Stars. Evans had starred in college at the University of Kentucky.

The 66ers had some other good-looking rookies. Phil "Red" Murrell, was a 6'4" forward, a collegiate All-American from Drake University and a teammate of Bobby's for the East-West All-Star Game. Dallas Dobbs, a 6'0" guard from the University of Kansas, had twice been a collegiate all-conference selection. Ray "Shag" Warren was the Air Force's Most Valuable Player in the 1957-58 season. Pete Gaudin was a 6'5" forward who'd played at Loyola University of the South. Bob Gingrich had played for the University of Colorado.

Plus, the 66ers had six other returning veterans from their 1957-58 NIBL championship team: guards Arnold Short, Dick Miller, and Gary Thompson and forwards Bill Darragh, Tom Fuller, and Jim Spivey. All in all, it was a talented, if not terribly tall, bunch of players.

Their lack of height would catch up with them. After a strong start, the 66ers had a tough NIBL season, finishing third at 15-15. The Denver Truckers took the title with a 21-9 record. Overall, the 66ers finished 33-20.

Height wasn't the team's only problem. Forward Jim Spivey missed the National AAU tournament and Pan-American Trials because of an emergency appendectomy. Billy Evans missed the AAU tournament with a sprained knee. Injuries plagued Gary Thompson for the second year in a row, as well; a broken wrist put him out of action for six weeks.

In spite of the difficulties, the 66ers charged to the finals of the AAU tournament before losing to the Wichita Vickers. They also finished a strong second in the Pan Am Games.

Burdie Haldorson had another spectacular season, winning his second straight NIBL MVP award and nearly winning the scoring title again with 1,155 points and a 21.8 point per game average.

And Bobby Plump? All the injuries gave Bobby a chance to break into the 66er line-up on a regular basis. He played in 52 of the team's 53 games, in which he averaged 5.9 points. Not surprisingly, he also led the team in free throw percentage: .804.

Bobby enjoyed himself immensely. The 66ers ended their season with a 17-day tour of Mexico, so he was seeing parts of the world he'd only imagined. And he was getting paid for playing the game he loved. Phillips paid him $6,000 a year — only about half of what he could have made in the NBA, but not bad for a kid from Pierceville, Indiana. The 66ers' traveling expenses where actually higher than NBA standards. "They were only getting eight bucks a day for meals. We were getting ten," Bobby said. "That doesn't sound like much, but you could eat pretty well on that — everywhere but in New York City."

Phillips always flew the players' wives to tournaments. But Jenine didn't get to do much traveling that year. Nevertheless, she was responsible for the highlight of Bobby's season. On April 18, 1959, the

Plumps became the proud parents of Tari Marie.

"When I first held Tari in my arms, it was the first time I'd ever held a baby. She was the most beautiful thing I had ever seen," Bobby said.

It wouldn't be too long before he'd get another beautiful surprise. In the summer of 1959, Jenine announced that the little Plump family was going to be one child bigger again. Kathryn Keleen, who has always been called Kelli, was born almost exactly a year after her sister, on April 8, 1960.

In between the births of his girls, Bobby had another basketball season to play. This one was just a bit better for the team, which this year included Arlen Clark, an All-Big Eight forward from Oklahoma State; Jerry Shipp, who was twice named Outstanding Player in the Oklahoma Collegiate Conference while playing for Southeastern Oklahoma State; H.E. Kirchner, a 6'10" center and unanimous All-Southwest Conference player from Texas Christian University; Tom Robitaille, a two-time All-Southwest Conference forward from Rice; and Don Matuszak, an All-Big Eight Conference guard from Kansas State University. After a one-year absence from the NIBL throne, the 66ers regained their title with a season-closing 117-115 overtime victory over arch rival and runner-up Wichita. Phillips finished 24-8 in the league and 41-13 overall. Bobby again played in all but one 66er contest, finishing with a 5.1 points per game average and two NIBL records: a 93 percent free throw mark and a string of 47 charity tosses without a miss.

1960 was also an Olympic year. In those days, the American Olympic team was chosen through a tournament process controlled by the AAU. The NIBL champion automatically qualified for the tournament and often won. And the winning team automatically placed at least five players on the Olympic squad.

The 66ers were looking to win. In fact, Phillips had already made reservations for their players in Rome. Bobby was a starter for the 66ers and looked to be a shoe-in for a gold medal.

But this was the year that the AAU decided to open the Olympic trials to college underclassmen. Up until 1960, only seniors could try out for the team. This meant that the Collegiate All-Stars would be extremely talented — they'd have Jerry West, Walt Bellamy, Terry Dischinger,

Jerry Lucas, John Havlacek, Darrel Imhoff, and a young whirlwind from the University of Cincinnati by the name of Oscar Robertson.

It was the 66ers' misfortune to draw the All-Stars in the first round. The youngsters proved too hot to handle. The narrowly defeated the 66ers, and Bobby's Olympic hopes were dashed. His teammate Burdie Haldorson did make the team, though, becoming only the third American ever to play on two Olympic basketball squads. The other two, Bob Kurland and Bill Hougland, were also Phillips alumni.

This was to be Haldorson's last year as a 66er. Five straight years as an All-NIBL player and a slew of scoring records were enough for the big man. His services were still much sought-after by the NBA. But he was ready to retire from basketball.

Bobby and Burdie were great friends, as were most of the players on the 66ers. "My wife Kay is still a good friend of Jenine's, too," Haldorson said. "Bobby was just an ordinary guy from Indiana — very basic, very strong. He was always interested in the team."

Jim Spivey, another Phillips teammate, said the 66ers were like family. "We'd be gone for up to 20 days at a time. The guys would be close, and so were the wives. And, I don't know if it's because we all returned at the same time, but it seems that all of our kids are about the same age, too."

Bobby played one more year with the 66ers — another strong team whose new players included guard Kermit Gentry from West Virginia Tech; Wally Frank, an All-Big Eight forward from Kansas State University; Jim Hagan, twice a unanimous selection at center for the All-Ohio Valley Conference team while at Tennessee Tech; and Al Bunge, Maryland University forward and two-time All-Atlantic Coast Conference selection. Although Jenine wasn't pregnant this year, she had two small children and still couldn't travel with the team. And Bobby did a little less traveling himself. A collision with John Barnhill, a Cleveland Pipers player who later played in the ABA, put Bobby on the sidelines with a collapsed lung.

"We ran into each other pretty hard. I didn't think much about it, but I couldn't get my breath," Bobby said. In fact, Bobby made two trips up and down the court before collapsing and crawling off the floor.

The injury caused Bobby to miss a good part of the season. And it contributed to his decision to hang up the gym shoes.

Bobby did stay with the 66ers for one more year as assistant coach to Bud Browning. He took over the team when Browning missed a six-game stretch and retired immediately thereafter, undefeated as a head coach.

After his playing days were through, Bobby had time to reflect on his professional career. "It was a very high caliber of basketball. Could we have played in the NBA? We probably didn't have the depth. But four or five players on each team could have played at that level," he said.

Was Bobby among them? Jim Spivey thought so. "The NIBL got the players who could have played on the lower division NBA teams. Bobby was a tremendous competitor. He could have played in the NBA."

Publicity Director George Durham agreed. "Bobby Plump was one of a kind. He was one of the finest guards we ever had. He was very good defensively, and, of course, at the free throw line. Bobby was a great hustler and a team leader. You can't do what he did in high school and not be a leader."

Bobby's final season was capped by a seven-week tour of the Middle East — a dream come true for a young man from Pierceville, Indiana. Near Jericho, the 66ers played an exhibition for Palestinian refugees, who, in spite of a lack of just about everything but heart, built an asphalt basketball court just so they could watch the team play.

The traveling taught Bobby not only how big the world is, but also how small. Once in a cafe in Beruit, Lebanon, a man walked up to him. The man had recognized the name and the face. "He asked me if I was Bobby Plump from Milan, Indiana. I think the other guys on the team were in shock," Bobby said.

It was that sort of experience that taught Bobby a lesson he never forgot. "People all over the country and all over the world have the same concerns we do. We're not really all that different. People want the same things in Pierceville and Milan, Bartlesville and Denver, Mexico City and Cairo," he said.

It had been a great run. But Bobby was tired of traveling, tired of being away from his growing young family. And, in the summer of 1962, Jenine was pregnant again. "It seemed like a great time to make a change," Bobby said.

The change was to involve more than basketball. Bobby's and

Jenine's families were getting older. The Plumps wanted to share their lives with the dearest people in the world to them. They wanted Lester Plump and Jack and Marie Ford to get to know their grandchildren, and vice-versa. Oklahoma was a great place. But, even after four years, it wasn't home. Bobby and Jenine decided it was time to pull up stakes and head back to Indiana. This time, there was no sunburn. And the Indians were Tari, Kelli, and one to be announced.

CHAPTER TWENTY TWO

BACK HOME IN INDIANA

"When you went to work for Phillips, you had a job at Phillips for life, if you wanted it," said Jenine Plump. Even, apparently, if you wanted to move back to Indiana. In the fall of 1962, Phillips offered Bobby a job as Indianapolis city sales manager. He accepted, and the Plumps were on their way home.

Still, the move was hard for Jenine. "We'd lived in Bartlesville for four years — some of the best times of our lives. In a way, I really hated to leave."

Having lived in Indianapolis only during their college years, Bobby and Jenine weren't quite sure where to locate their family. But they quickly found a comfortable and familiar spot: right next to Marvin Wood.

In 1962, Marvin and Mary Lou and their two kids, Doug and Dee, were living near Castleton, on Indianapolis's Northeast side, just 15 minutes or so from Butler University. Woody had had an interesting and sometimes difficult road since he'd been the toast of Indiana as coach of the Miracle Men of Milan. He'd left Milan the next year for the head basketball coaching job at New Castle, a perennial power in the prestigious North Central Conference that later produced Indiana University All-Americans Kent Benson and Steve Alford (not to mention Dwight "Ike" Tallman, who, as coach of Muncie Central in 1963, broke Marvin Wood's record as the youngest head coach ever to win the state tournament). New Castle had a big enrollment and plans to build the world's largest high school gymnasium. Although they were only 5-17 in the 1953-54 season, their history included a state championship in 1932, Final Eight appearances in 1936, 1940, and 1949, and a Sweet Sixteen run in 1950. All of which looked pretty good to a young coach who already had a state title under his belt.

But New Castle was a tough place for Coach Wood. Expectations were high, and Woody put plenty of pressure on himself to perform. In his first year at New Castle, the Trojans were 14-11, a dramatic improvement over the prior season, and won their sectional championship. The next year, the team was a dismal 6-16. After just two seasons at New Castle, Wood decided it was time to look for another job. He found it at a brand-new school: North Central High School in suburban Indianapolis.

North Central was no picnic, either. Wood was now in the center of the biggest media market in the state. His schedule was at least as tough at North Central as it had been at New Castle. His talent pool wasn't as big, either. And he didn't find anything like the talent he'd found back in Milan.

Still, Wood was up to the challenge. And he was happy to hear that his old friend and star player was coming back home to Indiana.

It just so happened that the house next door to the Woods, at 75th Street and Chester Avenue, was for sale. Bobby and Jenine called the owners to ask about the possibility of renting. The owners agreed, and the Woods and the Plumps were Indianapolis, Indiana neighbors.

Moving in next door to the Woods helped smooth the transition for Bobby and Jenine. Remarkably, they found the pace of life in Indiana somewhat faster than it had been in Oklahoma. Once, while listening to a conversation, little Tari asked Jenine, "Mommy, why do those people talk so fast?"

"I thought, 'My God, I'm raising an Okie,'" Jenine laughed.

Soon, though, Jenine and Bobby became parents of a genuine Hoosier. Jonathan Plump was born on April 8, 1963 — three years to the day after the birth of his older sister Kelli. The Plumps now had three small children to raise.

Meanwhile, Bobby was trying to adapt to life in the eight-to-five world of business. He spent his days calling on Phillips 66 stations around Indianapolis. But it wasn't long before he realized that this job wasn't going to be the challenge he was seeking. And, ironically, both he and Jenine were finding that the regular hours were an unexpectedly tough adjustment. "Basically, when he was with the team, Bobby left in October and didn't come back until April. We just weren't used to keeping business hours," Jenine said.

Since coming back to Indiana, Bobby had found a number of friends in the insurance business. It seemed to be an interesting and challenging career. And it definitely wasn't eight-to-five. The more he explored the idea, the more he like it.

But it was a little scary. About this time, Jenine was planning to go back to school at Butler. It didn't seem to be an ideal time to make another big career change. "It was terrifying," Jenine said. "It would have meant giving up the paycheck we depended on for something that was a lot riskier." And there was a small matter of loyalty. Phillips had been good to the Plumps. And Bobby was a fiercely loyal person.

The first time Bobby was offered a position with the Fidelity Union Insurance Company, he turned them down. "I still just wasn't sure about leaving Phillips," Bobby said.

But the people at Fidelity Union proved to be as persistent as Bobby Plump. They flew him out to their corporate headquarters in Dallas to meet with founder, president, and CEO Carr P. Collins. Collins convinced Bobby that he was offering a challenge worthy of the aspirations of this ambitious young man, and Bobby accepted. With a mixture of excitement and sadness, Bobby said good-bye to Phillips and accepted the challenge of opening his own insurance business. It was another giant step for the former Pierceville Alleycat.

Bobby's challenge was to break new ground in Indiana for Fidelity Union. His target market was college students preparing to enter the workplace. For every $10,000 life insurance policy he sold, Bobby made $109.48.

With the desk and chair the company sent him, Bobby set up an office in his home. His first day on the job was his birthday: September 9, 1963. (Believe it or not, that same desk and chair are still in service today.)

He soon found out that his challenge was going to be even greater than he expected. On November 22, 1963, President John F. Kennedy was assassinated while riding in a Dallas motorcade. While the world mourned, insurance business competitors spread rumors that, because of all the turmoil in Dallas, Fidelity Union was going out of business.

Once again, Bobby found himself in the familiar position of underdog. "I didn't think I was ever going to make it. I must have thought about quitting 30 or 40 times in those first few months," he said.

But he didn't. And he had the help and support of Jenine, his best friend and partner, who was trying to balance motherhood and school at the same time. "I used to come home from class and hold the baby in one hand while typing with the other. I'm not sure how we did it all," she said.

Having good friends and neighbors helped, too. Ralph and Sally Preble, friends from Ripley County — Ralph played with Bobby on Milan's 1953 team — were good friends, as were their new neighbors,

Jim and Betty May. The Plumps were also close to Mike Hafenbritle, who'd been the basketball coach in Jenine's hometown of Holton, and his wife Joan. The Hafenbritles had no children, "but our kids regard them as second parents," Jenine said. The Plumps made it a tradition to attend state tournament games with the Hafenbritles. "We've seen all but one state tournament since 1964 with them," Bobby said.

And, although it surprised Bobby, he found that he was still in demand as a speaker. People remembered his heroics, although ten years had passed since his shot had won the championship for the Milan Indians. He traveled all around the state speaking to civic organizations and schools and youth groups, and, in the process, met many other people who were to become friends for life — among them *Indianapolis Star* sports editor Bob Collins, ex-Crispus Attucks star Bailey Robertson, Jr., and Bailey's little brother Oscar, who was in the middle of his Hall of Fame career with the Cincinnati Royals of the NBA.

And there was Woody, right next door. The Woods were good friends, and Marvin loved it when Jonathan came over to play — usually.

"Once, I was just standing in the kitchen, and I heard someone scream, 'Jenine!' from next door," Jenine said. She knew Woody was home recuperating from back surgery, so she rushed outside. She found him on all fours, with Jonathan on his back.

"He'd been doing some work in the garden, and Jonathan wanted a horsy ride. Woody couldn't get him off his back, and he couldn't stand up. He was stuck," Jenine laughed.

Another time, Jonathan got into Woody's golf clubs. which Woody didn't mind. "It was Jonathan hitting rocks with his clubs that he minded," Jenine said.

The mid-60s were a great time for the Plumps. Tari and Kelli, and later Jonathan, went to school at St. Pius X, the Indianapolis Northeastside Catholic church to which Jenine belonged. "Even though my Dad was a devout Lutheran, and I often attended the Methodist church in Pierceville, there was never any question about raising the kids in the Catholic church," Bobby said.

The Plumps valued their family time. Every summer, they vacationed with Jenine's parents, Marie and Jack Ford, down on the Ohio River, which never failed to bring back memories of the Haven of

Rest and camping with the Pierceville gang. "Jack had a bread truck that he'd converted into a camper, and we had a station wagon we used to sleep in," Bobby said. On weekends, the entire Plump family would pile into the wagon and drive down to Southeastern Indiana to Brooksburg, to float down the Ohio on their pontoon boat. Often, friends and family would visit. "I think we went just about every weekend from May through October. All of our kids have since told us how nice it was, how much it meant to them," Bobby said.

In 1965, while Bobby's business was growing and the Plumps were becoming firmly rooted in Central Indiana, Marvin Wood was getting restless. He had coached at North Central High School for nine years and won the Marion County tournament four times. But Wood's Panthers never won a sectional. And he was frustrated with the school district's lackadaisical commitment to basketball. The high school program was fed by three junior high programs, each with its own coach and its own system. And the superintendent of schools refused Coach Wood's request for a unified youth program that would help young people develop their basketball skills before high school. The bottom line was, Wood thought he could make a bigger difference somewhere else. So when the head coaching position at Mishawaka High School in Northern Indiana became available, he applied and got the job.

Actually, it was about time for the Plumps to move, too. The house they'd been renting was getting a little small for their growing family. But with the girls in school, and Bobby's success in business, they didn't want to move too far. Fortunately, they found a home for sale just a couple of blocks away on 71st Street, just down the road from St. Pius, with a big yard for the kids and a driveway just perfect for a basketball goal.

But one morning before the move, in January of 1966, Bobby got a phone call from his sister Dot. Sometime during the night, Lester Plump had become ill. Dot tried calling Lester at home, but got no answer after three tries. She and her husband Carl were concerned about the unanswered calls and decided they'd have to drive to Pierceville to investigate.

Lester Plump had had a stroke. When Dot found him, he had already passed away. It was the second time Dot had been on hand for the death of a parent at the house in Pierceville.

Bobby was devastated, "more devastated than I'd ever been in my life. A couple of months before Dad died, I went home to see him. It felt so comfortable to be at home. I sat down and we talked about things we'd never talked about before — his dad, growing up. Dad went upstairs and pulled out a box of things that had belongs to his dad, which he gave to me.

"We must have talked for four or five hours. I don't think we ever talked that long in one sitting in our lives. It was really special.

"But I never thought about Dad dying. He'd had a stroke five or six years earlier, but I never thought about it even then. It was a long time after he died before I could talk about him. I just figured he'd always be there."

Although Bobby couldn't talk about him, he certainly heard a lot from others about Lester Plump. "Everybody told me what a great man he was. Dad had such a positive influence on so many people's lives. Sometimes you don't realize how many lives you touch."

Throughout the years after Mable Plump's death, Lester Plump never dated. "Once my father-in-law, Jack Ford, told Dad he wondered why he'd never taken up with another woman. Dad got so angry, he nearly punched him. He still felt that strongly about my mother, years and years after she'd died," Bobby said.

Lester Plump was only 66 years old when he died. But Bobby's brothers were even younger when they passed away. Bill died of a heart attack in 1977 at age 54, shortly after marrying; in fact, his heart attack occurred at the hospital, where he was visiting his wife. Les was only 57 when he lost a lengthy battle against cancer in 1984.

"Bill was such a sweetheart, such a good, simple man. And Les was one of my favorite people in the world, one of my best friends. We used to do a lot together," said Jenine. "I really miss them."

Losing his father and brothers at such young ages caused Bobby to become philosophical about living and dying. "I finally came to the realization that it's all part of the process of living — that you can't die if you don't live. Funerals shouldn't be sad affairs. You should be happy for the time you had with friends and relatives, and for all the experiences you shared."

It's a philosophy that has served Bobby well over the years and helped him deal not only with the passing of family members, but the inevitable tragedies that touch one's life through the years. In 1972, Bobby's Butler teammate Ted Guzek had just been named principal at Southport Middle School when he was killed in a terrible automobile accident. Ted's wife Peggy was in a coma for more than a year before she died. Several years later, in 1979, Marvin Wood's son Douglas was killed in a motorcycle accident after a prolonged battle with alcohol and drug abuse.

The Plumps' religious faith has always been a rock, as well. Much like his father, Bobby never wore his religion on his sleeve. But his faith was unmistakable. Father Marty Peter, one of the Plumps' closest friends since he arrived at St. Pius X as a newly ordained priest in 1967, said, "One of my strong beliefs is something I heard years ago from a great theologian, who said that there are a lot of anonymous Christians out there, people who don't talk about it, but live it. That's what real Christianity is all about. That's what I see in Bobby. He is a deeply kind and caring person. He lives the Christian message of love of God and love of neighbor."

It was evident in the way Bobby treated his children as they were growing up, always encouraging, never pushing them to perform. Bobby taught all of them to shoot jump shots and lay-ups. "He told us to just lay it up like an egg," Tari said.

Both girls played basketball at St. Pius, and Kelli played a bit later at Chatard High School. Once in eighth grade, Kelli found herself in a position to make two clutch free throws to win a game. She hit them both. Kelli was then surprised at the fuss surrounding her feat — "another Plump pulling out a last-second victory."

"The kids knew Bobby had played basketball, but he never bragged about anything. It wasn't until the kids were older that they knew he'd done anything remarkable," Jenine said.

Tari agreed. "When I was in kindergarten, there was a little boy who used to tease me all the time. 'Bobby Plump, Bobby Plump, he made that last second shot.' I asked mom what he meant, and she told me he was just jealous. She showed me her scrapbook, but it didn't seem like such a big deal to me. The older I got, though, the more people I met who knew about it."

In 1972, there could have been little doubt. At a special banquet to raise money for the Indiana State Chapter of the National Cystic Fibrosis Research Foundation, Bobby was honored as a member of Coach Tony Hinkle's All-Time Indiana High School Dream Team. Other members included James Bradley (East Chicago Roosevelt), Bob Ford (Evansville North), Willie Gardner and Oscar Robertson (Indianapolis Crispus Attucks), George McGinnis (Indianapolis Washington), Homer Stonebraker (Wingate), John Townsend (Indianapolis Tech), Robert "Fuzzy" Vandivier (Franklin), and John Wooden (Martinsville).

The Plump girls were decent basketball players, although their Chatard teams were never very good. Kelli also starred in volleyball, twice making it to the Final Four with Chatard, once losing to a team from South Bend on which boys had petitioned the school to be allowed to play girls' volleyball. Bobby never missed a game. "He was wonderful about supporting me," Kelli said. "He was always there, and my freshman year, we were horrendous."

Being a dad with young girls in the house wasn't always easy for Bobby. One night, the girls were having a slumber party down in the basement with several friends. In the middle of the night, Bobby heard a loud noise and rushed downstairs. He flipped on the lights to see what was the matter.

Unfortunately, he'd forgotten to put on any clothes.

"The girls' friends still tease me about that," Bobby laughed. "They want to know when I'm going to go streaking again."

Both Tari and Kelli graduated from Purdue University. They lived together for a couple of years on campus. "They were like twins," Bobby said. "They were best friends, always together."

Through the 1960s, Bobby's business became another success story in his life. Bobby Plump and Associates expanded beyond his ability to manage it at home. Bobby needed an office — and a partner.

He found one in Dave McCollum. Dave was a native of Lynn, Indiana, a little town north of Richmond, about 80 miles from Milan and 30 miles from Muncie. He was 10 years old when Bobby hit the winning shot in 1954. "I had a Bobby Plump scrapbook," he said.

Dave was a good high school basketball player and a smart coach;

his Randolph-Southern junior varsity team was 37-2 his last two years there. He met Bobby when he purchased an insurance policy from him. "It was like meeting Joe Namath," said Dave. The two became friends, and Bobby convinced Dave to join his agency in 1970.

It proved to be an excellent move for both men. Together, they made Bobby Plump and Associates a strong, respected insurance and financial planning firm.

In the late 1970s, Fidelity Union Life became part of Allianz Insurance, a German company that is the sixth largest insurer in the world. Bobby and Dave made a smooth transition. Phil Wheat, director of the Midwest for Allianz, said of Bobby, "His client base is very loyal. I never saw him perform athletically, but he probably has some of the same attributes in business, including sneaky speed — you know, someone who's so smooth you don't realize they're fast until they turn it on. Bobby's creative and intelligent, and you don't always get that combination."

It was also around this time that Jack and Marie Ford came to live with Bobby and Jenine in Indianapolis. The Fords had made a good life farming in Holton until 1941, when Jack decided to learn to become an electrician. For years, he not only did electrical work, but also plumbing, building, carpentry, and general repairs. But Jack's eyesight began to fail him. Bobby and Jenine added onto the house so the Fords could live close to their family in retirement.

Fifteen years of weekends traveling to Brooksburg ended, as well. Bobby and Jenine decided to sell the boat and invest in a house in the country. Beginning in 1979, their weekends would be spent at their cabin in scenic Bartholomew County, just west of Columbus and east of Nashville in Southern Indiana. It was a sanctuary and a gathering place, a wonderful benefit of hard work and a successful career in the insurance business.

Everything seemed secure for the Plumps. But there was a dark cloud on the horizon — another challenge that would test the mettle of the entire family. Especially their son, Jonathan.

Memories

of a

Small Town Hero

and his

Classmates, Teammates, Coaches,
Family and Friends

Carr Street in Milan around the turn of the century.

The iron horse pulls out of the station in Milan.

Carr Street in Milan around the turn of the century.

The iron horse pulls out of the station in Milan.

B. & O. S. W. Pumping Station, Milan, Indiana.

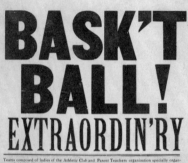

Poster promoting a women's basketball game in Milan, February, 1924.

Old Milan High School.

Milan Indians, 1928. Front row, from left: Francis Nocks, Louis Coffee, George Lewis. Middle: Elmer Laws, Orville Hodson, Walter Krick, Vernon Tucker, Walter Voss, Verle Rumsey, Bum Wagner, Russell Butt. Back: Dr. Bauer, Jess Conyers, Dorotha Laws, Noble Laws, a player identified only as "pitcher from Indianapolis,' Tommy Thompson, Murray Bruce.

The 1947-48 Milan Indians. First row: Ralph Blanken, St. Mgr., Earl "Bub" Bonfer, Dave Ridenour, Arnie Droge, Jim Coyle, Wayne Caplinger, Alvin Busching; second row: Jim Jackson, Coach, LeVon Winters, Don Pettit, Bill Kohlerman, Kenny Wuellner, Chet Nichols, Ray Bergman, George Ammerman.

A rare photo of the entire Plump family, circa 1938. Front: Esther, Ginny, and Lester Junior. Rear: Dot, Lester, Bobby, Mabel, and Bill.

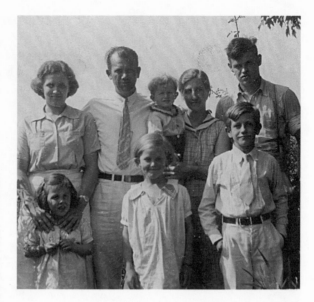

Louisa and John Plump, Bobby's grandparents.

Lester Junior enjoys an ice cream cone in the Plumps' side yard while young Bobby stands by in his wooden "play pen."

The Plump family home in Pierceville, Indiana, 1943.

Pierceville's one-room schoolhouse, circe 1930. Bill Plump is in the front row, third from the right; Dot is third row, far left. Helen Dunn, the girl who named Bobby, is second from the left in the fourth row. Teacher Joe Hill stands at the back.

Bobby, Whitey the cat, and Pierceville pal Glen Butte, 1944.

Al Busching and Lester Junior Plump, 1946. Les is astride the bike that was passed down through the Plump family along with the paper route.

Freshman initiation at Milan High School included wearing skirts, onions around the neck, and carrying a bucket. Pictured from left to right: Fred Busching, Roger Schroder, Gene White, Bob Tobrock, and Bobby Plump.

Sligo School. Bobby's mother Mabel is second row, fourth from right; her sister Carrie Dilla is third row, second from left.

Lester Plump at Prattsburg School 1906 or 1907. He is sitting on the ground in the first row, far right; his sister Catherine is second row, third from left. Also pictured are Harvey Call, who married Mabel Dilla Plump's sister Carrie, first row, third from right; and Mabel's sister Margaret Dilla, second row, second from right.

Cold irons used by Bobby's sister, Dot.

Marc Combs's eighth grade class at Milan. Bobby is pictured third row from the bottom, second from left.

Bobby proudly displays his trophy bluegill near the Haven Of Rest, 1950.

Bobby in his Pierceville Knothole team uniform, 1949.

Part of the Haven Of Rest gang. Front, from left: Lester Plump, Bill Plump, Leo "Pop" Dunn. Back: Roger Schroder, Bobby Plump, Fred Busching, Joe Mess.

The fabled Haven Of Rest at Versailles State Park, where the Plump men spent summer vacations.

Pierceville's Knothole League team. Front row, from left: Gerry McKittrick, Roger Schroder, Bobby Plump, Elmer Pollard, Bill Higdon. Fred Busching, George Brexshear. Back row: Gene White, Bernard Slayback, Lloyd Freeman, Wayne Smith, Bob Coffee, Ray Bergman, Gerald Allen.

The 1949-50 Milan seventh and eighth grade basketball squad. Front row, from left: Dan Bulloc, Roger Schroder, Bobby Plump, Ken Wendleman, Bill Jordan, Jimmy Nickell, Gerry McKittrick, Fred Spark. Back row: Ray Craft, Fred Busching, Bill Martin, Clifford Bushorn, Gene White, Ronnie Truitt, Bob Engel, Dale Smith, Bill Higdon, Coach Marc Combs.

The 1948 confirmation class at Stumpke's Corner's St. Paul Lutheran Church. The front row includes Wendleman (far left) Rollin Cutter (third from left), and Bobby Plump (fourth from left). Jim Wendleman is in the second row, third from left. Back: Rev. Stahl.

Lester Junior's birthday party at the Plump home in Pierceville, 1956. Bobby's brother Bill is wearing glasses, seated in front of the window; Les is seated to his left; Les's wife Ann, seated to Les's left is dealing the cards.

High school graduation photo,
Lester Junior Plump, 1946.

High school graduation photo,
Dorthea Mae Plump, 1939.

High school graduation photo, Virginia Lee
Plump, 1949.

High school graduation photo, Eloise Esther
Plump, 1951.

Lester Junior Plump after being called up to serve
during the Korean War, photographed in the
Plumps' back yard, 1951.

Bill Plump at Camp Atterbury, 1944.

Milan's 1952-53 freshman basketball squad. Coach Clarence Kelly is at the far left; Rollin Cutter is third from right, and Glen Butte is at the far right.

The car from which Bobby was thrown when it rolled off the road in October, 1952. Miraculously, none of the four teenager in the car was seriously injured in the wreck.

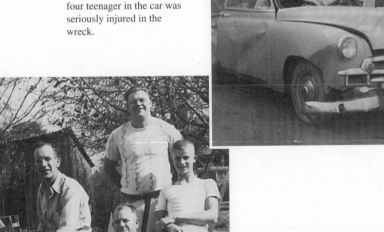

The Plump men in their side yard in Pierceville, from left: Lester Junior, Lester, Bill, and Bobby.

The 1952-53 Milan Indians. Front, from left: cheerleaders Virginia Voss, Joan Johnson, and Ellen Voss. Middle: Fred Busching, Dale Smith, Roger Schroder, Jim Call, Ken Wendleman, Bill Jordan, Bobby Plump, Ray Craft. Back: Assistant Coach Clarence Kelly, Assistant Coach Marc Combs, Bob Engel, Ronnie Truitt, Jim Wendleman, Ralph Preble, Gene White, Principal Richard Brollier, and Coach Marvin Wood.

Milan's 1953-54 junior varsity squad. Ken Delap is seated in the second row, second from right; the third row includes Rollin Cutter, Bob Wichman, and Glen Butte, second, third, and fourth from left, respectively.

Roger Schroder and Ken Wendleman being entertained by Bill Jordan at the piano.

Ray Craft tends to his duties at the family farm.

Gene White at work at the family feed store in Milan.

Country boys Glen Butte, Rollin Cutter, and Glen's brother Bill.

Ronnie Truitt and Bob Engel hard at work for Chris Volz.

Milan High School's Pierceville Alleycats. From left: Glen Butte, Roger Schroder, Bobby Plump, and Gene White.

Coach Marvin Wood shows the boys how it's done. Players, from left: Rollin Cutter, Glen Butte, Roger Schroder, Ken Delap, Ken Wendleman, Bill Jordan, and Bob Wichman.

Milan's senior basketball stars, photographed the week before their history-making victory over Muncie Central. Bobby is behind the wheel. Other, from left: Ronnie Truitt, Ken Wendleman, Ray Craft, Roger Schroder, and Gene White.

Milan against Crispus Attucks, 1954 Indianapolis Semistate, Bobby, with the ball, is guarded by Bill Mason, as sophomore sensation Oscar Robertson looks on.

Butler Fieldhouse, jammed to the rafters for the 1954 final game.

A dejected Muncie Central team after their defeat at the hands of Milan. Sitting, from left: Jimmy Barnes, Phil Raisor, Leon Agullana, John Casterlow, and Gene Flowers. Standing: Principal Loren Chastain, Assistant Coach Carl Adams, an unidentified school official, and Jim Hinds.\

The Shot Heard 'Round The World hits the bottom of the net. From left: Muncie's Jimmy Barnes, Jim Hinds, Gene Flowers, and John Casterlow and Milan's Ken Wendleman.

Gene White and Patty
Boelke after the Shot Heard
'Round the World

Playing cards at Schroder's in Pierceville. From left: Carl
Schroder, Tiny Hunt, and Marc Combs.

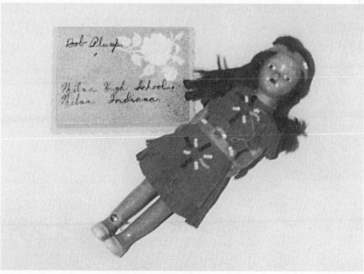

Little Indian doll sent to Bobby by Aline Anderson, a fifth-grade student at Sacred
Heart Grade School.

Bobby in his Indiana All-Star jersey with Angus Nicson, long-time coach of Indiana Central University (now the University of Indianapolis).

Bobby cuts down the nets in victory after the 1954 championship game.

Milan's seniors united in victory. From left: Ken Wendleman, Gene White, Bob Engel (with his championship ring box in his mouth), an IHSAA board member, Roger Schroder, Ray Craft, Bobby Plump, and Ronnie Truitt.

1954 I. H. S. A. A. State Champions

Front row, left to right: Principal Cale Hudson, Gene White, Ronnie Truitt, Coach Marvin Wood, Bobby Plump and Ray Craft.

Davy Jordan, the little Injun and the mascot of the team is sitting in front.

Back row: left to right: Assistant Coach Clarence Kelly Jr., Roger Schroder, Bob Engel, Glen Butte, Bill Jordan, Rollin Cutter, Student Manager Fred Busching, Kennie Wendelman, Student Manager Oliver Jones and Assistant Coach Mark Combs.

Milan High School Athletic Banquet
Honoring
Indiana State High School Basketball Champions of 1954

Friday Evening, April 9, 1954
7:00 o'clock

MILAN HIGH SCHOOL GYMNASIUM

MARVIN WOOD

—0—

Menu

Relish Dish
Turkey or Fish

Whipped Potatoes	-	Buttered Peas
Gravy	-	Dressing
	Cole Slaw	
Hot Rolls	-	Butter
	Coffee	
	Pie	

—0—

This dinner served by the Milan Mother's Club

Program

Milan High School Song

Prayer of Invocation..............................Rev. Ivan Morgan

DINNER

When the Indians Go Marchin' In

Introduction of Distinguished Guests
    L. V. Phillips..........................Commissioner of the I. H. S. A. A.
    Robert Hinshaw...........Assistant Commissioner of the I. H. S. A. A.
    and Others

Introduction of the Milan High School Superintendent and Principal

Introduction of Milan High School Coaches

Introduction of Milan High School Basketball Team and Cheer Leaders

Speech for the Team.................................Gene White

Overture, "Green Meadows" ....Hanson

Introduction of Guest Speaker

Address..........................Alex Clark, Mayor of City of Indianapolis

"Trombrero" ....Cofie'd

—0—

Music by Milan High School Band under direction of Mrs. Louise Snider

A happy victory scene over Shelbyville, final game of the 1953 Semi-State. Front, from left: Bobby Plump, Bill Jordan, Ralph Preble. Middle: Ken Wendleman, Roger Schroder, Ray Craft, Bob Engel, Ronnie Truitt, Gene White, Jim Wendleman. Back: Clarence Kelly, Marvin Wood, Fred Busching, Ralph Williamson, Marc Combs.

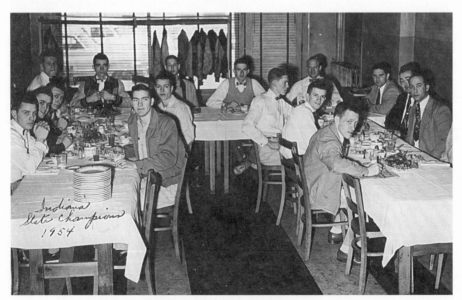

The 1954 champs dining at the Apex Grill, Indianapolis.

Milan's 1953-54 varsity basketball team. Front row, from left: team manager Oliver Jones; cheerleaders Marjorie Ent, Virginia Voss, and Patty Bohlke; and team manager Fred Busching. Middle row: Assistant Coach Clarence Kelly, Roger Schroder, Bill Jordan, Gene White, Bobby Plump, Ken Delap, Ray Craft, Coach Marvin Wood. Top row: Principal Cale Hudson, Assistant Coach Marc Combs, Ken Wendleman, Bob Wichman, Ronnie Truitt, Glen Butte, Rollin Cutter, Bob Engel, Superintendent Willard Green.

The Milan Fire Department takes part in the parade the day after their hometown boys brought home the state championship in 1954.

Indianapolis Star sportswriter Bob Collins addresses the crowd at Milan's victory celebration.

Standing room only – sometimes only on the roof! — at Milan's 1954 victory parade.

Another victory parade scene.

Connor Salm awards Bobby the 1954 Trester Award.

The 1954 Indiana All-Stars starting five. From left: Bobby Plump, Pete Obremsky, Larry Heddon, Ray Ball and Arley Andrews

Mrs. Beuna Kohlerman's advanced composition class at Milan High School, 1954. Front row, from left: Jimmy Nickell, Jo Anne Steinmetz, David Jeffries. Middle: Anita Womack, Bobby Plump, Roger Schroder. Back: Patsy Busteed, Carl Richardson, Virginia Voss, Gene White, Mrs. Kohlerman.

Arky and his sister, "Tootie" Herbst

Arky and Rosie

Arkenberg's Dining Room, corner Carr & Main Streets, Milan

Cover of Milan's 1954 graduation
program.

Bobby's 1954 Milan High School
graduation photo.

Milan's Class of 1954. Bobby is in the bottom row, second from left. Other Mighty Men of Milan include
Gene White, bottom row, third from right; second row from bottom, Ronnie Truitt (far left), Fred
Busching (fourth from right), and Roger Schroder (second from right); fourth row from bottom, Ray
Craft (far right); and top row, Ken Wendleman (far left), Coach Marvin Wood (fourth from left), Principal
Cale Hudson (fourth from right), and Bob Engel (far right).

A recruiting trip to Milan. From left: Ed Cassidy, Mark Peterman, Scott Chandler, Jo Anne Steinmetz, Bobby Plump

Butler University
INDIANAPOLIS 7, INDIANA
DEPARTMENT OF PHYSICAL EDUCATION
AND ATHLETICS

OFFICE OF THE ATHLETIC DIRECTOR

April 5, 1954.

Dear Bob:-
First may I congratulate and your team mates on winning the I.N.S.A.A. championship. I probably got as big a kick out of it as you boys did.

Bob, I want you to come to Butler. We have a swell school and I know you will be satisfied here. We have a bunch of good boys. Also I have a man who has taken an interest in you and wants to help you through school financially.

Some time when you get some free time, I want you to come up.
(over)

(2)
I want to introduce you to the man and get your application for admission filled out.

Many schools probably will be after you, but just make up your mind to be with us. You can't go wrong.

When can you come up?

Sincerely,
Tony Hinkle

P.S. If any of the other boys want to come with you, bring them up also.

Bobby's handwritten note from Coach Tony Hinkle.

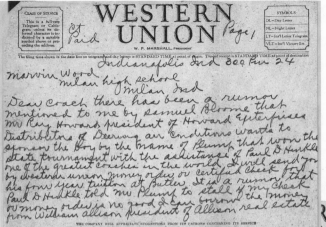

Coach Wood received this telegram offering Bobby a chance to play at Butler University.

What was left of Butler's Sigma Chi house after the boiler exploded in the autumn of 1955.

The Men of Sigma Chi at Butler University, 1958.

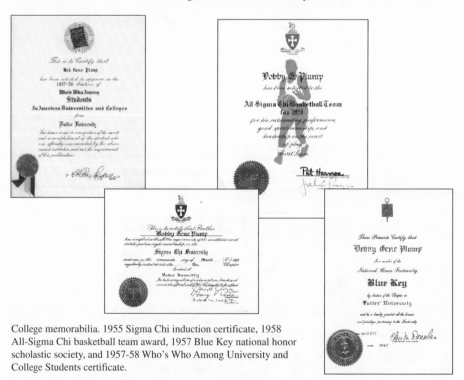

College memorabilia. 1955 Sigma Chi induction certificate, 1958 All-Sigma Chi basketball team award, 1957 Blue Key national honor scholastic society, and 1957-58 Who's Who Among University and College Students certificate.

Bobby in action
versus Fresno State.

The 1958 East All-Star squad.

Butler's 1958 graduating senior basketball stars. From left: Bobby Plump, Ted Guzek, Keith Greve, Ray Craft, Wally Cox, and Indianapolis Mayor Phil Bayt.

Bobby—junior year at Butler.

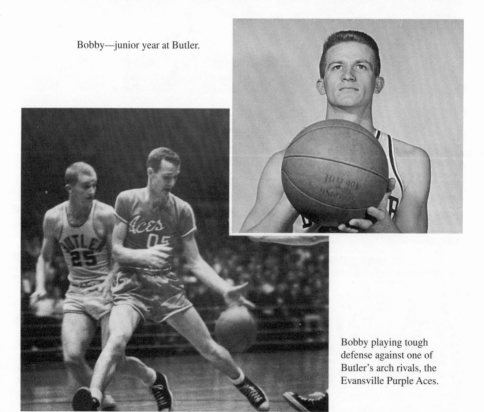

Bobby playing tough defense against one of Butler's arch rivals, the Evansville Purple Aces.

A program from the 1960 Hoosier Classic that was signed by all the participants and sent to Bobby in the hospital where he was recuperating from a collapsed lung suffered during a Phillips 66ers game.

Butler Medal Winner

Bob Gene Plump (center), president of Butler University Alumni Association, offers his congratulations to Otto N. Frenzel for being selected as a co-winner of this year's Butler Medal, while embracing Mrs. James H. Morris, who accepted the medal on behalf of her late husband. Frenzel, chairman of the executive committee of Merchants National Bank and Trust Company, and the late James H. Morris, Butler University trainer for 30 years, were chosen as winners of this year's award which annually recognizes loyal and unselfish efforts in the perpetuation of Butler University as a "great and cultural institution." The medals were presented Friday evening in the Hilton Hotel at the President's Club of Butler University 1976 dinner. (Star Photo)

The program from Butler's final home baseketball game in 1958 recognized the departing senior who led the Bulldogs to one of their finest seasons in history.

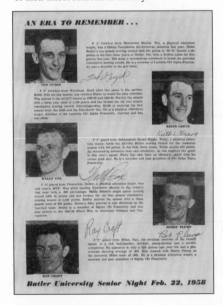

Butler University Senior Night Feb. 22, 1958

Bobby as president of the Butler University Alumni Association congratulating Otto N. Frenzel and Mrs. James B. Morris during the President's Club of Butler University 1976 dinner. Frenzel and the late Mr. Morris were named co-winners of the Butler Medal.

The Miracle Man from Milan on defense…

…and on offense.

A picture of great defensive form and concentration.

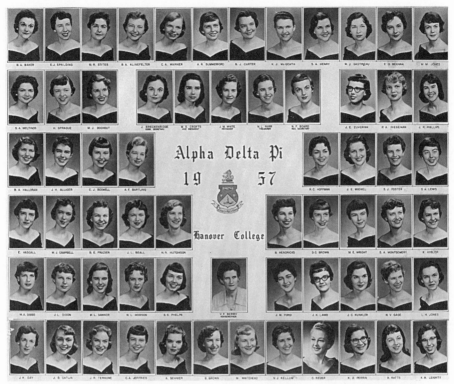

Jenine's 1957 Alpha Delta Pi composite at Hanover. Jenine is pictured second row, fifth from right.

This card was sent to Bobby to "Plump, Indiana" and was delivered. To this day Bobby hasnever cashed in on the five gallons of gas.

336 West Wash. St,
Fort Wayne, Ind.
Mar. 21 1954

Dear Bob;
    Congratulations, my
boy. You really came
through. That last
shot of yours was
beautiful to see.
    I suggest that you
run for mayor at
the next election. Your
game proved to be the
best television show
I have ever seen.
    There is 5 gallons of
Shell Gasoline for you at
Dexter's Shell Service at
above address. (L. L. Brumit)
Congratulation again.

John Ford with daughter, Jenine

St. John Catholic Church, Osgood

Marie Ford, Jenine, Bobby,
Dot and Lester

Back: Ruth Miller,
Gloria Furlow,
Patricia Ryan,
Jenine, Bobby, Jon
Ford, Glen Butte,
Mark Peterman;
front: Margie Flick,
Elmer Pollard, and
Ray Craft

The 1959-60 Phillips 66ers. Players, clockwise from lower left: Gary Thompson, Dallas Dobbs, Jerry Shipp, Jim Spivey, Arnold Short, Tom Robitaille, H.E. Kirchner, Burdie Haldorson, Arlen Clark, Phil "Red" Murrell, Bob Ginguard, Don Matuszak, Bill Evans, Bobby Plump. Front, from left: Assistant Coach Gib Ford, a representative from Mexico, and Head Coach Bud Browning.

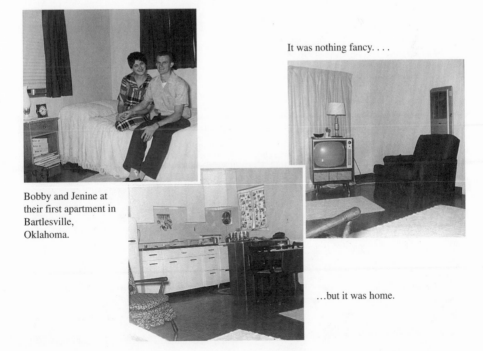

It was nothing fancy. . . .

Bobby and Jenine at their first apartment in Bartlesville, Oklahoma.

...but it was home.

The 1958 West All-Star squad at Madison Square Garden. Front Row, left to right, Red Murrall, Dave Gambee, Hube Reed, Archie Dees, Mike Farmer; back row, left to right, Bob Plump, Roy Dewitz, Gene Brown, Jack Mimlitz, Joe Stevens.

Jenine, Kelli, and Tari after a visit to the grocery store in Bartlesville.

Bobby and Tari in Pierceville, 1959.

The Plump family, circa 1963: Bobby, Jenine, Jonathan, Tari, and Kelli.

Bobby helped coach Phillips's 1962 National AAU Champion 66ers. Front row, left to right: Don Kojis, Gary Thompson, Ron Altenberg, Carl Cole, Charlie Bowerman, Jerry Shipp. Middle: Coach Bud Browning, Assistant Coach Bobby Plump. Back: Manager Andy Likens, Al Bunge, Jim Hagan, Tom Robitaille, Wally Frank, Charlie McNeil. Kneeling in front is mascot Stan Likens.

The 1955 Milan Indians. Kneeling, from left: Charles Shuck, Paul Voss, Jim Craft, Virgil LaFollette, Kenny Delap, Philip Tobrock. Back: Coach Jim Roush, Bill Jordan, Bob Bruns, Glen Butte, Bob Wichman, Rollin Cutter, Jackie Little, Willard McNees.

Bobby, right, confers with old coach Herman "Snort" Grinstead in 1967

Phillips Gymnasium,
Bartlesville,
Oklahoma.

Bobby at his "off-season" job
at Phillips.

Jenine at work in the Phillips engineering
department, Bartlesville.

Bobby participating as an honorary coach at
the second annual Phillips Holiday
Basketball Classic, 1991. Eight teams
competed in the tournament. Bobby was the
honorary coach of Borger, Texas, High
School.

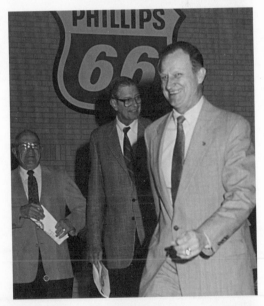

Phillips 66ers Reunion at the Shangri-La Resort, Afton, Oklahoma, 1981, attended by 98 former players
from 21 states.

The Broad Ripple Little League Braves. Bobby (center of back row) coached with Paul Federle (left) and Don Pickett (right). Jonathan is standing, third from right.

Another Broad Ripple Little League squad. Jonathan is standing, far left.

The 1977 State Champion AAU team just after their victory. Coach Red Taylor is standing far left, next to Bobby; Jonathan is standing fourth from left. James Murphy is kneeling, second from right.

The AAU champs pose with Indianapolis Mayor Bill Hudnut, far left.

Chatard's 1976 State Final volleyball team. Kelli is standing, fourth from left.

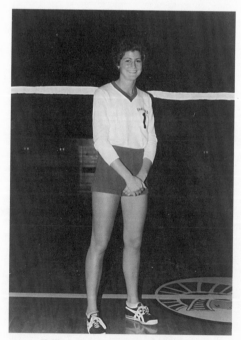

Kelli on the court and ready for action.

Cover of the 1976 championship program. Chatard was eventually beaten in the finals by South Bend Adams – a team that boasted several boys.

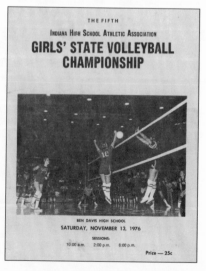

Jonathan shoots the jumper as a Cathedral sophomore.

Program from the 1978 Logansport Holiday Tournament, Jonathan's sophomore year.

Jonathan in action against Brebeuf.

A line of familiar faces cheering the hometown boys at Milan's 1973 Indianapolis Semistate appearance. From left: Ray Craft, Gene White, Bobby Plump, Ken Wendleman, Roger Schroder, and Milan Principal Bob Gardner, who later became IHSAA commissioner.

1981 Indiana Basketball Hall of Fame induction ceremony. From left: IHSAA Commissioner Ward Brown, Hall of Fame President Sam Scheivley, Bobby Plump, and inductee Earl Townsend.

Bobby entertains a reporter in his office – in what is now Plump's Last Shot restaurant.

Ray Craft's induction into the Indiana Basketball Hall of Fame. From left: Marvin and Mary Lou Wood, Ray and Virginia Craft, Bobby and Jenine Plump.

Bobby and Jenine decorate the tree.

Bobby autographing a program for a young basketball fan

Bobby's 1977 Scarborough Peace Games team. Jonathan is standing, second from right.

Plump/Ford family photo. On the grass, from left: Duffy the dog, Jaclyn Piechocki, Jenine, Baron the dog. Middle: Marie Ford, Pat Ryan, Jon Ford, Josh Piechocki. Back: Mark Ford, Judy Ford holding Benjamin Ford, Karen Ford holding Katherine Ford, Rose Taylor, Al Taylor, John Ford, Mike Piechocki, Kelli Plump Piechocki, Mike Ford, Valerie Ford.

Bobby with sisters Esther (left) and Dot (right).

Jenine and Bobby.

Bobby and boyhood pal Lloyd Freeman.

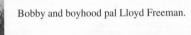

Hoosiers with the real Miracle Man. From left: Kent Poole, Bobby Plump, Maris Valainis, Brad Long.

Virginia "Jinky"
Voss Craft.

Clarence Kelly

Rollin Cutter.

Gene White.

Ray Craft.

Glen Butte.

First Annual

All--Star Basketball Game

Versailles Sectional Senior Stars

vs.

Lawrenceburg Sectional Senior Stars

Friday Night, June 4, 1954

8:00 o'clock EST

TYSON AUDITORIUM

Versailles, Indiana

La Societe des 40 Hommes et 8 Chevaux

Ripley Co. Voiture 1047

40
8

Sponsored by

**Ripley County Voiture 1047, 40 and 8 for
NURSES TRAINING PROGRAM**

Origin and Growth of the Forty and Eight

(By Paul Wycoff)

The Forty and Eight, La Societe de Quarante Hommes et Huit Chaveaux, (The Society of Forty Men and Eight Horses), was organized by a group of active Legionnaires shortly after the organization of the American Legion. Its purpose was to provide a meeting ground where more active members of the American Legion, in concerted action, could better support and augment the various programs of the American Legion. They took their name from the French boxcars in World War I that were designated to carry forty men or eight horses, and was the common means of troop transportation in France in 1917 and 1918; Hence, their officers, meetings, and so forth, all carry French titles.

The Forty and Eight is generally referred to as the Fun and Honor Society of the American Legion, which is an apt title, as they do have fun and membership is restricted to election as a reward for faithful and active service in the American Legion.

The Forty and Eight now has "Grande Voitures" (state organizations) in all forty-eight states and in many foreign countries. Its service to the Legion through membership drives, child welfare work and other Legion programs has grown to such magnitude as to wholly eclipse the hopes of its original founders.

Repeated reports of the extreme shortage of trained nurses, both in military service and in civilian service, at the beginning of World War II furnished the idea to some Indiana Forty and Eighters of sponsoring nurses' training. This program was started in Indiana at the beginning of World War II and immediately became a national program of the Forty and Eight. Thousands of nurses have since been graduated at Forty and Eight expense and are now serving throughout the world.

Ripley County Voiture No. 1047 was organized in 1928. Dearborn County Voiture No. 612 was organized a few years earlier, and each have and will continue to serve the American Legion, and the community, state and nation, effectively, though unobtrusively, in Southeastern Indiana.

The Nurses Training Program

In 1952 the Ripley County Voiture No. 1047 of the Forty and Eight instituted its program to provide scholarships to girls seeking a career in nursing. This program is being carried out by the 40-8 in every state of the nation and was inaugurated here in Indiana. Since its inception Indiana has led the country in numbers of nurses assisted in their education. Up to this year hundreds of nurses have been sponsored by the 40-8 in Indiana.

Here in Ripley County the program is new and had its start in 1952. We feel that in a manner of service we can do much to contribute to the best interests of our communities by providing assistance and encouragement to those who will undertake a career in

-1-

Membership Roster of Voiture No. 1047, 40 & 8

VERSAILLES	Post No.	BATESVILLE	Post. No.
Robert L. Akers	173	Milton J. Baas	271
Halstead C. Curry	173	W. W. Bloemer	271
Roscoe J. Finke	173	Edwin Boese	271
Melvin Fuehrer	173	Francis Doll	271
Charles F. Gardner	173	Dr. Edward H. Daley	271
Edgar L. Hayes	173	Malcolm Elzhaus	271
William D. Hill	173	Louis Ferringer	271
Arthur Hodges	173	Raymond Firsich	271
Cletus Holzer	173	Dale Freeland	271
Carl Lansing	173	John H. Frushour	271
Gilbert B. Michel	173	Bernard W. Gerdon	271
Harold L. McCreary	173	Gilbert Goyert	271
Orin Nowlin	173	William Greeman	271
D. D. Pangburn	173	Albert Green	271
William Raney	173	Herman Heldt	271
Dallas C. Robertson	173	Leo Hirt	271
Carl T. Smith	173	W. W. Huneke	271
Thomas D. Stephenson	173	Peter Karbowski	271
R. B. Sutherlin	173	Earl Kreinhop	271
Roger K. Tewksbury	173	Clarence Lampert	271
		Henry S. Lampe	271
MILAN		Luther Lindeman	271
Chester Baylor	235	Alfonse F. Mollaun	271
Robert Bode	235	Harold Narwold	271
Joseph LeGrand	235	Harry Narwold	271
James F. Shanks	235	William J. Neyer	271
Frank Smith	235	William Nordmeyer	271
John W. Stute	235	Dr. George Obery	271
		Richard H. Prentice	271
BROWN TOWNSHIP		Dr. M. J. Pfleffer	271
William Foley	247	Ed Picker	271
Dwight Lamb	247	Jerome J. Prickel	271
James A. Lemon	247	Tilford E. Reverman	271
Bruce Ralston	247	Howard Ricke	271
Jesse W. Taul	247	Aloys M. Roell Jr.	271
Harold Whitton	247	Irvin Schott	271
		Raymond H. Smith	271
OSGOOD		Harold Steinkamp	271
Lawrence Crum	267	Robert Stewart	271
Earl Littell	267	Robert H. Tekulve	271
Edward R. Oliger	267	Louis Thielking	271
Robert Peters	267	Dr. Robert Timmerman	271
William L. Peters	267	Philmer J. Ward	271
Edward Radican	267	F. H. Weigel	271
G. W. Schroder	267	John Wonning	271
John R. Thomas	267	Paul V. Wycoff	271

-2-

nursing. Little more need be said about the need for trained nurses. Each applicant is screened thoroughly for proper character, scholastic record and the desire to pursue a career in nursing. The two girls we presently have in training have been outstanding and have proved a credit to this program.

Applications for scholarships may be obtained from the high school principals in each of the Ripley county schools. Scholarships when granted may be used in any accredited school of nursing.

First Nurse of Ripley County Voiture No. 1047

Miss Faith Ann Hooton
Miss Faith Ann Hooton, daughter of Mr. and Mrs. Roland Hooton

COMPLIMENTS OF

W. M. HUNTER & SON
VERSAILLES, INDIANA

— 4 —

of Versailles, Indiana, is nearing her final year of Nurses' Training at the Bethesda School of Nursing at Cincinnati, Ohio. She is nineteen years old and graduated with the class of 1952 from Versailles High School. Faith Ann has three sisters, Mrs. Hope Fisse, a registered nurse, Mrs. Alice Swingle, and Miss Jane Hooton, also twin brothers, Dwight and Duane, who are Freshmen in high school.

Our Second Nurse

Miss Nancy Broerman
Miss Nancy Broerman entered the School of Nursing at The Good Samaritan Hospital in Cincinnati. Nancy lives in Batesville and graduated from that high school in 1953. Nancy was well chosen for her high scholastic standing in school and her earnestness to pursue a career in nursing. During this first year she has excelled in every phase of her training and has proved an excellent selection to receive the scholarship given her. Her parents are Mr. and Mrs. Ed Broerman of Batesville.

COMPLIMENTS OF

LEORA WEARE POST NO. 173
THE AMERICAN LEGION
VERSAILLES, INDIANA

— 5 —

R. F. "Dutch" Struck
Mr. R. F. "Dutch" Struck, athletic director and head football coach at Hanover College, will coach the Versailles Sectional All-Star team.

Mr. Struck graduated from DePauw in 1926, completed his Master's Degree from Indiana University in 1934, and secured in 1951 a Director of Physical Education Degree from Indiana University. During his playing days "Dutch" participated in four years of varsity football at DePauw from 1922 to 1925, serving as captain in his senior year. He played three years of varsity basketball, was selected as all-state guard during the 1925-1926 season and during the spring of 1924-25-26 Struck starred on the baseball diamond for DePauw.

Mr. Struck started coaching after graduation at Spring Valley, Illinois and coached all three major sports through the 1926 and 1927 seasons at Spring Valley. In 1927 "Dutch" moved back to Indiana and took a job as head coach at Wabash High School and remained until 1937. Mishawaka High secured the services of Struck as basketball coach for the 1937 season and he served the Mishawaka school until 1942 when he was called into the Navy where he served as a Navy athletic specialist for three years. After being released from the Navy Struck returned to Mishawaka for one more year, the 1945-46 season, and then he received the appointment to Hanover College. "Dutch" Struck has served as athletic director and football coach at Hanover ever since 1947.

— 6 —

Charles A. Henry
Charles A. Henry, head basketball coach at Hanover College, will coach the Lawrenceburg Sectional All-Star team. Mr. Henry graduated from Huntington High School in 1934 and from Michigan State College in 1940. During his senior year he was co-captain of the basketball team. He received his Masters Degree from Indiana University in 1947. He coached at West Branch, Michigan, high school from 1940 to 1942. He was Navy instructor at Gonzaga University (Spokane, Wash.), in 1943-44—his team winning the Northwest Collegiate Championship in 1944. During 1947 to 1950 he was director of physical education and head basketball coach at Washington, Indiana, high school.

Welcome to First Annual Nurses Training Benefit Basketball Game

Ripley County Voiture No. 1047 Forty and Eight welcomes you to this the First Annual All-Star Basketball Game between the seniors of Versailles Sectional and the seniors of the Lawrenceburg Sectional. The proceeds, after necessary expenses are paid will be used to pay the scholarships of the Nurses Training Program. The Voiture hopes to make this an annual event.

For the Versailles All-Star Sectional Team the Voiture All-Star committee selected Herman Streuwing of Batesville, James Gabbard of Versailles, Dale Linkmeyer of Cross Plains, John Wolford of Osgood, Kenneth Dunbar of Napoleon, Roger Ertel of Sunman, Ethan Jackson of Holton, Irvin Meierle of New Marion and the five senior members of Milan, who were the regular starting five of the I. H. S. A. A. state champions of 1954. They are Bob Plump, Ray Craft, Gene White, Ronnie Truitt and Bob Engel.

Pete Furnish and Newell Fox of Vevay, Donald Mathias of Dillsboro, Ronald Klingelhoffer and Donald McIntosh of Aurora, Donald Dale Mendel and Phillip Benning of Moores Hill, Bill Wuellner and Bucky Dennis of Lawrenceburg, Ray Swales of Bright, Willis Holland and Don Smithers of Rising Sun and William Rea of Patriot were selected to represent the Lawrenceburg Sectional

— 7 —

BOBBY PLUMP

Bobby Plump

Bob is the son of Lester G. Plump of Milan. He is 17 years of age, 5'10" tall and a graduate of Milan High School, class of 1954. Bob played three years varsity basketball at the position of guard, scoring 388 points for the past season for an average of 15 points per game. His foul shooting percentage was .712. Plump was a member of the 1954 Indiana high school basketball championship team, was chosen as a member of the all-sectional, all-regional, all semi-final and all-state team. He is "Mr. Basketball" of 1954, No. 1 man on the Indiana All-Star Team and the only player in the history of Indiana basketball who was a member of the championship team and also the winner of the Trester Award.

RED SMITH AGENCY
INSURANCE
MILAN, INDIANA
Red - Bill - Mary - Irene - Betty

— 8 —

RAY CRAFT

Ray Craft

Ray is 17 years of age, 5'8" tall, has played three years of high school basketball at Milan as a guard. He is the son of Mr. and Mrs. Roy Craft, a graduate of Milan high school in the class of 1954 and a member of the 1954 state championship team. He was chosen as a member of the all-sectional, all-regional, all-semi-final and all-state teams. He has scored a total of 230 points this past season for an average of 8.8 per game with a foul shooting percentage of .688.

COMPLIMENTS OF

CHRIS VOLZ MOTORS, Inc.
Pontiac - Buick - Oldsmobile - Cadillac - GMC Trucks
Sales and Service
MILAN, INDIANA

— 9 —

RONNIE TRUITT

Ronnie Truitt

Ronnie is the son of Walter S. Truitt of Milan, a graduate of Milan high school, class of 1954, and was a member of the 1954 state championship basketball team. He plays the position of forward, has scored a total of 210 points this past season for an average of 8.1 points per game with a foul shooting percentage of .500. Ronnie was chosen as a member of the all-sectional, all-regional, all-semi-final and all-state teams. He had a field goal shooting percentage in the four tournaments of .525.

W. H. STUTE & SON
Complete Home Furnishings
MILAN, INDIANA - PHONE 2601

—10—

BOB ENGEL

Bob Engel

Bob is the son of Cora Engel of Milan. He has played three years of varsity basketball at Milan at the position of forward. He is 18 years of age, 6'1" tall, a graduate of Milan high school, class of 1954, and was a member of the 1954 state championship team. Engel, although being handicapped by a bad back during most of the past season, has scored a total of 166 points for an average of 7.5 points per game with a foul shooting percentage of .623. He was chosen as a member of the all-sectional, all-regional and all-semi-final teams.

COMPLIMENTS OF

THE MILAN FURNITURE MFG. CO.
MILAN, INDIANA

—11—

GENE WHITE

Gene White

Gene is a graduate of Milan high school, class of 1954. He was a member of the state championship basketball team, selected as a member of the all-regional, all-semi-final and all-state teams. He is 18 years of age, 5'11" tall and has played three years for Milan at the position of center and forward. Gene has scored a total of 139 points this past season for an average of 5.4 points per game. He owns a foul shooting percentage of .603 for the past season. Gene is the son of Mr. and Mrs. Horace L. White.

CONGRATULATIONS
ALL STARS
MAY THE BEST TEAM WIN

KIRSCHNER'S DEPT. STORE

MILAN, INDIANA

—12—

JIM GABBARD

Jim Gabbard

Jim is 19 years of age, 6 feet tall and has played four years of basketball at the positions of forward and center. He played one year at Sunman before going to Versailles where he played three years, graduating with the class of 1954. Jim was chosen as a member of the 1954 all-sectional team of Ripley County.

Other sports which Jim excells in are baseball and track. He has scored a total of 370 points for an average of 17.6 points per game for the past season. Jim is the son of Mr. and Mrs. George Gabbard.

COMPLIMENTS OF

AKERS SERVICE STATION

Junction of U. S. 421 and 56
VERSAILLES, INDIANA

—13—

DALE LINKMEYER

Dale Linkmeyer

Dale is 18 years of age, 5'11" tall and has played four years as a forward for Cross Plains high school. He is a member of the graduating class of 1954. Dale has scored a total of 206 points for an average of 10.8 points per game during the season of 1953-54. He also has participated in track and baseball during his high school career. Dale is the son of Mr. and Mrs. Paul Linkmeyer of Cross Plains.

COMPLIMENTS OF

LAMB'S STORE

General Merchandise - Dry Goods - Wallpaper
Nationally Advertised Brands
CROSS PLAINS, INDIANA

—14—

JOHN WOLFORD

John Wolford

John is the son of Mr. and Mrs. Wm. L. Wolford of Osgood. He is 17 years of age, 6'4" tall and a graduate of Osgood high school, class of 1954. He has played basketball four years, two of which were on the varsity at the position of center. John also is an athlete in the sports of track, softball and volley ball. John has scored a total of 614 points in three seasons, 285 of which were scored during the 1953-54 season for an average of 12 points per game. He is admitted to Purdue University to study Vocational Agriculture and is working for a scholarship.

Compliments of		Compliments of
SOUTHEASTERN INDIANA R. E. M. C.	Compliments of SPORTSMAN BAR	RIPLEY COUNTY FARM BUREAU CO-OP.
Owned by Those We Serve		Osgood, Ind.

—15—

ROGER ERTEL

Roger Ertel

Roger is a graduate of Sunman high school, class of 1954, where he played basketball for four years at the position of guard. He also excells in baseball at Sunman high. Roger is the son of Mr. and Mrs. W. J. Ertel of Sunman. He scored a total of 234 points in 18 games the past season for an average of 13 points per game. His foul shooting percentage for the 1953-54 season was .750. He was a member of the all-county and all-sectional teams his junior and senior years.

COMPLIMENTS OF

OSBURN MOTOR COMPANY

SUNMAN, INDIANA

—16—

IRVIN MEIERLE

Irvin Meierle

Irvin is a member of the graduating class of 1954 of New Marion high school. He is 18 years of age, 5'11" tall and played at the position of guard for four years on the New Marion basketball team. He has scored a total of 273 points during the past season for an average of 13.6 points per game.

Irvin is the son of Mr. and Mrs. Charles Meierle of Holton R. 1. He was awarded both the athletic and scholarship awards from his school this past yeear.

COMPLIMENTS OF

HARMON'S GROCERY & TAVERN

Phillips "66" Service

Bacil Harmon

NEW MARION, INDIANA

—17—

KENNETH "KENNY" DUNBAR

Kenneth "Kenny" Dunbar

Kenny is 17 years of age, 5'11" tall and a graduate of Napoleon high school, class of 1954. He was a member of the Napoleon Bearcats for four years at the position of guard, earning a varsity letter in his junior and senior years. Kenny also participated in softball and baseball four years, playing at shortstop and third base. Kenny has an "A" average for his four years and has applied for a scholarship at Purdue University. His total points for the 1953-54 season are 212 for an average of 10 points per game. He owns a foul shooting percentage of .620 for the past season. Kenny is the son of Mr. and Mrs. Eugene Dunbar of Osgood R. R. 3.

Compliments of

**RADICAN
RURAL REPAIR**

Compliments of

**BEHLMER
HDWE. CO., INC.**
Hardware & John Deere
Farm Implements
Napoleon, Indiana

—18—

ETHAN JACKSON

Ethan Jackson

Ethan is the son of Mr. and Mrs. Eldon E. Jackson of Holton, a graduate of Holton high school, class of 1954, and was a member of the Holton Warhorses for three years. He is 17 years of age, 5'9" tall and played the position of guard during his high school career. Ethan broke the all-time scoring record for a single game in Ripley county which was held by Earl Triplett of Osgood with 48 points, when he scored 53 points against Guilford in a game this past season, which Holton won, 100-44. Ethan has scored 335 points the past season for an average of 15.25 points per game. He is also a baseball and track star.

COMPLIMENTS OF

KEETON & SON

Pure Oil Service Station
GARAGE   -   RESTAURANT
HOLTON, INDIANA

—19—

HERMAN "HAM" STRUEWING

Herman "Ham" Struewing

"Ham" is 17 years of age, 6'2" tall and a graduate of Batesville high school, class of 1954, where he was an outstanding member of the Batesville Bulldogs. He played the position of center and forward. Ham has scored a total of 443 points the past season for an average of 20 points per game and owns a foul shooting percentage of .700. He was chosen as a member of the all-sectional team in Ripley county in 1954. Ham is one of Batesville high school's leading scorers, if not of all time. He also plays baseball and his spirit and ability did most to carry the Junior American Legion baseball team into the finals of the state tourney last year. He is the son of Mr. and Mrs. George Struewing of Batesville.

COMPLIMENTS OF

Baesville Liquor Store   The Ship
Triangle "B"   Poske Hardware
Wycoff & Greeman   Stewart's
Picker Frozen Foods   Steinkamp & Co.
BATESVILLE, INDIANA

—20—

CHARLES "PETE" FURNISH

Charles "Pete" Furnish

"Pete" is 17 years of age, 5'10" tall and a graduate of Vevay high school, class of 1954 where he has played four years of basketball as a guard. Pete has scored a total of 267 points the past season for an average of 12.13 points per game. He was chosen as a member of the all-sectional team at Lawrenceburg this year. Pete also excells in softball, baseball and track. He is the son of Florence and Carl Furnish of Vevay.

COMPLIMENTS OF

WALTER E. GAUDIN

Lumber and Hardware

VEVAY, INDIANA

—21—

NEWELL FOX

Newell Fox

Newell is 18 years of age, 6'2" tall, 190 pounds. He is a graduate of Vevay high school, class of '54 where he played four years of varsity basketball as center. As a freshman Newell was a reserve but still averaged three points per game. During his next three years, he was leading scorer for each season for his team and captain of his team all four years. Fox was chosen as a member of the all-sectional team during his junior and senior years. During his senior year he was picked on the Louisville Courier Journal all-state team with over 150 coaches voting on the team. The choice was based on seasonal play. Ten teams of five men each were picked, the eighth of which he was a member. He has scored a total of 290 points for an average of 14.5 points per game this season. He is the son of Herman and Louise Fox of Vevay.

BEST WISHES

VEVAY DEPOSIT BANK

VEVAY, INDIANA

—22—

DONALD L. MATHIAS

Donald L. Mathias

Don is 18 years of age, 5'8" tall, and a graduate of Dillsboro high school, class of 1954 where he played four years of basketball, alternating between the positions of forward and guard. Don is also a great enthusiast of baseball. He has scored a total of 103 points during the past season for an average of six points per game. His top number of points in any one game was 15. He owns a foul shooting percentage of .490. Don is the son of Hubert and Ethel Mathias of Dillsboro R. R. 1.

Compliments of

**KLEINE
LUMBER CO.**

Phone 150-3

Dillsboro, Indiana

Compliments of

**Dearborn County
Farm Bureau, Co-op.
Ass'n., Inc.**

Dillsboro, Indiana

—23—

RONALD KLINGELHOFFER

Ronald Klingelhoffer

Ronnie is a graduate of Aurora high school, class of 1954, where he played three years of varsity basketball at the positions of forward and guard. He is 17 years of age and his great heighth of 6'2½" has been a valuable asset to the Aurora Red Devils during his basketball career. He has scored a total of 278 points for an average of 11.12 points per game during the past season. Ron was chosen as a member of the all-sectional and all-regional teams. He is also an excellent baseball player and track man. Ronald is the son of Raymond and Margaret Klingelhoffer of Aurora.

COMPLIMENTS OF

FIRST NATIONAL BANK
AURORA, INDIANA

Since 1864 - Our Ninetieth Anniversary

—24—

DONALD DALE MENDEL

Donald Dale Mendel

Dale is the son of Charles E. and Hettie M. Mendel of Moores Hill. He is a graduate of Moores Hill high school, class of 1954, where he played four years of basketball as a guard. He is 5'10" tall, 17 years of age and has scored a total of 329 points during the season of 1953-54 for an average of 15.7 points per game. Dale is also a fine baseball player and track man, both of which he participated in for his school.

Compliments of

M. L. PLATT

Bulldozer Service

Phone 272GO

Moores Hill, Indiana

Congratulations

MOORES HILL
STATE BANK
Moores Hill, Indiana

—25—

PHILLIP BENNING

Phillip Benning

Phillip is 19 years of age, 6'1" tall and a graduate of Moores Hill high school, class of 1954. He has played four years of basketball for his school at the position of forward. Phillip has scored a total of 80 points during the past season for an average of four points per game. He has also participated in baseball. Phillip is the son of Jesse Benning of Moores Hill.

Compliments of

PIEPER HARDWARE
and
SERVICE STATION

Phone 137

Moores Hill, Indiana

Compliments of

Floyd Becker Post
No. 209
American Legion
Moores Hill, Indiana

—26—

BILL WULLNER

Bill Wullner

Bill is 18 years of age, 5'9" tall and a graduate of Lawrenceburg high school, class of '54, where he has played four years of basketball as a guard. Bill is the holder of many records and trophies, such as the sectional scoring record with 35 points in one game, the Lawrenceburg high school record with 35 points in a single game, in 1952-53 he won the Krider Trophy for the best foul shooting percentage and the Hopper Trophy for the most improved player that year. In 1953-54 he won the Harold C. Crater Trophy for mental attitude and the Krider Trophy again for foul shooting. He has scored a total of 367 points for an average of 15.2 points per game the past season. He also holds letters in football, baseball and track. He was picked as a member of the all-sectional team in 1954. Bill is the son of Edith and Ivan Wullner of Lawrenceburg.

Compliments of

Edward's Grocery

Phone 642
Lawrenceburg, Indiana

TAYLOR BROS., INC.

Firestone Tires
Mobil Gas - Mobil Oil

Lawrenceburg 65

Rising Sun 192-R - Guilford 221-2

—27—

DONALD McINTOSH

Donald McIntosh

Donald is a graduate of Aurora high school, class of 1954. He is the son of Walter and Grace McIntosh of Aurora. Don is 18 years of age, 5'11½" tall and was a member of the Aurora Red Devils basketball team for four years at the positions of forward and guard. Don also participated in other sports for his school, such as baseball, football and softball. He scored a total of 80 points during the past season for an average of four points per game.

COMPLIMENTS OF

ULLRICH'S DRUG STORE

AURORA,   Phone 27   INDIANA

—28—

RAY SWALES

Ray Swales

Ray is 17 years of age, 5'10" tall and a graduate of Bright high school, class of 1954, where he played basketball four years at the position of forward. Ray scored a total of 284 points the past season for an average of 16 points per game. He also is very good at the game of baseball, which he played as a student at Bright. Ray is the son of Mr. and Mrs. John Swales.

COMPLIMENTS OF

RENCK BROS.

BRIGHT, INDIANA

—29—

WILLIS HOLLAND

Willis Holland

"Wid" is a graduate of Rising Sun high school, class of 1954, where he played four years of basketball as a forward. He is 19 years of age, 5'6" tall and makes up for his smallness in stature with his speed and coolness of head on the basketball court. Wid has scored 330 points this past season for an average of 15 points per game. He also played baseball and participated in track meets for his school. Willis is the son of Mrs. Hester Fancher.

COMPLIMENTS OF

BEN FRANKLIN STORE

RISING SUN, INDIANA
H. C. "Pelly" Poellman

—30—

WILLIAM H. "BILL" REA

William H. "Bill" Rea

Bill is 18 years of age, 6'1½" tall and a graduate of Patriot high school, class of 1954. He has played four years of basketball at the positions of center and forward. Bill has scored a total of 78 points the past season for an average of 4.87 points per game. He also participated in baseball and softball for his school. He is the son of Clarence and Lena Rea of Patriot.

COMPLIMENTS OF

THE FRIENDSHIP STATE BANK

Friendship, Indiana
COMPLETE BANKING SERVICE

—31—

DON SMITHER

Don Smither

Don is another Rising Sun basketball player who was chosen for this all-star basketball game, graduating from there with the class of 1954. He is 17 years of age, 6 feet tall, and has played four years for his school as a forward. Don has scored a total of 177 points the past season for an average of 10.7 points per game. He has also played baseball and participated in track for his school. He is the son of G. M. Smither of Rising Sun.

BEST WISHES

DANBURY'S

Appliances - Stoves - Washers - Refrigerators
Electric Supplies - Wallpaper - Paint
222 Main St., Phone 202

RISING SUN, INDIANA

—32—

"BUCKY" DENNIS

Bucky is a graduate of Lawrenceburg high school, class of 1954. He is 17 years of age and 6-3 tall. His great heighth has enabled him to be one of the outstanding basketball players for Lawrenceburg high school. He has played four years of basketball, three of which were on the varsity first five. Bucky was voted the most valuable player for his school in 1953-54, holds the record for the most rebounds in a single game, (26) and has earned 15 letters in four sports in his four years of high school, other sports being baseball, football and track. He has scored a total of 361 points for an average of 15 points per game the past season. Bucky is the son of Cecil and Alma Dennis. His position is center.

COMPLIMENTS OF

KNOTTY PINE

Mr. and Mrs. Carroll Hopper, Prop.

LAWRENCEBURG, INDIANA

—33—

Dick Farley

This 6-3, 21-year-old senior from Winslow is the unsung Hoosier and probably the Big Ten's most-underrated player. He's Indiana's jack-of-all-trades, able to step in anywhere and do an outstanding job. He regularly draws the opponent's top scorer on defense, if he doesn't have to give away too much height, and just as regularly bottles him up. Held Ohio State's great Paul Ebert to two baskets in one half and in return game limited him to seven points in three quarters of responsibility. Stopped Iowa's Deacon Davis cold in two meetings and earns McCracken's accolade as "one of the greatest defensive players ever to play in the Big Ten." On top of that he's a dangerous offensive threat—proving many baskets on his feeding game—and able to hit timely baskets on his own with deadly accuracy. His .457 shooting average last season set a new all-time Big Ten record and his eight buckets in nine attempts against Illinois set a new one-game mark. Great pressure man. Without any pivot experience since leaving high school, he stepped in when Schlundt got a fourth personal at Wisconsin and his ball-handling and cleverness paced Indiana to a 20-14 quarter, its best of the game. Third-high scorer on the squad. In four years at little Winslow he was the big man in making the Eskimos one of Indiana's top giant-killers, beating many high schools with greater enrollment than the entire population of Winslow.

—34—

Bob Leonard

The "Mr. Outside" to "Mr. Inside" Don Schlundt, Leonard, a 6-3, 21-year-old senior from Terre Haute Gerstmeyer has written a brilliant record into the book as one of Indiana's famed "one-two" punch. Were it not for Schlundt, Leonard would be the possessor of almost every I. U. scoring record—yet it's the team-minded Leonard who makes many of Schlundt's scores possible through his feeding game and by loosening up the inside defense with his long-range shooting. Fans remember fondly one night Leonard, by himself under the basket with a crip shot, passing off to a nonplussed Schlundt to boost Don toward his record-breaking total. A great outside shooter, who also can drive and otherwise make himself handy in a defensive role, Leonard has startled crowds with his ability to hit from far out. At Ohio State he hit his first six shots, missed one and connected on his next two. He hit seven of his first ten shots at Iowa and eight of his first 10 against LSU. He's generally acclaimed as the Hoosier "quarterback," setting up and engineering the Hoosier offense. Teammates voted him the honorary captaincy of last year's championship team. A unanimous choice on the All-Big Ten team and Chuck Taylor picked him for his All-American five ahead of Schlundt. Made the All-Tournament team at both the Chicago Regional and Kansas City final of the NCAA meet. Greatest tribute came from Jim Enright, well-known Chicago American sports writer and Big Ten court official, who wrote: "This fellow Leonard is to basketball what Robin Roberts is to baseball, Ben Hogan to golf and Eddie Arcaro to horse racing. Pound-for-pound, dribble-for-dribble, pass-for-pass and shot-for-shot, Bob is without question the game's greatest individual player in my book."

—35—

New Milan High School.

Golfing buddies Joe Wolfla, Dave McCollum, Purdue Head Basketball Coach Gene Keady, and Bobby Plump.

Good Morning PUBLISHING CO., INC.

Re-Order Form

Please Send Additional Orders To:
(Please fill out below)

Ship to:

Name _____

Address _____

City _____ State _____

Zip Code_____ Telephone (____) _____

Hardbound	$ 24.95
Indiana Sales Tax	1.25
Shipping and Handling:	6.00
Total Price	**$ 32.20**
Number of copies desired: _____	

Please enclose a check or money order payable to:

Good Morning Publishing Co., Inc.
P.O. Box 2366
Indianapolis, IN 46206-2366

Please allow 6 to 8 weeks for delivery.

Charge Cards: ❑ VISA ❑ MasterCard

Expiration Date ____/____

Account # _____

Name _____

Signature _____

Autograph:

Please fill out below how the book should be autographed:

_____

_____

Ship to:

Name _____

Address _____

City _____ State _____

Zip Code_____Telephone (____) _____

CHAPTER TWENTY THREE

JONATHAN

From the day he was born, Jonathan Plump was a special child to his father, "not any more special than the girls, of course. But neither of my brothers had any children. If we hadn't had a boy, the Plump line would die."

Jonathan would carry on the Plump name. He would also carry on the Plump tradition. Because Jonathan Plump was a pretty fair basketball player. He was always tall for his age and had lots of natural ability. But he never knew he'd have to live his young life as an athlete in a bubble, being compared with the kid who hit the biggest shot in Indiana high school basketball history. Life as the son of a famous athlete might seem desirable. But there's a lot of pressure that goes with the territory.

"The first I remember thinking about basketball was when I was in second or third grade. I used to watch the fourth and fifth and sixth graders at St. Pius play. I was already dribbling around, and I knew I wanted to do that," Jonathan said.

Bobby encouraged his son. But he never put any pressure on him. "Dad never talked about what he'd done. I guess the first I ever thought twice about it was when I found a reel of film in his bottom dresser drawer. He told me it was a film of Butler's NIT game against St. John's," Jonathan said.

Bobby was a good coach, though. He spent hours with his son at the basketball goal in the driveway, teaching him to dribble and shoot. "He told me that if I learned to do these things, I'd be able to play when I got older," said Jonathan. "There weren't a lot of kids in the neighborhood, so I spent a lot of time at the basketball goal. I enjoyed it."

He spent a lot of time dribbling in the house, as well. "I used to drive Mom nuts bouncing the ball off the door waiting for Dad to get home to take me to practice."

It was in his middle school years that Jonathan first began to realize that his dad had been a big deal. He pieced together various clues: the Trester Award, the bushel baskets full of trophies in the attic, the Hall of Fame banquets the Plumps attended every year. "I always thought it was fun to go, but I never knew Dad had done anything special. I was always looking at all the other great ballplayers," said Jonathan.

But it was at basketball practice that Bobby really began to make an impression on his son. "He used to sit us down at the free throw line and talk with us. While he was talking, he'd shoot the ball. He wouldn't even turn around to look at the basket, and they'd always go in. It was obvious how good he was."

Bobby served as assistant coach for the St. Pius team from the time Jonathan was in fourth grade all the way through eighth grade. "He had a great impact on everybody. A lot of the guys still get together at the restaurant (Plump's Last Shot) and talk about grade school as if it were yesterday," said Jonathan.

Jonathan's head coach at St. Pius was Bob Anderson. Anderson was a student of the game, passionate about basketball; in fact, he was also a high school referee and once officiated a boys' state final game. To inspire his boys, he'd take them to watch Indiana University scrimmages. Jonathan also played on an AAU team coached by Red Taylor. Both teams were loaded with good ballplayers — including Jonathan's best friend, James Murphy.

To Jonathan, his sixth, seventh, and eighth grade years were the best basketball years ever. "Mr. Taylor always made practice fun. His drills were always interesting. And we were playing against kids who were bigger and stronger than we were, yet we were still competitive. Basketball was just so much fun. I couldn't play enough," he said.

In the summers, Jonathan would nearly get his fill. He and Murph were both sought-after athletes, Murph more for his budding talent as a runner than as a basketball player. Two Northside Indianapolis Catholic schools, Cathedral High School and Chatard High School, were hoping to recruit both boys. Both schools' basketball coaches, the late Tom Steavson of Chatard and Ron Steward of Cathedral, would pick up the boys and take them to summer leagues.

"From my point of view, it was great," said Jonathan. "It was twice the basketball."

(The Catholic schools weren't the only ones interested in Jonathan. The Plumps lived in Washington Township, where North Central High School was the public school. North Central boys' basketball coach Arlen Lickliter certainly coveted Jonathan's basketball skills — as did Coach Ernie Cline of Indianapolis Tech. Once after a high school game, Cline approached Bobby and said, "Heck, everybody else in this town recruits. I may as well throw my hat in the ring. If you ever want to move Jonathan, we'd love to have him here.")

On the surface, the decision about where Jonathan would go to school looked to be no contest. Most of his friends from St. Pius would be going to Chatard. Tari and Kelli were already at Chatard. And Bobby was on Chatard's athletic board.

But Jonathan had other ideas. "My sisters were there, and all the teachers knew them, and they were both such good students. I thought the teachers were going to have expectations of me that I wasn't sure I wanted to try to live up to."

"You could always see Jonathan was smart," said his sister Kelli. "He was wonderful in math and science. But it never seemed to show up in his grades."

Jonathan was a smart kid. But even in his early elementary school days, he'd had trouble with school work. When he was eight, Bobby and Jenine decided to have him tested. They took him to a specialist and watched through a one-way glass as Jonathan tried to work puzzles with blocks. At one point, he became so frustrated, he swept the blocks off the table.

"I knew how to do the puzzle. I knew exactly how it was supposed to go together, But I just couldn't do it," young Jonathan told his parents.

Jonathan was diagnosed with dysgraphia, an impairment of the ability to write. "I always knew his handwriting wasn't very good, but mine wasn't very good, either. I never thought anything about it," Bobby said. Jonathan was able to absorb information. But there was a disconnection between his brain and his hands.

Bobby and Jenine pondered what this meant. Their doctor suggested that perhaps Jonathan could take his tests in school orally. But the Plumps decided not to pursue this option. "He was already a head taller than all the other kids, and he was a good athlete, so he was already getting lots of attention. We wanted to make sure he fit in with his class," Bobby said.

Jonathan *was* tall. Today, Jonathan stands 6'6", and he'd achieved most of that height by the time he was ready for high school. It was little wonder that he was attracting so much attention on the basketball court.

Ron Stewart was clearly interested. He was a young, aggressive coach who had big plans for his program at Cathedral. Jonathan saw Stewart a lot that summer before high school. "Once he came over to talk with Mom and Dad, and I was shooting around in the driveway. He told me to stand in front of the bucket and try to take it off the bankboard — said that was one of the hardest shots in basketball. I worked on that shot for two weeks. When he came over again, he saw me shooting it, and he walked by and patted me on the butt. 'Looks like you're coachable,' he said. I was flattered. I could see he was interested in me," said Jonathan.

Bobby liked what he was hearing from Ron Stewart, too. "It seemed like he was really building a good program," he said. He and Jenine decided to look into sending Jonathan to Cathedral. Bobby made an appointment with the late Robert V. Welch (a good friend of the late *Indianapolis Star* sports editor Bob Collins, who happened to be a good friend of Bobby's).

"Bob Welch told us right away that he knew there were rumors that they paid people to go to school there, but that simply wasn't true. They didn't recruit anyone with money, and they didn't offer scholarships, except for a few based on need. But we weren't expecting any kind of financial assistance. We just wanted what was best for Jonathan," Bobby said.

So did everyone, it seemed. And nearly everyone else thought Jonathan would be better off at Chatard.

"We got a lot of phone calls from people who'd heard Jonathan had started to lean toward Cathedral. They told us it would be a mistake to send him there, that Cathedral wasn't our type of crowd. But it sure didn't seem like a mistake to us," Bobby said.

Jonathan had made up his mind. "Red Taylor's son Rob was going to Cathedral, and Red was scouting for them. I could really relate to his scouting reports, and I had a lot of respect for him. So, although he never talked to me about going to Cathedral, that was a factor.

"I also had a crush on a girl who was going to Cathedral. When I played in the driveway, I used to pretend she was sitting up in the stands watching me. She was older than me, and I knew she would never notice me unless I did something dramatic on the basketball floor.

"And I really liked Coach Stewart. I knew I could play for him," Jonathan said.

So late that summer, the decision was made: Jonathan would go to Cathedral. Bobby and Jenine was comfortable with the decision. And Jonathan was happy.

Some people at Chatard apparently weren't so happy. "My first three years at Chatard, my principal, Steven Noone, was just a terrific guy. He knew the names of all the kids and made you feel important. But the new principal, Larry Bowman, was never very nice to me, and I could never figure out why," said Kelli.

Chatard Coach Tom Steavson, though, wasn't bitter. It wasn't until after school started that Bobby talked with Steavson. "He came into my office one day and said, 'Bobby, I just wanted you to know that I wanted to stay out of this. Jonathan has a right to go wherever you think is best. I hope you made the decision that's going to turn out best for him.' We talked for a long time that day. Tom and I got to be pretty close friends." Years later, when Tom was dying of cancer, Bobby called him in the hospital and Jenine and the girls wrote to share their love. His passing was a sad event for the entire family.

"He was always nice to me — one of my favorite teachers ever," said Kelli.

Judging by the way Jonathan's freshman year went at Cathedral, it looked as though he'd made a good decision, indeed. He played with the varsity and even started a game, and ended one with the patented Plump flair for the dramatic: his last-second shot beat Indianapolis Tech High School, whose star was future Indiana University starter Landon Turner.

"Mr. Stewart was a heck of a coach. I was really developing quickly. And we had some big kids who used to beat the crap out of me in practice — Kenny Walton, who was a McDonald's All-American, and Matt Webber, who was 6'7", strong, and mean. Those guys taught me how to play," Jonathan said.

Basketball was his top priority. Coach Stewart took him to several camps that summer, including one at the University of Kentucky. At Kentucky, Jonathan twisted his knee and had to call Bobby to come get him. "No one from Kentucky ever called me. I thought that was pretty irresponsible," said Bobby.

Jonathan's knee wasn't improving. At the beginning of his

sophomore year in school, it was decided that surgery was the best option. The doctors thought Jonathan would recover fully, and would be playing for Coach Stewart again in no time.

But while Jonathan was still in the hospital, Coach Stewart dropped a bombshell.

"I'll never forget Jonathan's face when Stewart told him. He was sitting up in bed eating taco chips. Stewart told us he was leaving Cathedral to accept an assistant coaching position at the University of Nebraska. Jonathan had a chip halfway up to his mouth, and he just froze and turned white as a sheet," Bobby said.

"My first thought was, 'who's taking his place?'," said Jonathan. "Of course, I wanted the best for him. I thought it was great that he was going to coach in college. I just knew he'd be a head coach in a couple of years."

But inside, Jonathan was shattered. "I saw him on TV not long ago, and thought to myself that I was one of the people he dropped along the way," he said.

Stewart's leaving left Cathedral in a bind. The school year had already started. and they needed to find a coach. They eventually hired Dave Cartow, who was willing and interested — but not the caliber of coach Jonathan was expecting.

"I remember him coming up to me and asking me what kind of offense we played. I was floored. I never had a coach ask me about the game before. I just didn't know what to think," he said.

Jonathan's game began to suffer. "I felt like my life had fallen apart," Jonathan said.

Jonathan's coach and mentor had left. And his troubles were only beginning.

Jonathan's best friend James Murphy was the best young miler in the city, perhaps in the entire state. His future was bright. Maybe he'd even make it to the Olympics some day. But that year, doctors found a dime-sized spot deep in James' leg. They feared it was cancerous — and that they might have to amputate a leg.

"I don't think his doctors and his parents wanted him to know that. We just couldn't imagine it. Murph losing a leg? It was part of our identity, part of everything we did. If Murph had to have a leg taken off, where would he be. We decided that if that was going to happen, we'd both run away," Jonathan said.

Jonathan was in the hospital waiting room during James's surgery. When Jenine came in crying, he feared the worst. Then he realized she was crying tears of joy. The operation had been successful. James was going to be okay.

But Jonathan's life didn't stop sliding. Bobby and Jenine began to catch on to the fact that they had a major problem developing. They considered pulling him out of Cathedral, thinking a change might be best for him. But there were other things happening at Cathedral. At the start of Jonathan's junior year, Bob Welch and the Cathedral administration were looking for another new basketball coach — a coach with a bit more experience. They found Tom O'Brien, who had grown up in a large Irish Catholic family on the east side of Indianapolis. O'Brien was a graduate of Cathedral and Butler University, and had spend several years as an assistant coach for the University of Evansville Purple Aces under Coach Arad McCutcheon.

O'Brien knew he had a kid with a problem, and tried to motivate Jonathan to get his mind back on basketball. On the bus on the way to a game against Tech, he announced that Jonathan would be playing for the junior varsity. "That was an embarrassment — especially at Tech. That was where I'd made the last-second shot against Landon Turner as a freshman." Jonathan had a terrible game. "I just didn't know how to act," he said.

Soon, Jonathan's funk became clear even to him. "Once at the end of a game, we were up by three, and I fouled a guy coming down the lane. He made the bucket and the free throw, and we went into overtime. It was such a stupid play, such a dumb mistake on my part.

"A few days later, I was in my street clothes, and Coach O'Brien pulled me into the gym and said, 'Jonathan, I want you to show everyone what you don't do at the end of the game.' So he sent a guy down the lane, and I fouled him again. I was so confused, so embarrassed. At that point, I would have quit and never played again."

And Bobby and Jenine at last were certain they were dealing with a very troubled young man. In an attempt to get their son's life back under control, they made a tough decision: they'd remove him from

Cathedral and try to find a slower environment for him.

"We decided the best thing to do would be to get out of Indianapolis altogether. We had some good friends up in Peru, Lee and Susie Holmes. And the head basketball coach at Peru High School was Bob Macy, whom I respected," Bobby said. Macy's son Kyle was an Indiana Mr. Basketball and part of Kentucky's 1978 NCAA championship team.

Cathedral hated to see Jonathan go. But they, too, wanted what was best for him and his family. The basketball program would get along without him. Indeed, in the years that followed, Coach O'Brien brought the respect back to the Cathedral Irish basketball program, taking his team to the Final Four in 1982. The Irish lost that year to eventual champ Plymouth and their future Michigan State and NBA star guard, Scott Skiles.

Bobby and Jenine decided to rent an apartment in Peru. At least one of them would be there with Jonathan at all times. Bobby went to talk with the IHSAA about their decision and make sure there would be no problems with the move.

The late Charie Maas, IHSAA assistant commissioner, didn't beat around the bush. "Would you still move if we make him ineligible?" he asked.

"Yes," said Bobby.

"Have you talked with the principals?" Maas asked.

"Yes," Bobby said. Maas told him that the IHSAA wouldn't get involved unless the principals complained, and called in Commissioner Ward Brown to hear Bobby's story.

"Are you going to sell your house?" Commissioner Brown asked.

No, Bobby told him, that wasn't part of the plan. The Plumps had just finished the addition to their house for Jenine's mother and father and didn't want to put them through moving again. But Bobby assured Commissioner Brown that he or Jenine would always be in Peru with Jonathan.

The plan was set. The Plumps were off to Peru. That was the last they heard from the IHSAA — until about a month later, when the phone rang in their Peru apartment one day around 10 a.m. and Bobby answered.

It was Commissioner Charlie Maas. "What do you want, Charlie?" Bobby asked.

"Nothing else. You've answered my question by answering the phone," Maas said.

Basketball rumors are bound to start whenever a talented player moves from one school to another. When that player is a 6'6" senior named Plump, you can bet the rumor mill was working overtime, and it seemed that someone from nearby Maconaquah High School had told the IHSAA that Jonathan was living in Peru by himself. The Plumps were careful to keep Jonathan's troubles in the family. But someone from Maconaquah was trying to look in the windows.

The move seemed to pay off for Jonathan. He had an excellent senior year as a basketball player. NCAA Division I schools from across the country, including Indiana, began to show some interest in this kid who seemed to have beaten the odds.

The games were becoming fun again. "Coach Macy's style fit me. He didn't yell, but he had a way of getting his point across. I respected him," Jonathan said.

Once Coach Macy made Jonathan sit out the first half of a game because he wore blue jeans — a violation of team rules. Another time, he sent Jonathan to the locker room after he cursed while questioning an official's call right in front of an open radio microphone.

That same year, Jenine nearly got sent to the showers early one game, as well. "We had seats near the front, right under one of the baskets," Bobby said. "Jenine was angry at the officials one game. Well, one of them called a one-and-one foul and he backed up toward us with his fingers in the air. Jenine was so mad at him, she reached up and grabbed his finger. They nearly threw her out for that one."

And, in spite of Jonathan's success on the court, the move to Peru did nothing to reverse his personal problems. "I didn't realize that if I wanted to excel in basketball there were sacrifices I was going to have to make," Jonathan said.

Bobby used to spend hours talking with Jonathan. "I used to tell him, 'I can't control your life, but I hope you will. And I hope you understand the consequences of what you're doing.'"

When you're 18 years old, the consequences don't always leap right out at you. Jonathan was still living life on the edge. But he was still playing well on the court. It didn't seem to matter.

Just before the sectional tournament in Jonathan's senior year, Bobby got a call from Milan: his brother Les had had a heart attack. Bobby rushed off to be by his brother's side and told Jonathan he'd be back for the game.

Jonathan had plans of his own. He took a jug of whiskey from the Plump home in Indianapolis and hid it in the garage in Peru. The jug was for a post-game victory celebration. But as he was taking the jug up to the apartment, a man called to him from the nearby Moose Lodge parking lot.

"How old are you," asked the man.

"Eighteen," replied Jonathan.

"Then you're under arrest," the man said.

The officer put Jonathan in his car. "He put handcuffs on me. Then, from his car, he called my principal. I was suspended, not from school, but from basketball," said Jonathan.

Next, Jonathan was hauled over to school, where the team bus was waiting to take the boys to Kokomo for a practice session. The officer took him out of the car in handcuff in front of all of his teammates.

Coach Macy thought it was a joke and told the officer to take off the cuffs. But it was no joke. The officer informed Coach Macy that Jonathan was under arrest. The bus left without Jonathan.

Then, for some reason, the officer unlocked the handcuffs and told Jonathan he was free to go.

"He just took off the cuffs and told me to leave. There were never any more consequences. But that was enough," Jonathan said. The team bus had left without him. There would be no sectional victory celebration for Jonathan. Basketball in Indiana can sometimes be a strange game.

And that was the end of any major college interest in Jonathan's basketball skills. The next year, he decided to play junior college ball at Sheridan, Wyoming, but came home before the season even started. He tried to play at Vincennes Junior College, but his personal problems again got the better of him. Jonathan's once-promising basketball career was on hold until he could put his life back together.

Through it all, Bobby was there for him.

"Sometimes, it was hard to be Bobby Plump's son. There were a lot of expectations. I'm sure that contributed to my confusion.

"But I've seen the resentment and rebellion in the sons of athletes and other famous people. I wasn't like that. Dad never pressured me. I always knew I was loved. He was always there for me," Jonathan said.

"I tried to use a sort of non-judgmental judgmental approach with him," Bobby said. "I always let him know what I thought. But I never wanted to get too tough with him. I thought it would only drive him away.

"I guess I fell back on how I was raised. I tried to keep an attitude of forgiveness and good will and trust. And I knew Jonathan had great instincts. I felt like if he could just hang around, everything would work out."

In many ways, it was just hanging around Dad that had a big impact on Jonathan. "I particularly remember Uncle Les's funeral. We were at the service, and I was sitting behind the rest of the family. Dad had his arms around Mom and Grandma, and he was touching Tari and Kelli, too. They were all crying, but Dad wasn't. I had a lump in my throat. I didn't know how to act.

"Well, back at the house, Dad was walking around smiling and shaking everybody's hand. I'm sure I looked sad, maybe angry. Dad said, 'Hey, your Uncle doesn't care. If he was here, he'd be the first one to be having a good time.'

"But later that night, we were walking around back behind Uncle Les's house. And it finally occurred to me what he was doing. 'You're really hurting, Dad, aren't you? You're just doing this for us. You know that everyone's looking to you, so you have to be strong. But it's okay now, Dad.'

"He grabbed me and started to cry. He was so hurt. But he was trying to be strong to help us. I learned a lot that day. I grew up a lot right then," said Jonathan.

Indeed, Jonathan has grown up a lot. Today, he's married to Lynne Beatty, owner of the Jazz Cooker restaurant in Indianapolis; their son Garrett was born in 1992. Jonathan and Bobby own Plump's Last Shot, another restaurant just a couple of blocks from the Jazz Cooker. Plump's Last Shot has proven to be a great success. "I always felt afraid to fail before. But I'm not afraid any more. I know now that failing doesn't mean the end of your life," he said.

"He's been a great success story," said Jonathan's uncle, Jon Ford. "There were lots of expectations placed on that kid — the son of Mr. Basketball, Bobby Plump, he was tall, and he had lots of talent. It's great to see him come through it all. And Bobby was always there to provide love and understanding."

"There are things in life that being involved with sports and having a strong family teach you to accept. Things don't always happen the way you want them to. I would have loved to have seen Jonathan play, but it's better to grow as an individual. There were crises that he overcame that are more important than sports," Bobby said.

And Jonathan knows that it was his dad's inspiration that helped him get through the toughest battles of his life. He's not alone. As the years passed, Bobby proved to be an inspiration to kids across the state. That shot, that game, that achievement now 30 years in the past, was becoming legend. But it was still a local legend — a turning point and an important event in Indiana high school basketball history, to be sure, but more than anything just a pleasant Hoosier memory. Yet, in 1986, the Milan legend was revitalized, repackaged, and introduced not only to a new generation of Hoosiers, but to people around the world. It wasn't anything Bobby Plump did. It was the movie *Hoosiers*.

CHAPTER TWENTY FOUR

HOOSIERS

Back around 1977, more than 20 years after the Mighty Men of Milan made Indiana basketball history, Gene White was serving as athletic director at Milan High School. He received a letter from a recent Indiana University graduate named Angelo Pizzo. "The letter said he thought the team we played on might be the source of a story for a film or a TV film, and he was seeking some information. I kept the letter, just in case it was true."

It was true. A decade later, *Hoosiers* debuted in movie houses across the nation, delighting fans and film critics alike. The film was the realization of a dream for Pizzo, who co-produced and wrote the screenplay, and David Anspaugh, Pizzo's fellow Hoosier and college buddy, who directed. The two were familiar with the Milan story and, as Indiana University students, had decided it would make a great film.

That said, the movie *Hoosiers* is not the story of the 1953-54 Milan High School Indians, but of the 1951-52 Hickory Huskers and their improbable rise from small town obscurity to win the Indiana state championship. As far as the story is concerned, the championship is one of the only similarities between the two.

Hoosiers is the story of enigmatic Coach Norman Dale, and his rag-tag basketball team. Dale takes over the Huskers from a popular coach who died the year before. Along the way to the state championship game, he molds his boys into a tough team, dealing with skeptical townspeople, rabid fans, and a drunken assistant coach.

No one who has ever seen a Hollywood sports movie should be surprised at how *Hoosiers* ends. The Hickory Huskers win close games against good opponents in dramatic fashion, overcoming all kinds of adversity along the way, to reach the state finals against South Bend Central. South Bend is much bigger and more experienced. They are the defending champs. They are heavily favored.

But in the end, they are sitting on the floor at Butler Fieldhouse, sobbing, their dreams shattered by a last-second Jimmy Chitwood jump shot. Hickory wins, glorifying "all the small towns that never got here," as one of Dale's players says before the game.

Hoosiers stars Gene Hackman, the Oscar-winning star of scores of films in the '70s, '80s, and '90s, as Coach Norman Dale. Hackman, who grew up in Danville, Illinois — just across the Indiana state line

— was reportedly so enamored of the script, he agreed to make the film for considerably less than his $3 million fee at the time. Sources close to the film said Hackman received $500 thousand for *Hoosiers*.

Hackman said that playing in *Hoosiers* was like going home. Actually, it *was* a lot like going home; the film was shot entirely on location in Indiana, much of it in New Richmond, only about 60 miles from Danville.

Dennis Hopper plays Shooter, the former Hickory basketball star and current town drunk who becomes Coach Norman Dale's assistant. Hopper once said that Shooter was "a role I've rehearsed for years," and that the character, "has his own story with. . .a beginning, a middle, and an end. Most supporting roles simply drift in and out."

Other actors in the film included Barbara Hershey as Myra Fleenor, Coach Dale's love interest; Sheb Wooley as Cletus, the Hickory principal who hires Coach Dale; Fern Parsons as Opal Fleenor, the old women who befriends the new coach; and Chelsie Ross as George, the Hickory resident and interim coach who's none too happy with the way he sees Dale running his program.

Surprisingly, most of the Hickory Huskers themselves were not Hollywood pros, but Hoosier basketball players. It was in the producers' plans all along to find basketball players and try to teach them how to act — not vice versa. It proved to be the right decision. The high quality of basketball playing in the film sets *Hoosiers* apart from many other sports movies in which the actual playing is sloppy and unrealistic.

The one professional actor in the bunch was David Neidorf, who plays Everett, Shooter's son. Neidorf has also appeared in such films as *Platoon* and *Bull Durham.*

Maris Valainis plays the part of Jimmy Chitwood. Valainis was an Indianapolis kid who was cut from his basketball team at Chatard High School, the school Tari and Kelli Plump attended. But he loved the game and continued to play. By the time the film started shooting, Valainis was probably skilled enough to play small college ball. *Hoosiers* inspired Valainis to go to Hollywood, where he landed small roles in several TV series and films.

The rest of the Huskers ranged in age from 18 - 23. Rade was played by Steve Hollar, a DePauw University student and basketball player at the time of the shooting who is now a dentist in Warsaw, Indiana. At the time the film was made, Hollar's appearance in the film was cleared by the NCAA; later, he was reportedly suspended from playing and had to pay back part of the money he earned for the film.

Strap was played by Scott Summer, a high school player from Bethesda Christian in Brownsburg. Whit was played by Brad Boyle, who attended Ball State University.

The cast even included two real-life farmers. Wade Schenck, now a farmer near Pittsboro, plays Ollie, the little kid who hits two clutch free throws to clinch a regional victory. At the time, Schenck was a senior at L&M and was given permission by the IHSAA to appear in the film.

Kent Poole, who plays Merle, was a farmer near Lebanon and a teacher at Hamilton Heights High School. He was a member of a Western Boone High School team that reached the Sweet Sixteen.

Brad Long plays Buddy, a player who early in the film smarts off to Coach Dale and quits the team. (He later rejoins.) In reality, he may have been the best ballplayer of the bunch. Long graduated from Center Grove High School in 1981 and received letters of interest from several NCAA Division I schools. Unfortunately, he suffered a finger injury halfway through his senior year. Long settled for Division II ball at Southwestern College in Winfield, Kansas.

Basketball ran in Brad Long's family; his father Gary was an Indiana University basketball player. Brad saw a lot of his father's world in *Hoosiers*. "What made the movie neat for me was that my father always said what a special time the 1950s were for Indiana basketball. Then, it was the only thing in town. Everybody went to the games. It was neat to relive his era."

In the middle of the Hickory Huskers' season, Coach Dale was looking for a way to build Shooter's confidence as his assistant. Shooter was deathly afraid of having to make decisions if Dale was ejected from a game. So Dale promised he'd take it easy — then proceeded to get himself ejected on purpose.

The referee who tossed Dale was played by Ken Strunk, owner of Bogie's Cafe in Ft. Thomas, Kentucky, just across the Ohio River from Cincinnati. Strunk is a long-time local actor who has appeared in numerous commercials, industrial films, and several other movies. He was also a semipro football player who had little interest in basketball — and none in officiating.

"It was supposed to be a one-day shoot in Knightstown, about a three-hour drive for me. I got there at a quarter 'til nine. I'd been drinking coffee all the way, so I was ready to go. Gene Hackman and Dennis Hopper were just getting out of bed from their RVs. They hadn't even had coffee yet.

"We had a rehearsal. Hopper pulled out a napkin with his lines written on it. Then we got made up and into costume.

"Then we were told they weren't going to shoot us. They had a crowd that day, and they wanted to shoot crowd scenes. Hackman said, 'Anyone for a poker game?' So we played poker all that day and the next. I made about $60. There were a few guys there who could stand to lose some money."

Strunk said the scene was finally shot on the third day. The director ended up choosing the very first take for the film.

"I've had a lot of people recognize me from the film," Strunk said. "I was in downtown Cincinnati once, and a guy driving a garbage truck started screaming at me about being the referee in *Hoosiers*. When I told him I was, he told me it was the best scene in the movie."

In addition to the New Richmond and Knightstown locations, parts of Hoosiers were shot in Ninevah, Danville, and Lebanon. Of course, the big finale was shot at Hinkle Fieldhouse in Indianapolis — the place all the real-life action occurred more than 30 years earlier.

Bobby Plump was on hand for the action at Hinkle. No one had asked him to attend. In fact, he'd received only one call from anyone connected with the film, who asked questions about the team's uniforms. But Bobby decided it would be fun to sit in the stands and watch the recreation of the central event in his life.

When Gene Hackman heard Bobby was at the fieldhouse, he insisted on meeting him and discussing the actual events with him. "Gene Hackman was standing at one end of the floor, and they were filming at the other end. They were having a heck of a time getting Jimmy Chitwood to hit the shot. I walked over and said, 'Mr. Hackman, I'm Bobby Plump.' He said, 'Get over here! This is who the movie's all about.'" Bobby proceeded to show them how the events really transpired.

Hoosiers was many months in the editing and finishing. When, in 1986, the film was about to be released, Bobby was asked by editors of *The Indianapolis Star* to attend a private screening and give his opinions. He arrived armed with a notebook and a prejudice that it probably wouldn't be much of a movie. "I'd read the script and didn't think it sounded interesting at all," he said.

His experience was much different. "I started looking at it, and I wrote about two lines. And then I got so engrossed in the movie that I never wrote another line at all. I laughed. I cried. I felt good when it was over. I think that's how a lot of people reacted."

Angelo Pizzo was also in attendance at the screening. He asked Bobby whether, in spite of the movie's fictionalization of the Milan story, the last 18 seconds of the championship game were right.

"I told him they had it just about exactly right," Bobby said.

Not everyone loved the film. Some of the film's harshest critics are the people you might expect would have been its biggest fans: the people of Milan.

Folks around Ripley County first got to see *Hoosiers* at a debut in 1986. The film was shown in Batesville. Most of the original Indians gathered in Milan and rode to the premier in Cadillacs. Even Ronnie Truitt, who had lived in Houston since college and become a successful coach and principal in his own right, turned out for the event.

There was some resentment that Milan was never mentioned in the film, and that none of *Hoosiers* was shot in Milan or anywhere in Ripley County. In truth, Milan may not have looked small enough anymore to play the 1950s version of itself. The original Milan High School had been torn down to make way for a bigger, more modern high school. Others involved in the production said that Hollywood lawyers were concerned that the town or certain characters who were part of the real story would demand a piece of the low-budget film's pie. But, according to writer Angelo Pizzo, the real reason the Hickory story is not the Milan story is that the true story had very little controversy. "The very essence of all drama is conflict, conflict between people," he said.

Apparently, Pizzo wasn't familiar with the very human drama of the Pierceville Alleycats, Snort Grinstead, Marvin Wood, the Downtown Coaches Club, the clock incident against Morton Memorial, the Aurora rivalry. . . .

One of the film's most outspoken critics was Bill Jordan. Ironically, Jordan spent many years as a Hollywood character actor and had socialized with Gene Hackman over the years.

"I mean, here I am in the city where they do the film, and they know I live here, they know me. I thought, how stupid. Why would you not ask a guy who was on the team? I've known Hackman for years. He knows I was on the team."

Jordan has never been able to watch the film in its entirety. "It had nothing to do with reality. It was Hollywood hokum. If they wrote the real story, it would be wonderful, something true to what it was."

Gene White's mother Genivieve's opinion was mixed. "It was a good movie. But it was not the story of Milan. It was excellent, because we don't see many good, wholesome pictures anymore. But we didn't have a drunk for an assistant coach. That was unthinkable. It just wasn't true to Milan."

Milan resident Jim Boyd expressed stronger resentment. "The movie didn't do justice to the town or the team at all. Coach Marvin Wood is a religious guy. He never swore in his life. In the movie, the coach was playing footsie with a teacher. That just wouldn't happen."

Hollywood hokum? Undoubtedly. The Hickory story is not the Milan story. But, as film critic Roger Ebert (who gave *Hoosiers* four stars) observed, "What makes Hoosiers special is not its story, but its details and its characters."

He is right. The details feel right. The small town men fiercely loyal to their team, living and dying with every shot. The crackerbox gyms. The lines of cars stretching into the distance, following the team bus to an away game. The screaming fans. The coach measuring the distance from the rim to the floor at Butler Fieldhouse, assuring his intimidated young charges that it's the same everywhere.

There are other details that feel right, too. Although Marvin Wood was asked to consult on the film, he couldn't break away from his coaching duties. But the official who welcomes the Huskers to Butler Fieldhouse is played by none other than Milan's own Ray Craft. South

Bend Central is coached by Ray Crowe, whose Crispus Attucks Tigers lost in the semi-state to Milan in 1954 — and won the tournament going away the next two years. And there is Tom Carnegie on the public address system, and Hilliard Gates announcing the game on the sidelines.

"The Milan legend has been kept alive and made important to America through *Hoosiers*," Gates said. "It's worth seeing every once in a while."

"The thing that gives me a thrill is when I run into people who were at the Milan game, or who say 'that's what it was like.' We did have the barbershop scenes. People did huddle around radios and listen to games. The movie was an honest portrayal of Indiana basketball," said Brad Long.

Although not everyone in Milan loved *Hoosiers*, practically everyone else did. The movie was a huge box office success in its initial release, and has gone on to win big audiences around the world. It has long been a big seller on video cassette, a movie people want to own.

The Academy of Motion Picture Arts and Sciences loved *Hoosiers*, too. The film received several Oscar nominations, including a Best Supporting Actor nomination for Dennis Hopper and Best Original Screenplay for Angelo Pizzo. Ironically, Pizzo didn't attend the Oscar ceremony. His beloved Indiana Hoosiers were battling (and defeating) Syracuse for the national championship the night of the awards.

In March of 1993, Pizzo and David Anspaugh were guests at "39 And Holding," a first-ever reunion of the 1954 Milan and Muncie Central teams. The event was a fundraiser for the Indiana Kidney Foundation, and was held at — where else? — Hinkle Fieldhouse.

Pizzo told the crowd that it struck him that if they could capture the passion, energy, and enthusiasm of Indiana basketball on film, he and Anspaugh would really have something special.

"The quintessential basketball story in Indiana is the Milan and Muncie Central game. I didn't know what I was going to do, the exact story or what kind of version. I wanted to capture the spirit and the feeling," he said.

And, although Milan was never mentioned in the film, Pizzo always let people know that Milan was the film's inspiration. In a press release about the film, Pizzo said, "The story seemed to be the classic Hoosier folk tale. The period, early '50s, really appealed to me, as well. It was the last vestige of true innocence. And, naturally, there is that unique phenomenon called Hoosier Hysteria."

Anspaugh agreed. "When Angelo and I were in college, we talked about what a good film it would make. Of course, neither of us thought at the time that we would be in a position to realize that dream."

The Muncie Central players may have provided the biggest surprise of the evening. They said they were disappointed in their loss in the finals. But, to a person, they thanked the Milan Indians for that game in 1954. Because of the Milan victory, the 1954 Bearcats were better-known in their community than even the members of Muncie Central's many state championship teams! (Bearcat Coach Jay McCreary may not have been so forgiving. When McCreary died years later, his daughter told Bobby that, for the first twenty years of her life, she thought Bobby's first name had only four letters.)

And what did the other Milan Indians think of the film? Asked if anything about the movie sent a chill up their spines, here's what several of them had to say the morning after *Hoosiers* premiered:

Gene White: "I thought the opening scenes with the country roads, the guys shooting along the highway on the side of the barns. That was very accurate."

Ray Craft: "I think the gymnasiums. We used to play in those, believe it or not. They weren't all like Butler Fieldhouse."

Rollin Cutter: "The crowds. The fans. Standing up, screaming and yelling during the whole game."

Bobby Plump: "In the scene where they came out in the first game in that small gymnasium, and Gene Hackman says. 'Welcome to basketball in Indiana.' Everybody is screaming and standing.'"

Jenine Plump still gets choked up when she hears the music of the film. Bobby and Jenine watch the movie occasionally, and are big fans.

"I think it has been fantastic," Bobby said. "I know some people in Milan are disappointed, but I think they did a tremendous job. The population knows the movie was based on Milan. The bottom line is, it's been great for Milan, great for Indiana, and great for basketball."

Give Bob Hammel, *Bloomington Herald-Times* sports editor, the last word. "Angelo Pizzo is a big IU fan. He's even traveled with us. I told him, 'The movie was really good. But the real life story is better.'"

CHAPTER TWENTY FIVE

HONORS
AND ACCOLADES

The success of the movie *Hoosiers* did nothing but add to the power of the already mythic Milan Indians story, and to the legend of the one shot that brought down a giant and provided kids in small towns everywhere with a sense that their dreams of basketball glory could come true. So it was only fitting that, when the new Indiana Basketball Hall of Fame was dedicated on June 30, 1990, Bobby Plump, his teammates, Milan High School, and the Milan fans were big parts of the festivities.

The Hall of Fame had been housed in a small space in Indianapolis since 1962. But the new, 14,000-square-foot museum was in New Castle, Indiana. Although there was some resistance to move the Hall of Fame to Henry County — Bobby originally opposed the move, thinking it would be less accessible to visitors — the Hall of Fame's board members voted unanimously for the move.

It's a fitting site for an Indiana basketball shrine. The museum sits right beside New Castle High School and the world's largest high school gymnasium (9,314 capacity) — the same gym that was promised but never built during Marvin Wood's tenure as New Castle's head basketball coach. And New Castle is itself a storied name in Indiana high school basketball circles, having produced Kent Benson and Steve Alford, both of whom won the title of Mr. Basketball and went on to win NCAA Championships with Bob Knight at Indiana University.

And it's a downright beautiful facility. More than six thousand bricks forming the State of Indiana greet visitors near the front walkway. The marquee above the entrance is shaped like an enormous backboard. Overhead fly 37 flags: the American flag, the Indiana flag, the Hall of Fame's own banner, the reigning boys' and girls' champions, and the previous year's Sweet Sixteen for both the boys and girls.

Inside, the museum resembles a great arena, surrounding visitors with the sights and sounds of an action-packed ball game. It is an impressive, beautiful facility, a fitting shrine to Indiana's favorite sport and the people who have played it.

The day of the dedication included a basketball game at the nearby gym. Although the crowd was far short of the gym's 9,314 capacity, the folks on hand saw a memorable game. The opponents: the 1954 Milan Indians and the cast of *Hoosiers,* appearing as the Hickory Huskers. Marvin Wood was on hand to coach the Indians. Angelo Pizzo coached the Huskers.

As the game began, the actors brought the ball down the floor and missed a couple of good shots. Gene White finally grabbed a rebound for the Indians. Bobby dribbled to half court and call time out. Then the Miracle Men proceeded to recreate the shot that ended the season and brought the state title to their little Southeastern Indiana town.

Ray Craft took the ball out of bounds. Bobby dribbled. He faked left, dribbled right. He shot.

Two points. Just like in 1954.

As it turned out, the Hickory Huskers were not the equal of the Milan Indians on the basketball floor. In five minutes of play, the Indians posted a 16-10 victory. Gene White, never much of a scoring threat in his high school days, had six points. Glen Butte had two. Bobby led all scorers with eight.

The opening of the Indiana Basketball Hall of Fame provided a great opportunity to reflect on basketball's place in the history of Indiana — and Indiana's place in the history of basketball. At the dedication ceremony, Indianapolis broadcaster Tom Carnegie, one of the founders of the original Hall of Fame, said, "In no other state would this be possible. Indiana stands above the rest in its love of the high school game. We feel a surging sense of pride."

"Basketball is more than just a sport," said Indiana Governor Evan Bayh. "It's teamwork. It's community spirit and community pride."

U.S. Senator Dan Coats gave his thanks and congratulations to the 250,000 Hoosiers who had played varsity basketball. "We value tradition. Each one has contributed to the tradition. We pray the dream will go on and on."

Then the great Oscar Robertson expressed his feelings from a player's standpoint. "To be honored in your home state by people who know you and love you is very special. Sixteen Indiana Hall of Famers are in the National Hall of Fame. This gives justice to our heritage."

Basketball heritage runs deep in Indiana, and the story of the Milan Indians is a major reason why high school basketball has remained such a big draw in the Hoosier State. The boys' State Final game was sold out for an incredible 57 years in a row. The same year that the Hall of Fame was dedicated, a national record 40,000 people turned out to watch Damon Bailey and Bedford North Lawrence win the title —

even though the game was televised across the state (and nationally on ESPN). California, the most populous state in the union and a hotbed of high school basketball, can't come close to matching Indiana's numbers. In their 1984 tournament, considered one of the state's most successful ever, 200,000 Californians watched the Division I, II, and III tournaments. That same year in Indiana, more than one million people turned out to see the boys' tournament — a number that's even more impressive when you consider that Indiana has 18 million fewer people than California and only one third the number of high schools.

A lot of people have attributed the long-time success of Indiana basketball to the idea that "there's nothing else to do in Indiana in the winter." Certainly, back in the middle of the century, that was true. Small town pride and a long, cold winter were important factors in the growth of interest in basketball in Indiana.

But that doesn't explain the continued interest in the game. While snobs on both coasts would probably contend that there's still nothing to do in Indiana, Hoosiers know better; given modern transportation, even the most remote farm in the state is close enough to a major American city that every Hoosier has access to practically everything under the sun. And the small town schools aren't what they used to be. School consolidation has steadily reduced the number of high school teams in Indiana, grouping formerly bitter rivals into bigger schools with higher enrollments. And yet, the game is still strong. There are still scores of small town gyms that hold twice as many people as there are in the town itself.

Why? Look to Milan.

At the Indiana Basketball Hall of Fame, you don't have to look too far to find Milan memorabilia. You'll find a taped welcome from Bobby Plump (as well as one from Warsaw's Judi Warren, the first Miss Basketball). You'll find postcards featuring photos of the Indians in the museum gift shop. You'll even find an interactive exhibit that lets you play Bobby Plump. You stand alone, basketball in hand, crowd roaring while the clock ticks down to zero. Can you hit a jump shot to win the game for your team before the buzzer sounds? If you miss, it costs only a quarter to try again.

But the display of Milan memorabilia is, as much as anything, what draws visitors. "The three questions people most ask when they come here are, 'What do you have on Bobby Plump and the Milan Indians? What do you have on the movie *Hoosiers*? And what do you have on Larry Bird?' It's especially remarkable when you consider that 40 percent of our visitors are from out-of-state and 10 percent are from out of the country. It shows that the Milan story isn't just an Indiana phenomenon, but a story that captured the nation and the world," said Hall of Fame Director Jason Crowe.

What the museum has about the Milan story is part of its Time Line Exhibit, a 72-foot corridor of Indiana basketball history. Along one side of the hallway are displays of trophies and uniforms and memorabilia from many different schools. Along the other are four permanent displays.

One is for Crawfordsville, where basketball was first played in Indiana. Another is for Muncie Central, whose eight championships are a state record. But right in the middle of those state championships came the game for which the Bearcats are even more famous: their loss to the 1954 Milan Indians.

The Indians have an exhibit all their own. It includes a taped presentation, game film, pictures, and team memorabilia — including a piece of the old Milan gym floor. The exhibit was funded with money raised by Milan fan Bill Thompson. According to his wife Mary Gray Thompson, it was the last great accomplishment of his life.

"Bill wasn't well at the time," she said, "but he always loved Milan and basketball so much. The 1954 team was a once-in-a-lifetime experience."

Former Hall of Fame Director Ron Newlin agreed. "Milan is here because they were the small school that won it all. No other small school has been able to do it since."

But the dream persists. In 1982, Plymouth High School, led by future Michigan State and NBA star Scott Skiles, won the tournament. The Pilgrims chose their team from an enrollment of just 894, and bested giant Gary Roosevelt 75-74 in double overtime. (Bob Collins wrote, "For years, I've believed that 1954 — Milan 32, Muncie Central 30 — never would be duplicated. Well, folks, it was tied Saturday night, I won't live to see a better championship game — I hope, because if I do I won't live through it.")

"Every few years, a Cloverdale or a Logootee or an Argos will get to the Final Four, or an L&M or White River Valley will get to the Final Eight, and they'll look like they have the stuff to go all the way. They look like they're the next Milan, but none of them has quite gotten over the hump," Ron Newlin said.

"Remember, when Milan won the tournament, it had been forty years since a small school had won (Thorntown, 1915). In reality, a small school getting that far was more rare in the 1950s than it has been in the forty years since then. For a small school to get to the Sweet Sixteen, you have to win four or five games. Back then, with around eight hundred schools, you had to win eight or nine games to get that far. And the small schools back them were really small. Today's small schools are consolidations themselves."

So Milan was the last really small school to win the crown. But Milan was also the last of another important aspect of Indiana basketball history. The fourth permanent exhibit at the Indiana Basketball Hall of Fame is for a high school team that doesn't even exist anymore: the Flying Tigers of Crispus Attucks. The Crispus Attucks Tigers were the first all-black high school to win the title — maybe the first all-black high school team to win any kind of integrated tournament in America.

In 1954, the Milan Indians beat Crispus Attucks 65-52 in the Indianapolis Semistate. It wasn't the first time the Indians had played against African-Americans; although no blacks lived in Ripley County at all, many of the schools in nearby Dearborn, Jennings, and Jackson Counties had black players on their teams. But Attucks was the first all-black school the Indians had ever played.

Remarkably, the loss to Milan was the worst defeat a Ray Crowe-coached Attucks team would ever suffer. In fact, it was one of the *only* losses they would ever suffer. In the next two years, the Tigers would win sixty-two games and lose only one, and that by only one point, en route to two consecutive state titles. That streak was due in large part to the presence of a young man who would later become one of Bobby Plump's closest friends, Oscar Robertson.

"We knew Milan was a good team," said Oscar. "I had read about them in the newspaper, and Mr. Crowe told us about them. They were more seasoned than we were. They played up to their capabilities, and we did not."

But then, Oscar was just a sophomore. After losing to Milan, he went on to dominate the game at every level as no one ever had before.

Oscar Robertson was quite possibly the greatest basketball player in history. Not even Michael Jordan can surpass Oscar's individual accomplishments: a 28-point average and a 62-point single game performance to go along with his two state titles at Attucks; three years as a collegiate All-American at the University of Cincinnati, where he averaged 33.8 points, set 15 school records, 16 conference records, and 14 NCAA records, and led his team to a 79-9 record; captain of the gold-medal-winning 1960 U.S. Olympic team, considered by most to be the best basketball team ever assembled up until the Dream Team; and 11 NBA All-Star appearances in 14 seasons, three Most Valuable Player awards, nine playoff runs with the Cincinnati Royal and Milwaukee Bucks, one world championship, a career point total of 26,710, and NBA records for assists (9,887) and free throws (7,694).

The end of the all-white era of Indiana basketball was a long time coming. Indiana was a Ku Klux Klan stronghold during the 1920s and 30s. When Attucks was opened to isolate blacks in 1927, nearly a half-million Hoosiers claimed membership in the Klan. Even though it was built to keep blacks separate, the KKK was none too happy about the school's existence. They staged a rally outside Attucks to protest its opening. Neither Attucks nor any other all-black school was allowed in the IHSAA Tournament until 1943. And, although the first Indiana Mr. Basketball, George Crowe, was black, the fans were reluctant to let blacks compete. Even in their glory years, the Crispus Attucks Tigers wore hand-me-down uniforms and played all of their games away from home; after all, who wanted to travel to an all-black school for a basketball game?

"Those were very, very troubled times, although, back then, I didn't realize what was going on," Oscar said.

But more and more people across Indiana were seeing for themselves what African-American players could do. Beginning in 1951, the IHSAA Tournament was televised for the first time, bringing images of such stars as Hallie Bryant, Willie Gardner, and Oscar's older brother Bailey into homes across the state.

These images weren't always well-received. When the Milan Indians came to Indianapolis to play Attucks in 1954, they found to their surprise that many Indianapolis basketball fans were rooting against the Tigers — because they were black.

"As we were going up toward the fieldhouse, we went past lots of people who were encouraging us to 'go and beat those n——-s,'" Bobby said.

The racial slurs were disturbing and confusing to the Indians players, who were there not to compete in an exhibition of racial superiority, but to play basketball. "It was upsetting to us," Bobby said.

Lester Plump had always taught his children to love and respect people of all races. Bobby knew that all men were created equal, but that sometimes they were treated differently. "Dad said that if another team had a black kid, you had to figure he was really good or he'd never get a chance to play."

Once, while Lester was in school at Hanover, he and Mabel lived next door to an African-American couple who had a child about Dot's age. Lester often told Bobby the story of how the two kids played together in the sandbox outside their home, "a white kid and a black kid, just having a great time. Dad always told us that was evidence that you had to be taught to hate," Bobby said.

In 1954, the Indians prevailed. But in the very next year, the final game featured not one, but two all-black teams: Attucks and Gary Roosevelt. The Tigers' lineup of Oscar, Willie Merriweather, Sheddrick Mitchell, William Scott, William Hampton and Johnny Brown outscored Roosevelt, whose stars included Dick Barnett and Wilson Eison, 97-74, setting a tournament record for points scored — a shocking contrast to the previous year's 32-30 Milan victory.

Oscar gave Coach Ray Crowe the credit for making the Tigers a great team in spite of all the adversity. "He'd played in an all-white environment (Whiteland, Indiana). I had been around blacks all my life. Fate threw us together."

The game had changed before the fans' eyes. And, again, a lot of the fans weren't too happy about that. Oscar still feels bitter about the decision of some local politicians to keep the Attucks victory celebration contained in the black neighborhoods, even though no Indianapolis or Marion County team had ever before won the state basketball tournament.

"I will never forgive that as long as I live. They took us out by the black park and had a bonfire. Did they think that because we were black we were going to tear up something? We were young and naive and didn't know what was happening. Because of the color of our skin, they thought we were less than human. I will never forgive them," he said.

Busing and school consolidations would integrate the game to a greater degree than ever before in the years ahead. Crispus Attucks itself graduated its first integrated class in 1974. Since 1954, only seven all-white teams have won the boys' state basketball title (Fort Wayne South, 1958; Evansville Bosse, 1962; Lafayette Jefferson, 1964; Carmel, 1977; Plymouth, 1982; Warsaw, 1984; and Bedford North Lawrence, 1990).

Still, racism in basketball was persistent. In college, Bobby remembered hearing about, "semi-imposed quotas that you could have no more than a few blacks on a college team, and you couldn't have an odd number so a black guy and a white guy wouldn't have to room together. I'm sure there was some truth to that. You didn't see many blacks on teams in the 1950s, and never more than two or four." He emphasized that the African-Americans he played with at Butler, including Henry Foster, Sheddrick Mitchell, Sam Rice, and Bill Scott, were always treated fairly and equally by Coach Hinkle.

Bobby and Oscar got to know each other as tough competitors on the basketball floor. But it wasn't until many years later, when they were traveling together to promote a book on the life of Ray Crowe, that they realized they had a lot more in common than they would ever have suspected.

"I've always considered Oscar a friend, but we developed a real closeness. We started talking about home life. They grew up on a farm in Tennessee, which wasn't much different from Pierceville. They didn't have electricity or running water, either. Oscar and Bailey pitched hay on the farm, just like I did.

"It just doesn't make sense to hate somebody because they're different. A lot of energy that could be used for very positive things is used up in anger. Unfortunately, some of the greatest players in the game never had a chance. There were a lot of wrongs. At least now it's open," Bobby said.

Oscar agreed. "Basketball is a sport where, no matter what your color, you can get out there and play. Basketball is king."

It probably always will be in Indiana, in spite of the fact that it's no longer the only game in town. Herb Schwomeyer, the former player, coach, official, and broadcaster whose *Hoosier Hysteria* documents each tournament since the first in 1911, agrees that the Milan story is a big reason for the game's continuing popularity.

"It's the kind of thing I talk about when I give speeches. Hoosier Hysteria is the name of the game in Indiana, primarily because the little guy can beat the big guy."

And that's been the real lasting appeal of the Bobby Plump story. "Milan is still one of the defining stories of Indiana basketball. Indiana is coming up on its hundred basketball anniversary. When it has its two hundredth, Milan will still be one of the top five or ten stories," said Ron Newlin.

"Bobby Plump and Milan are to the myth of the small school what Damon Bailey was to the myth of the individual. Forty years from now, people will believe that a one-man team can win a state championship, because Damon did it. Just like we'll believe a small school can win because Plump and Milan did it."

That particular myth may no longer exist. In the mid 1990s, the IHSAA was seriously considering a multi-class basketball tournament. Bobby and his friends would lead a strong effort to inform the public and arrive at a consensus about what Hoosiers really wanted. But first, Bobby and his family had even more important fights on their hands — not for the game they loved, but for their very lives..

CHAPTER TWENTY SIX

LIFE'S
REAL STRUGGLES

Cancer. The Plumps had dealt with it before. Bobby's brother Les and Les's wife Ann — and his brothers-in-law, Carl Sullender and Bill Schwing — died after long battles with cancer. They'd had other friends and acquaintances who'd fought the dread disease. But Bobby and Jenine never thought it would happen to them.

Then, in 1990, Jenine went to her doctor for a routine checkup. The doctor found a lump in her breast, and was concerned that it might be malignant.

"Bobby was working down in Evansville that day. I called him and told him I was getting test results that afternoon. I told him he didn't have to come home, but he came right away," Jenine said.

Together, Bobby and Jenine went back to the doctor. The news was not good: Jenine had breast cancer.

Typically, Jenine was initially more concerned about telling her family about her cancer than she was about her own state of mind. "I knew I had to tell Mom and Dad right away. Mom is usually a rock, but she couldn't handle this very well," she said.

Telling the kids was hard, too. But that weekend, the Plumps all gathered at the family cabin near Columbus and talked about Jenine's condition. "We had friends who volunteered to watch the kids that weekend," said Kelli. "But Mom said to bring them along. She said they'd help put things in perspective."

"Tari and Kelli and Jonathan were great. They were very protective of me," said Jenine.

Sadly, Jenine wasn't going to be fighting cancer alone. Two of her best friends, Sally Preble and Betty May, were diagnosed with cancer at about the same time. The three became a mutual support group, friends who could lean on each other in their most difficult hours.

And Jenine and her friends found their battle to be difficult in ways they never expected.

"I'd go to church and see people I'd known for years, and they'd shy away from me. I remember once seeing some people I knew in the grocery store. They pretended they didn't see me and walked the other way. I know it didn't have anything to do with me personally. People just don't know what to say when you have cancer. They find it easier to just avoid you," Jenine said.

Still, Jenine said she thought that her cancer was scarier for Bobby than for her. "I know he worried about me," she said, "and he doesn't worry about much of anything."

Together, Bobby and Jenine weighed their options. They spoke with surgeons and decided that a lumpectomy, along with a course of radiation and chemotherapy, was the path that seemed to offer the best chance for recovery.

The operation and chemotherapy were painful and difficult. But, never one to feel sorry for herself — or to give up without a fight — Jenine persevered. Every day, she felt a little stronger. Still, there were times when depression began to get the best of her.

"Once I was sitting in the bedroom, looking at myself in the mirror, and I just looked awful. I was right in the middle of radiation therapy, and I'd lost a lot of weight, and I had an awful scar.

"'I look terrible,' I said. Bobby looked at me and smiled and said, 'Well, you do. But you don't look like you have cancer.'

"That helped me a lot, because it was true. It would have been a lie if he'd told me I looked great, because I knew I didn't. What he said made me laugh and feel better," Jenine said.

Jenine's sense of humor helped her get through many tough times. "Once Kelli was in the bathtub with her baby girl Jaclyn, and I was playing with my grandson Joshua. I called into her that he was feeling my breast, and Kelli called back, 'Probably just the good one, eh, Mom?'" Jenine laughed.

"Mom was always so strong," said Tari. "Her battle with cancer really made me appreciate that."

Jonathan agreed. "I know it was important to Mom that everyone have a positive attitude, but I was scared to death for her. She's a fighter, though. She's one tough lady."

Slowly, Jenine's health began to recover. She was soon well enough to resume most of her normal routine with a new understanding of the stigma of cancer, and the burden it places on an individual and a family. Her sense of compassion has led her to become a guiding light and a helping hand to many others afflicted with cancer in the years since her own battle with the disease.

One of those was Marvin Wood. Soon after Jenine was diagnosed with breast cancer, Coach Wood learned he had lymphatic lymphoma. "I distinctly remember what I thought when the doctor told me," Wood said. "First, I thought, 'Why me, why now?' No one in my family had ever had cancer. And I was going to retire in a couple of months. The next thing I thought was, 'How am I going to tell my wife and my family?' And third, I thought, 'I wonder if I'll live to see another Christmas?'"

But Wood's doctor told him that lymphatic lymphoma was a treatable form of cancer. He prescribed a rigorous course of chemotherapy, which seemed to work. Wood's cancer was in remission.

Not, as it turned out, for long. "The relapse was even more devastating," he said.

This time, Wood's doctors thought a bone marrow transplant would be the only solution. The transplant held the possibility of a longer remission — and perhaps a cure. The problem was, at age 63, Wood wasn't a very good candidate for the procedure.

"Indiana University Hospital refused to take me, I would guess because of my age. My next shot was at Methodist Hospital in Indianapolis. About fifteen minutes into the interview, they told me they'd take me. When later I asked them why, they said they liked my attitude. In the interview, I'd told them I just wanted to get it over with and get on with my life. They told me that was the kind of patient they were looking for," Wood said, although nurses told him later that "they wondered why they were bringing in a 63-year-old man just to kill him."

But the transplant didn't kill him. Wood was in isolation for 28 days after the transplant. "My faith, family, and friends got me through. I talked with the Lord every night. I felt He was with me, that He had His hand on me the whole time."

Wood's body responded remarkably to the treatment. Day by day, he got stronger and stronger.

And through it all, he had the love and support of his old players. "Bob Engel came to stay with me for a couple of days when I had chemotherapy. Bobby Plump was in and out of the hospital with me, like a son. They'd all come to see me, then relay word about how I was doing to each other, like a big family. I'll never forget the first time Bobby hugged me. It was like it was from everyone, and he was the one expressing it."

Notes from Jenine raised Wood's spirits. "It seemed like I always got the right note at the right time from Jenine. Sometimes the smallest things do the greatest good. When you drop pebbles of kindness, you never know how far the ripples will expand."

Wood himself has been an inspiration to others. Part of his own recovery was encouraging other cancer patients whenever he was in the hospital. "I wanted to let them see that it wasn't a death sentence, that you could beat it," he said.

Jenine's friend Betty May wasn't so fortunate. Betty had surgery just two days after Jenine, but her recovery didn't go as smoothly. A couple of years later, while Bobby and Jenine were on vacation in Florida, they learned that Betty had had a stroke, from which she never fully recovered.

"I had planned to be on vacation in Greece, and Betty was in the hospital," said Jenine. "I didn't know what to do. So I went to see her. We talked and we cried, and I told her I didn't want to go, but she told me to go — that I couldn't hold up my life waiting for her to die. So I went. I prayed the whole time that she wouldn't die while I was gone."

Upon her return, Bobby met Jenine at the airport with the sad news. Betty had died the night before. "I was thankful that I was able to be there for the services. I still miss her," Jenine said.

Bobby had another piece of sad news for Jenine, as well: his old college coach, Tony Hinkle, had passed away at the age of 94. Bobby had been chosen to be one of the great coach's pall bearers. After the funeral, a note from the Hinkle family said that Bobby had always been "one of Dad's favorite kids."

Tony Hinkle hadn't coached in more than twenty years. But his passing was front-page news in Indianapolis, and a major sports story across the nation. From 1921 to 1970, Hinkle won 1,060 games in three sports at Butler University. Five hundred sixty of those wins came in basketball, which is why he is a member of the James Naismith Basketball Hall of Fame. And why the site of so many of those victories, Butler Fieldhouse, was renamed Hinkle Fieldhouse during his lifetime.

Less than two years later, the Plumps were faced with the cancer-related passing of another close friend and Indianapolis basketball legend: Bailey Robertson, Jr. Again, Bobby was a pall bearer.

Bailey "Flap" Robertson was not only a standout player at Crispus Attucks High School, but at Indiana Central University (now the University of Indianapolis). He was the Greyhounds' Most Valuable Player for three consecutive years, and was a three-time Hoosier College All-Conference selection. He owns numerous Greyhound scoring records that still stand: career points (2,280), points in a season (754), career scoring average (23.2), season scoring average (28.7), and others.

After college, Bailey played for the Harlem Globetrotters and for the U.S. Army, traveling around the world to entertain the troops. Even more important, Bailey was a tireless worker for the betterment of youth. Until his death, he was a respected community leader and a member of such organizations as the Indiana Black Expo Sports Commission and Big Brothers and Big Sisters of Indiana.

So cancer was a familiar, if unwelcome, presence in Bobby Plump's life throughout the '90s. But the battle of Bobby's life would be something different.

Bobby knew he had some heart problems. Back in 1990, he had a couple of episodes of feeling ill at work. "The first time, I asked Dave McCollum to drive me to the hospital. He was on the phone, and didn't know it was an emergency. Well, I nearly passed out on the way to the car. I thought I was dying. But I threw up, and then I felt better. I learned, though, that when you have to go to the hospital, you don't mess around. You call 911."

In the summer of 1991, though, Bobby took himself to the hospital when he began having chest pains. The doctors at St. Vincent Hospital in Indianapolis decided to keep him overnight and perform a heart catheterization, which showed he had 40 percent blockage of the left anterior descending artery. "My doctor, Dr. Dickos, told me they weren't worried about it until it was about 80 percent blocked. He told me to come back in a year to have it checked again," Bobby said.

But the year came and went. Bobby felt good, and had other priorities.

It was sometime later, when Bobby and Jenine were vacationing in Florida, that Bobby developed chest pains again. "He was just taking out the trash, and all of a sudden he had these pains," Jenine said.

Everything began happening at once. "I called 911, and we went to the emergency room. I was terrified," said Jenine.

Jonathan and Kelli flew down the next day to be with their parents. "I wasn't sure I should go,' Jonathan said. "But a friend, Julie Cohen, convinced me I should. She said she'd lost her father, and I'd never forgive myself if anything happened and I didn't go see him. Julie convinced me that nothing I was doing was more important than seeing Dad."

Bobby was going to be okay. The doctors found some blockage in his arteries, and performed an angioplasty, after which they declared him to be in good health.

But Bobby's doctors in Indianapolis thought otherwise. "They said it looked as if the doctors in Florida hadn't done anything," Jenine said. Bobby's doctors recommended a heart catherization and rotoblader, or stint. "Doctor Dickos told me that, if I'd come back to see him as he'd asked, maybe we'd have had some different options," Bobby said.

But once inside, the doctors knew that major repairs were needed. Bobby's arteries were 90% blocked. Without a double bypass operation, he was a prime candidate for a major heart attack. The surgery had to be performed immediately.

Bobby didn't think he had anything to worry about, even though his surgeon told him there was a chance he wouldn't make it through the operation.

"I know some people don't make it through open heart surgery. But they're usually the ones who aren't in very good physical shape, aren't they?" Bobby asked.

The doctor shook his head. "Being in shape isn't really the problem, Bobby. The problem is, we have to stop your heart. And sometimes when we stop a heart, we can't get it going again."

It was a shot of mortality to a guy who was 58 going on 17 — a six-foot tall man still often referred to as "Little Bobby Plump."

"In athletics, you can lose a game, but there's always another game to play. If you lose this game, there are no more games left," Bobby said. "I wasn't afraid of death. I just knew there was a possibility it was going to be there."

Once again, the Plump family gathered together. Bobby was frank with them about his wish not to be put on life support if the situation arose. "It was difficult to discuss. But it was reality. We had to prepare for it. They knew that."

A friend of the family's, James (J.W.) Thomason, took Jonathan aside. "Your Mom and your sisters are exhausted. Why don't you go home and get five or six hours of sleep, then come back and spend the night with your Dad?"

That sounded like a great idea. "It was exactly what I needed to hear. I don't think I'd have figured it out on my own, and I don't believe Dad would have asked me to stay," said Jonathan.

But Bobby wanted some time alone with Jonathan before the surgery. That night, Tari went home and Jenine and Kelli went back to the Plumps' house. None of them got much sleep.

Jonathan stayed at Bobby's side. "He told me that if anything went wrong, it was my responsibility to make sure he wasn't kept on life support. And he told me that Mom and Tari and Kelli were going to need my support. I gave him my word. I didn't know if I could handle the responsibilities, but I gave my word, and I knew there was no running away from that. I think I grew up a lot that night.," said Jonathan.

The next morning, Jenine and Tari and Kelli came back to see Bobby one last time before surgery. They all kissed him, "and Mom held his hand," said Jonathan. "She didn't want to let him go. He hadn't been making too much sense since they'd given him a shot. But as they were wheeling him toward the operating room, I grabbed his hand and kissed him and started to walk away, and he said to me, 'Don't you forget anything I told you last night.' It was almost eerie."

Bobby's family waited anxiously at the hospital while the surgery was performed. "We were all scared," said Tari. "We knew it was possible that they wouldn't be able to start his heart again."

But Bobby pulled through the operation. When his family finally got to see him, he looked terrible. He had tubes down his throat and four tubes coming out of his stomach for drainage. He was also on a respirator.

"Mom and I both kind of lost it at that point," said Kelli. "Dad was coming out of anesthesia and fighting it, pulling at his tubes. We called Jonathan for help."

Bobby's doctors thought that putting him on life support for a short time would help ease the transition from surgery to recovery. But Jonathan was concerned his dad would think he was dying. In the first few hours after the surgery, Jonathan leaned over Bobby's bed and told him, "It's okay. It's not what we talked about last night."

But as the days went by, Jonathan could see that Bobby was getting better. "He told me that every time he came to see me, I looked a little less dead," Bobby said.

"I remember when I knew he was going to be okay," said Kelli. "I was visiting him at the hospital. He was flat on his back with his eyes closed, still covered with a thermal blanket. I was telling him, 'Oh dad, I talked with Dr. Deeckos, and Dr. Deeckos was saying how well you were doing.' Without opening his eyes, Dad said, 'It's Dickos.' That was my old Dad."

Bobby wasn't quite out of the clear yet. Just four days after his release, he was back in the hospital with diverticulitis, an intestinal inflammation. The condition kept him on IVs for another eight days.

Bobby's recovery was the most difficult time of his life. Just getting out of bed was a project. Brushing his teeth seemed a struggle. Physical therapy was a day's work. It was frustrating for an athlete who'd led such an active, on-the-go life to not be in control of his body.

"He got depressed sometimes, kind of frightened of the pains he was having. I remember talking to his doctor about it once, and the doctor said, 'Well, you don't have to get up every morning and look in the shower and see the scar running down your chest.' I said, 'No, I just have to get in the shower and see that I have only one breast,'" Jenine said.

But being an athlete helped Bobby's attitude toward his recovery. "I don't think there's any doubt about it. If there's a challenge, I want to meet or exceed it," Bobby said.

"But this has been tough, especially mentally. It still is. There's depression you have to fight, and there's always a nagging feeling in the back of your mind: every little tick, you wonder if you're okay. But I'm getting that good feeling back. I'm getting that high you get from exercising and feeling good."

In spite of the difficulties, Bobby quickly surpassed the physical goals his doctors set for him. Along the way, he started to take a hard look at the things that were important in his life. "You start with breathing. That's pretty darn important. Then, just walking and being with the people who love you. I've always known that, but you can get caught up with things going on in society, or money, or other things.

And they're okay. But they're not what are really important. If you could get down inside the people who have money or fame and find out what's really important to them, it would be health, people who love them, family. We do a lot in our lives that overshadow those things. And I found that I was doing a lot of things that just weren't as important as I thought they were. Now I'm back to the important things."

Bobby's faith has also helped him recover. "I've always had a feeling that there's a supreme being. I've always felt that there's somebody there. I would have to say that somebody up there does like me. Life has been just fantastic to me. It has been almost like a dream world. Every once in a while, I feel like pinching myself. So many good things have happened. There has been some adversity, but nothing compared to the kindness and good things that have followed me through my life."

Bobby discovered he had a lot to live for. Like Jenine, he reached out to friends in need: Bailey Robertson, Tom Steavson, and many others. When Danny Lehane, the ex-Butler University football player whom Bobby had known only briefly in college, was diagnosed with throat cancer, he was surprised to get a call from Bobby. "I hadn't seen him in years. But he called to see how I was. That shows what kind of a guy Bobby Plump is," Lehane said.

And Bobby's family had gotten bigger. Kelli married Michael Piechocki in 1984 and had two children, Joshua, born in 1987, and Jaclyn, born in 1988. Jonathan married his wife Lynne Beatty in 1990, and their son Garrett was born in 1992. Tari married Kevin Farley in 1994. Their daughter Annaleigh arrived in May of 1996. So Bobby had four young grandchildren to get to know.

The important things in life — faith, family, and friends — have helped keep Bobby focused on recovery even through many complications: diverticulosis, an infection of the colon; pericarditis, an inflammation in the lining of the heart; and two other minor surgeries.

It *has* been a struggle. But perhaps Jenine said it best: "If you spend every day worrying about death, you might as well die, because then your life's not worth living. You have to be positive and strong."

CHAPTER TWENTY SEVEN

THE END OF AN ERA?

In March, 1996, the 86th IHSAA Boys State Basketball Final between Ben Davis High School and New Albany High School was a game not only worthy of the great tradition of Hoosier Hysteria, but a white-knuckle affair for even the most casual basketball fan. Nearly 22,000 fans in the RCA Dome — and countless thousands of others in their living rooms — watched the lead seesaw back and forth between two evenly matched teams. Ben Davis was up by two as the clock ticked away. New Albany's Reginald Wheeler let fly a baseline jumper at the buzzer. Two points. Overtime.

Again, the momentum swayed back and forth. With the clock winding down to zero and the score tied once again, Ben Davis's Jeff Poisel put up a high-arcing three-point shot. It sailed through the hoop as the buzzer sounded. Ben Davis 57, New Albany 54, in one of the most memorable finals in history.

The hoop gave Coach Steve Witty's Ben Davis Giants their second straight title. This one was more than a little unexpected. The Giants had a mediocre regular season, and were unranked going into the tournament. Most pundits didn't expect them to get out of their sectional. But they put together the victories when they counted most. When the smoke cleared, more than 380 high schools had been defeated in the tournament, and the Giants from Ben Davis stood alone.

The big question was, what did the game say about the state of the IHSAA Boys Basketball Tournament?

Did it mean that any Hoosier high school team, in spite of the odds, could play together, persevere, and end up a champion? Or was it another example of two big schools battling for the crown while the little schools sat on the sidelines?

And why were these odd questions even important?

Because just a little more than one month later, the IHSAA board of directors was set to vote on a proposal that would scrap the 86-year-old single-class tournament in favor of a new, four-class tournament designed to give more high school athletes a shot at a state championship. But at what cost? Was it worth destroying the nation's most popular and profitable high school basketball tournament, a tournament that was widely admired and routinely made national news? Was it worth tampering with an 86-year-old tradition of giving big guys and little guys alike a shot at ultimate glory?

Was it worth dismantling a tournament that had given the world the story of the Milan Indians and Bobby Plump?

Talk of multiclass-class basketball was nothing new in Indiana. The day after the Milan Indians won the title in 1954, the *Indianapolis Star* suggested that this should forever put to rest the idea of class basketball. Still, the issue was debated throughout the '60s and '70s. An IHSAA Board vote in 1979 defeated the idea 14-0.

At the time, Nyle Fox, who was principal at Tri County High School, said, "We are willing to wait. Any time we feel we can make a move toward it successfully, we'll do it."

And with a five-class system in place since 1975 for Indiana high school football, class basketball has been a natural topic of conversation every fall. And the fact that nearly every other state in the union had adopted a class system made people wonder whether it would work in Indiana, as well.

There were also financial questions. For more than thirty years, attendance at the sectional and regional levels had shown a steady, but not disastrous, decline. The lower attendance figures can almost certainly be attributed to societal changes, not the one-class system. In Indiana, high school basketball still draws more fans than any other state. Attendance at the state final peaked at 41,000 in 1990, the first year the Final Four was held at the Hoosier (now RCA) Dome. Would going to a class system encourage more fans to turn out for the tournament? Would small-school fans be more inclined to cheer for their teams if they were competing against schools their own size?

In 1994, the IHSAA appointed a committee to study the idea of class sports. The committee would study classes for all high school sports for eighteen months before releasing its report.

At first, it didn't seem to be too pressing an issue. New IHSAA Commissioner Bob Gardner, a former football coach and principal at Milan, was quoted in *The Indianapolis Star* as being in support of keeping the system the way it had always been. "I remember going to Hinkle Fieldhouse as a kid and seeing it packed for basketball. It was a great moment for me. I want all of our state tournaments to be a great moment for our youth.

"I've always believed that if it isn't broke, don't fix it. I can say without reservation that I like our one-class system. Our success has been phenomenal, something we can be proud of," Gardner said.

Still, a story by Mark Gardner in *The Indianapolis News* seemed to leave an avenue open:

> Gardner said if a change ever comes, the IHSAA might look at a big and small class at the early stages of the tournament. . . . "and then possibly come together and play for one championship," he said.

As late as April of 1995, a story by Walter Grable in *The Indianapolis Star* advised, "Traditionalists can rest peacefully. The boys' and girls' basketball tournaments as we know them will stay the same. For the last couple of years, class basketball has gained more and more interest, especially among smaller schools. But the IHSAA board will not discuss the issue this year, even though a committee has been formed to further study class sports."

But the issued refused to go away. And in September of 1995, the IHSAA dropped a bomb: its committee concluded its study with a recommendation that multiclass-class tournaments be adopted for a number of high school sports, including basketball, saying that principals overwhelmingly supported the change. An October survey of boys' basketball coaches conducted by the Indiana High School Coaches Association indicated that 53 percent supported the move to class basketball. The committee recommended a maximum of three tournament classes.

Commissioner Bob Gardner was quoted in the *Star*: "I believe this committee's study is the most thorough ever done in our state on this issue. This issue involves strong opinions on both sides."

But how thorough was the study? And where were the opposing opinions?

Bobby Plump had questions as soon as he saw the report. "We immediately saw several red flags. The first was that six of the eight members of the committee studying class sports were from small schools. Where was the representation for big and medium-sized schools? There were no women or minorities on the committee, either. Where was their representation?"

He was right: the committee studying class sports was loaded with white males from small schools. The committee included chairman Bruce Whitehead, athletic director at Crawfordsville (687 students); James Babcock, principal, Paoli (518); Curtis Casbon, principal, Morgan Township (162); Jim Feist, principal, Eastern (460); Phillip Gardner, principal, Wes-Del (313); Blake Ress, athletic director, Martinsville (1,661); John Spoonmore, assistant principal, Brownsburg (1,280); and Elmer Strautman, athletic director, Woodlan (514). One of the committee members, Blake Ress, removed himself from the committee before the completion of the study when he was named an assistant IHSAA commissioner.

The second red flag was raised when Bobby asked the IHSAA to see a breakout of how schools would be assigned to classes. "They told us it wasn't relevant — that they couldn't project what the enrollment of schools would be for the 1997-98 season, when the classes would go into effect. But we thought schools should know where they stood."

Bobby also had other questions: "The major one being financial. We feared for small schools' funding of their athletic programs. And we wondered what would happen to traditional rivalries? What would happen to schools' travel expenses? We envisioned situations in which larger schools would refuse to schedule smaller schools during the regular season because they wouldn't meet them in the tournament. How far would schools, both large and small, have to travel to play their games? And how would the tournament be affected?"

The biggest problem Bobby and his friends saw was a lack of information. To fill the void, Bobby, his old teammate Gene White, and Indianapolis attorney Richard Tinkham, Jr., a former high school player from Hammond High School and a college player at DePauw University, formed Friends of Hoosier Hysteria. Plump's Last Shot, Bobby's restaurant in the Broad Ripple area of Indianapolis, was the worldwide headquarters.

Response to the group was immediate and overwhelmingly positive. Among the first to join were John Wooden, Oscar Robertson, and *Hoosiers* screenwriter Angelo Pizzo. Such Indiana basketball luminaries as Damon Bailey and George McGinnis weighed in with negative opinions about a multiclass system. Requests for information and pledges of support came from all across the nation. To finance its work, the group began selling T-shirts that said, "Indiana Sports Already Have Class." Their membership swelled to more than 2,000 single-class die-hards.

"We weren't trying to stop class basketball. Our real purpose was to get information to the public and the schools, to the administrators and coaches and athletic directors. We thought they were voting out of context — that the issues weren't clear. Of course, we weren't in favor of class basketball, and if we stopped it, that would have been the outcome we wanted. But if enough people, after having all the information, made a decision to go with the class system, that was fine with us."

It simply didn't seem to be a possibility. "Oscar Robertson came into the restaurant one day. He said, 'Bobby, it's just not going to happen. We've got too good a thing here.' That was the same thing we were hearing all over," Bobby said.

The *Star*'s Bill Benner was one of the most vehemently opposed. In October of 1995, he suggested that the response he'd gotten to a column denouncing class basketball ran at least 25-1 against changing the system. Still, the newspaper reported on a straw poll taken among principals and athletic directors:

> The tally thus far is:
> 170-24 in favor of the end-of-season, multiclass basketball tournaments.
> 188-7 against a proposal for multiclass tournaments in December.
> 137-51 in favor of class tournaments in all sports, both team and individual.

"It's pretty apparent to me where we're headed," Commissioner Gardner said.

But what did the players think? What did the fans think? And why wasn't more information being made available to the public?

Friends of Hoosier Hysteria swung into action. Obtaining a complete list of school enrollments and gym sizes from the IHSAA, they crafted their own classes and a hypothetical tournament, held a news conference, and published the results. The Friends were concerned about the committee's report, which suggested that the three-class system would reduce sectionals from 64 to 48, regionals from 16 to 12, and possibly eliminate semistates altogether. (The IHSAA committee's rationale said, "A maximum of three classes are recommended based on the studies of other states. They showed greater success with a class system when the number of schools per class was a minimum of 128.") The Friends also cautioned that the change could leave the majority of the state's largest gyms without a piece of the tournament. Remember, Indiana is home of 15 of the 16 largest high school gymnasiums in the country, and most of them would be vacant come sectional time. All the schools in the tournament shared in the sectional revenues. In other words, the Friends projected the change to a class system to have potentially serious financial consequences, let alone the damage it would cause to traditional tournament sites and post-season rivalries. The Friends thought a non-binding public referendum on the issue was in order, and said so. They also invited the IHSAA to join in an independent financial impact study.

The Friends' report caused a major uproar and elicited an immediate response from the IHSAA. Soon after the report appeared, the committee dropped its support for a three-class system and voiced support for four classes — even though, in the IHSAA's area meetings, 70 percent of principals favored a three-class system if class sports were adopted.

"Once we started to get out the information, we saw a lot more support for keeping things the way they were," Bobby said. "A second Indiana High School Coaches Association poll of coaches three weeks after our news conference showed 61 percent support for a one-class system."

Students seemed to support the one-class system, too. Results of student forums commissioned by the IHSAA and published in *IHSAA Update* showed that, among male players, support was 60-40 for one-class basketball. Among girls, 52 percent supported the current system. Commissioner Bob Gardner would later dismiss these figures, saying he couldn't be certain that the students interviewed — one male and one female player from each high school — were speaking for the majority of their teams.

In late February, *Indianapolis Star* reporter John Krull traveled to

Milan to interview some of the boys on the 1996 Indian team. The story quoted Milan kids as bemoaning the fact that they just couldn't compete with bigger schools — and that they were tired of being compared with the 1954 Indians.

The article was a disappointment to Bobby. "I think the kids had gotten some bad information. The people who wanted class basketball had done such a good job of selling their side of the story that kids were believing that, if we only had a class system, they could win a state championship. The fact is, that Milan team wasn't going to win any championship. They'd won only eight games in the past four years, and their schedule was primarily against schools about the same size."

Still, Bobby thought the players' complaints about being compared to the 1954 team had some validity. "I know there are some fans in Milan who tell these kids that if they just worked a little harder, they could be just like we were. That's wrong. Those fans are doing a heck of a disservice to the kids and the community. Working hard is important, but it doesn't guarantee a state championship. It still takes a lot of talent and a bit of luck along with hard work and sacrifice.

"If athletics is taught correctly, it mirrors life. The emphasis shouldn't be only on winning; while winning is important, it seems that especially early on there is too much emphasis placed on it. Kids get the idea that if they don't always win, they're a failure. The difference in a true winner is the way in which wins and losses are handled. A true winner handles both on an even scale and always strives to do better," Bobby said.

All kinds of things were happening. State Senator Luke Kenley of Noblesville filed a bill calling for a non-binding referendum on the issue in Indiana's May 1996 primary election. IHSAA officials, concerned that such a vote would not fairly represent basketball fans, persuaded Kenley to drop the bill provided they would make an economic impact study and have some kind of public vote on the issue.

The IHSAA decided it would poll fans at basketball games. The plan called for fans to be allowed to vote on class basketball at one home game at each school. Again, Bobby saw red flags.

"For one thing, we kept hearing that is was not really a basketball issue, but a class sports issue. Yet, there were no votes at softball games or baseball games or at any any other sporting events

"Second, there were no controls. What was to stop a fan from voting dozens of times? And there were no guidelines for voting. Schools could pass out the ballots however they wanted. Plus, by that time, some of the girls' teams didn't even have a home game left. So some fans wouldn't get to vote at all."

The other big problem? The IHSAA's insistence on tallying the results as one school, one vote. If 500 fans at School A's game voted, and 251 voted for class sports, that was one vote for class sports; if 4,000 fans at School B's game voted, and 3,000 voted for the current system, it would count as one vote for the single-class tournament. The issue would be tied 1-1, even though the current system would be ahead 3,249-1,251 in the popular vote. "So even if the popular vote was far ahead, the one-class system could lose," Bobby said.

Which is exactly what happened. When the IHSAA released poll results in early April, the single class system lost, 167-159. But the results from 31 Indiana schools were not released, and eight more schools were listed as "did not participate in the survey of fans."

"We heard all kinds of stories about voting improprieties. Some schools' votes were apparently lost. And from the reports we heard, the single-class system won the popular vote hands down."

All of the studies and polls and opinions, though, were essentially meaningless. The fate of class sports in Indiana would be decided April 29 at the annual meeting of the IHSAA board of directors.

As the day of the meeting neared, talking about class basketball became a full-time job for Bobby. He was besieged by phone calls, requests for interviews, offers for TV appearances and speaking engagements. Class basketball had become a national issue. Bobby appeared on ESPN and CBS Evening News. He was quoted in *USA Today, Sports Illustrated, The Washington Post, The Chicago Tribune, The Cincinnati Enquirer, The Detroit News, Los Angeles Times,* and many other newspapers across the nation.

After seeing no economic impact study from the IHSAA, the Friends of Hoosier Hysteria commissioned their own study with Clifton, Gunderson & Co., Certified Public Accountants & Consultants. The firm's study suggested that smaller gyms with less seating capacity would contribute to lower revenues if the switch were made. CPA Randy Effner, who was the outside auditor for the Wisconsin Interscholastic High School Association before joining Clifton, Gunderson, found that, in a four-class tournament, the revenue loss would be $185,000 if attendance remained the same on a percentage basis. Because of fewer games played, a three-class system would have even more dire financial consequences — a $650,000 total loss.

And these figures were for attendance alone. They didn't take into consideration money from television and corporate sponsorships. Would the schools still be interested in the class system if they knew all these implications? "We thought they should know the financial consequences ahead of the vote," said Bobby.

April 29, 1996. The day of the vote. It was no contest. The IHSAA board voted 12-5 in favor of going to a multiclass system. Proposals to have the class system feed into a playoff of champions were soundly defeated, as well, by a 15-2 vote.

Here's how the vote went:

For class sports: James Babock, Paoli (377), principal; Mike Blackburn, Northwestern (435), athletic director; Dale Crafton, New Washington (135), principal; Frank DeSantis, Bremen (337), athletic director; Priscilla Dillow, Indianapolis Ben Davis (2,715), assistant athletic director; Phillip E. Gardner, Wes-Del (245), principal; Bill Griffith, Churubusco (314), principal; David L. Kaser, South Bend Washington (904), principal; Larry Pinkerton, Plymouth (815), principal; Don Sakel, Floyd Central (1,045), New Albany-Floyd Co. Schools; Oren A. Sutherlin, North Vermillion (235), principal; and Bruce Whitehead, Crawfordsville (687), athletic director.

Against class sports: Larry Gambaiani, Indianapolis North Central (2,385), assistant superintendent, Washington Township; Janis Qualizza, Merrillville (1,526), athletic director; Steve Riordan, Jennings County (1,067), principal; John Robbins, Muncie South (821), principal; and Lezlie Winter, Muncie Burris (286), athletic director.

"I don't think it will change the image of Hoosier Hysteria," said Commissioner Gardner in *The Indianapolis Star*. "I choose to think the game is bigger than the way the tournament is set up."

Others weren't so sure. Former NBA star and Indiana Mr. Basketball George McGinnis, Ben Davis Coach Steve Witty, Marvin Wood, Steve and Sam Alford, Damon Bailey, Oscar "The Big O" Robertson, and many others expressed their sorrow. Brownsburg Coach Steve Brunes said it was, "the saddest day in basketball history."

The Friends of Hoosier Hysteria had one remaining hope for the single-class tournament: a vote on the board's decision among the Indiana high school principals. The principals had the power to overturn the decision. It was the first time in the history of the IHSAA that a referendum was required, although such a referendum had been possible since the IHSAA's founding in 1903.

The results of the voting were released September 17, 1996. Principals for multi-class basketball: 220; against: 157.

The *Star*'s Bill Benner spoke for many Hoosiers when he wrote:
In the plush, northside Indianapolis headquarters built with the money she raised, Hoosier Hysteria was laid to rest Tuesday. She was 86. Cause of death was assisted suicide. She died at the hands of feel-gooders in the education business, but prosecutors declined to press charges because killing tradition is legal in Indiana. True, she hadn't been in the most robust health lately, but the feel-gooders convinced Hoosier Hysteria the only way to save her was to slay her and create something new in her image. It was a Dr. Kevorkian meets Dr. Frankenstein kind of thing.

The game would never be the same. And, according to Indiana Basketball Hall of Fame Director Jason Crowe, the decision leaves Milan forever sitting atop Indiana basketball history. "The first tournament was in 1911. Milan won it 43 years later, in 1954. Another 43 years after that, in 1997, we'll have our last single-class tournament. It makes Milan the pinnacle of Indiana high school basketball, both literally and spiritually."

Bobby Plump and Friends of Hoosier Hysteria had fought the good fight. They still questioned the process and were dismayed with the result. But finally, they accepted defeat with grace. "We still believe in the one-class system, and we're sad to see it go. In the end, I guess I can only hope that we were wrong — that class basketball will be the best thing for everyone. In fact, we hope the class system works so well that we can still legitimately call it Hoosier Hysteria and legitimately keep our claim of having the number one high school tournament in the nation. I will gladly say I was wrong.

"On the other hand, if it doesn't work, I hope the people in power will have some system ready to put Humpty Dumpty back together again," Bobby said.

Perhaps class basketball was inevitable. But one final comment, from an editorial in the *Kokomo Tribune:* "Single-class basketball — by its brutal acknowledgment of only one champion — allows kids and fans to enjoy well-fought games and surprising runs without making a state title the only measurement of success. That is what high school sports should be about."

CHAPTER TWENTY EIGHT

CLASS OF 1954

At this writing, it is the summer of 1996. For the second year in a row, a high school student with no collegiate basketball experience was made one of the top picks in the NBA draft. Salaries in the NBA are spiraling upward at a dizzying pace; Glenn Robinson's "ridiculous" request for a $100 million, long-term deal just a year ago is looking more modest every day. (And remember Bobby Plumps first-year salary of $6,000 at Phillips?) The Dream Team has its Olympic gold medals.

And this could well be the last season ever for a one-class basketball tournament in Indiana.

A lot has changed since 1954. In many ways, 1954 was like another world. Muhammad Ali, whose presence in Atlanta electrified the 1996 Summer Olympic Games, was a kid in Louisville named Cassius Clay, just learning to fight because someone had stolen his bike. Senator Joseph McCarthy was finding communists everywhere he looked — funny and even more tragic today in light of the collapse of communism around the globe.

In 1954, Bobby Plump and the Milan Indians played in front of one of the largest television audiences up to that time for a sporting event. Today, the media blasts larger-than-life images of professional sports superstars into hundreds of millions of homes.

It *is* a different world, better in some ways, worse in others. And the nature of progress is such that it's impossible to turn back the clock.

But we can turn it back here, just for a few moments. Not all the way back to 1954 and kids in crew cuts celebrating at the Milan Country Club, but just two years, September, 1994, and those same people all grown up, holding their fortieth class reunion at the same place. It's the place the 1954 Milan Indians have held a reunion of their own nearly every spring since their victory over Muncie Central.

There were 31 boys and girls in the Milan High School Class of 1954. Seventeen of the 31 attended college, thanks in part to the commitment the Milan teaching staff made to the basketball team. Knowing their kids would have scholarship offers, they stepped up the academic curriculum — a benefit not just for the team, but the school as a whole.

Fourteen of the 31 graduates are here on this evening. Five played basketball: Plump, White, Craft, Engel, and Schroder. Most have brought spouses and pictures of children and grandchildren. Fred Busching, the

Pierceville kid who was the team manager for the 1954 team, is showing off not only his eight grandchildren but a great-grandchild.

Four members of the class are deceased. Doris Pilz and Jake McKitterick both died of natural causes. Bill Raynor, another of Bobby's good friends, who drove the car that flipped in the fall of Bobby's junior year at Milan and was driving again when Bobby missed curfew that New Year's Eve, was killed in the line of duty as an Indiana State Trooper. "He just stopped a guy with a bad light. Turned out the guy was a felon, and he just shot him. We were all shocked," said Roger Schroder.

Ronnie Truitt is not here, either. He lost a fight with cancer that no one in this room even knew he was battling. The last time his friends saw him was in 1986, at the premier of *Hoosiers* in Ripley County. Ronnie knew he had cancer, but didn't tell anyone.

The trip to Milan for the *Hoosiers* premier wasn't the first time Ronnie had been back to Indiana since making a life for himself in Houston, Texas. Years earlier, when Ronnie's father died, Ronnie came back to make the funeral arrangements and pay off any debts Peck had incurred.

"Peck Truitt and Arky Arkenberg were good friends," said Tootie Herbst. "In fact, old Peck died right there at Arkenberg's. Ronnie was probably embarrassed by Peck's drunkenness, but he was always gentle with him."

As the *Hoosiers* get-together was breaking up, Ronnie walked to his car with Marc Combs, his junior high coach and teacher, a man who had made it his business to look after Ronnie and inspire him to rise above the difficulties of a broken home. Before getting into the car, Ronnie turned to Marc Combs and said, "Marc, I just wanted you to know that everything I've ever done, everything I am today, I owe to you."

"It was the greatest compliment anyone ever paid me," said Combs. "I told him he was wrong, that he'd done it himself, but he insisted I had been his inspiration."

It was an act of devotion by a man who knew he was dying. He passed away about a year later. It's a passing that still deeply affects Ronnie's teammates.

The evening's hostess is Mary Meyers, whose father, Chris Volz, provided the shiny new cars in which the Indians rode to their tournament games. There are teachers from the old days here, too. And there is Marvin Wood, who also left Milan after that great year so long ago, another graduate of the Class of 1954. Woody has had an interesting and at times difficult life since leaving Indianapolis for Mishawaka High School. His mother suffered a heart attack in Woody's first season at Mishawaka, so he resigned after just one year to move back to Central Indiana to be closer to her. For the next three years, he was athletic director and ticket manager for Shelbyville High School.

But he wasn't happy. Life on the bench was the only life for Marvin Wood. So when the Mishawaka head coaching job opened up again, Woody was there. He coached the Cavemen for another 11 years with some success, although Mishawaka won only one South Bend Sectional title during his tenure.

Again, Woody tried to retire from coaching. Again, it didn't stick. John Taylor, Mishawaka's girls basketball coach, suffered a heart attack, and Woody was asked to fill in. In his first experience coaching girls' basketball, Woody led the Mishawaka Lady Cavemen to a Sweet Sixteen berth.

Taylor returned the next year. But Woody had a new coaching bug. So when St. Mary's College in South Bend called in 1982 to see if he'd be interested in moving up to women's collegiate basketball, Woody was ready for the challenge.

The 1954 class reunion began earlier in the day with a golf outing. After golf was a cocktail hour. This is not a flashy affair. No one is out to impress anyone else. These are people who grew up together, who enjoy each others' company, and who realize that time is slipping away.

"It's a good time for me," Gene White says. "I really enjoy getting back together with these people. We had absolutely great times in high school. Our thirtieth reunion lasted five days."

Virginia Voss, the high school cheerleader who married Ray Craft, agrees. "We've always been close-knit. We're all good friends."

Her husband takes it one step further. He considers the whole class to have been part of the team that everyone remembers. "They decorated the cars to raise money for the prom and the senior class trips to Washington, D.C. and New York City. Sure, we played on the floor, but they were an integral part of it, and I'm sure we all felt that way. That closeness has continued over the years. We cherish each time we get together."

Fred Busching was certainly part of the team. Knowing he wasn't good enough to shoot jump shots, he passed out towels. Tonight, he still can't quite fathom the Milan Miracle. "I'm still surprised we won. I feel like, if we played them ten times, we'd lose nine. I just think Woody was a smart enough coach that he caught the other team off guard. Woody was the big stick. It was unbelievable."

Jo Anne Steinmetz is here. It has been a long time since most people who knew them thought she and Bobby Plump would be married some day. But she, too remembers that shot as if it were yesterday. "I was thinking it was going in. I had a lot of confidence in Bobby. After the game, I ran to the floor and gave him a hug."

Of course, basketball and grandchildren aren't the only topics of discussion this evening. Bobby and Bob Engel are talking both. Both are also showing off their scars from heart surgery. Gene White's hearty laugh roars above the din. "It's an exceptional group," says 1952 graduate Wayne Smith. "Winning has contributed to that."

Corinne "Corky" Denari Casey contributed to that, too, as a Milan High School teacher. She's seeing a lot of her former students for the first time since 1954. "It's like I just saw them yesterday," she says.

"I came here right out of college, and it was a great experience. The class was phenomenal. They were wonderful kids, the most respectful I ever met, and they weren't any different the Monday after they won the championship."

She looks at Bobby Plump. "He was such a shy young man. Interested. Responsible. He took care of things. A very neat kid."

Roger Schroder, who still looks as if he could play a few quarters without breaking a sweat, is working the room. But even he pauses to reflect. "I can't explain why all the ties are here. Maybe they're no greater than other small school were everybody knows everybody and all their sisters and brothers. We have the special occasion of winning the tournament that ties us together. Everybody grabs hold of that, too.

"We're just fortunate to have the time together. Bill Raynor was my best friend, you know. I'd even ridden in his squad car with him a time or two. I still think about him a lot. But that's part of the way life is. Some of us are favored to get through, others meet their maker a little sooner."

After dinner — chicken or steak, cooked on the grill outside — Gene White begins his duties as unofficial master of ceremonies. He introduces a couple of special guests: former Milan first grade teacher Geneva Wildman Myers and fourth grade teacher Kathryn Turner. Corky Denari Casey says a few words. She says she probably got several jobs over the years by discussing her warm memories of Milan High School and the Class of 1954 at her interviews. Of course, she says, she never tried to get a job in Muncie.

Marvin Wood gets the biggest round of applause. His former players and fans have prepared a cake and presented it to him "as a token of our love." They know that this night is Woody's forty-sixth wedding anniversary. Unfortunately, Mary Lou Wood was unable to attend this evening; she's home babysitting a grandchild. "You know, we did something a lot of people didn't think would happen. It almost happened a couple of times. It wasn't just the coach, it was the team, the town, the community. I'm just thankful to have been part of it," Woody says.

Next, Gene White reads a letter from Donald Jessie, another graduate who wasn't able to make it. Everybody gets a good laugh.

Then, one by one, the members of the class stand and introduce themselves and tell about their lives. Bob Engel, the toughest guy in the class, looks as if he might cry. Anita Womack, who married Gene White, says, "I can't believe it's been forty years. It's all gone by so quickly."

A man stands. His hair is lighter now, and thinner, and longer than it was when he sported a buzz cut in 1954. But the face is still recognizable — perhaps one of the most recognizable in the State of Indiana.

And yet, he introduces himself as if nobody knew him. "I'm Bobby Plump. My wife Jenine is here. We live in Indianapolis. We have three grandchildren. It's a pleasure to see all of you. . . ."

On this night, Bobby Plump is a happy man. That single shot he made so long ago was a defining moment in his life, and in the lives of all of these people. It would have been easy for them to live in the past, to forever see themselves in terms of that stunning victory. But none of them has. They are teachers and coaches and farmers and businesspeople, husbands and wives and fathers and mothers, grandfathers and grandmothers.

Bobby Gene Plump has come a long way from the house by the railroad tracks in Pierceville. He has been a professional athlete and a successful businessman. Perhaps more significant, he has, almost since the moment after the shot fell through the hoop, been a much-sought-after speaker at school and civic affairs across Indiana and beyond. Bobby Plump's story and his message of inspiration have made a significant impact in the lives of the young Hoosiers in his audience.

"I know I've touched a lot of kids," he says with a tear in his eye.

It is approaching midnight, and everyone has had a chance to speak. Gene White turns to classmate Carl Richardson, a Lutheran minister in Iowa City, Iowa, and says, "Since it's your business, how about a benediction?"

Richardson stands. All bow their heads.

"Thank you, Lord, for taking care of us. Thank you for the friendship we have known over the years. May the Lord bless and keep us this day, and the days to come. Amen."

And with that, it is time to leave. Hugs and kisses and handshakes are exchanged, as well as promises to see each other again soon.

Some have only a short way to go. Others came from across the State of Indiana to be here this night. Bob Engel now lives in Kalamazoo, Michigan, and has a long drive ahead of him. David Jefferies has to drive all the way to Alabama. But some of the local folks are hanging around for a while, listening to "Judge" Gene White hold court in the bar.

Bobby and Jenine walk out to the car, arm in arm. "Just to get together with people who were so meaningful forty years ago, and relive the memories, tell a few stories, have our teachers and Coach Wood there — they were so important in our lives, and they get more important every year. It was great to hear about their successes, and how happy they are," he says.

How happy. How nice to be able to look back to a time when life was simpler, when kids played basketball and baseball for fun and to defend the honor of their little towns, their rural county. How melancholy to see the smiling kids of forty years ago become, as if by magic, the older adults of today, all in an instant, as if no time had passed at all.

That, after all, is the significance of the Milan Miracle and the most famous schoolboy shot in the history of basketball. It is one of those rare events that allows us to stop time, if only for a moment. And it belongs, in a very special way, to the group leaving the Milan Country Club on this cool September evening in 1994.

But in another way, it belongs to all of us. It belongs to everyone who's ever lived in a small town, every man and woman who's fought for our freedom, everyone who's ever been an underdog. It's the achievement of the American dream.

And, perhaps most important of all, it belongs to every kid who ever held a baseball bat and swatted an imaginary grand slam to win the World Series, every kid whose kick into the upper right corner of the goal wins the World Cup for the USA, every kid who slams through the line on fourth and one for the touchdown, and, especially, every kid who's ever dreamed of eying the hole as the clocked ticked away, faking left, dribbling right, shooting, hearing that sound, that "swish," that "plump." The buzzer sounds. The game is ended. The good guys win again.

THE TEAM TODAY

Indianapolis sportswriter Bob Collins once said that if Bobby Plump hadn't made the shot that won the Indiana state high school basketball title, he'd have ended up pumping gas back in Pierceville, Indiana. He was being facetious, of course. But that shot, that title, changed Bobby's life in powerful ways. And Bobby was not the only one changed. Being part of the 1953-54 Milan Indians has made a difference in the lives of every member of the team. Each has done extraordinary things that may otherwise have been unthinkable if not for their schoolboy achievements.

Ron Truitt

Ron Truitt is the first member of the '54 Indians to have passed away. He died of cancer on March 12, 1988, at the age of 52. His obituary appeared not only in Ripley County and Houston, Texas, where he'd lived since high school, but in *USA Today*. They wrote:

Ronald D. Truitt, a member of Milan's 1954 basketball team, died of cancer at the age of 52. The victory by Milan, with 161 students, was the basis for the movie *Hoosiers*.

That championship season had a significant impact on Ronnie's life. A little more than a year before he died, he told a *Cincinnati Post* reporter, "I would never even have considered college, never even thought about it. That's what winning did for me. It changed my life. It was more than just a miracle on the basketball floor. It was a miracle of living, too."

Ronnie attended the University of Houston and played basketball for a young coach named Guy Lewis, who later coached Akeem (now Hakeem) Olajuawan and "Phi Slamma Jamma" to the NCAA finals. After college, he married Joan Thompson. The Truitts had three children: Tim, Tommy, and Terri.

Ronnie became a teacher and coach. He was the only Milan player to win a state championship as a coach. He took his Cypress-Fairbanks High School team to a Texas state big-school championship in 1971.

When *Hoosiers* was released, Ronnie was surprised by a group of 400 friends in Houston who turned out to preview the film and honor him as a hero. Ronnie was certainly one of the heroes of the Milan Indians. For example, in the regional final against Aurora, Ronnie's clutch shooting tied the game and gave the Indians the lead for good.

Said Gene White, "If you notice early on in the championship game, he threw up some crazy shot, and it went in. Turned out to be the difference in the game."

The last time most of his Milan teammates saw Ronnie Truitt was at the debut of *Hoosiers* in Ripley County in 1986. At the time, no one knew Ronnie had been diagnosed with cancer. Not even his mother knew. "She wondered why Ronnie was taking so long in the bathroom, and it turned out he'd had a colostomy. No one knew about it," said Tootie Herbst.

Best friend Bob Engel remembered their last conversation. "We stood out there in a driveway and gave each other a big hug. I said there'd been too much water under the bridge. He agreed. We both said we'd have to get together. He said he'd call me. I never saw him again."

Bobby Plump noticed some subtle differences during the visit. "Looking back now, it seems like he was reaching out to us and the Milan community."

Ronnie Truitt died about a year after his visit to Milan. Funeral services were held in Texas. A memorial service was held the following evening at Milan United Methodist Church. A team picture leaning against the alter, Rev. Scott Johnson eulogized the passing hero. Many of Ronnie's friends and teammates attended.

Bobby Plump will never forget Ronnie Truitt. "As a player, Ron was the type of guy who, when we were running our four-corner offense, if you were barely open, he was going to get you the ball. You would get it in the back of the head if you weren't ready. He could get on hot streaks. He was instant offense."

But his basketball skills were only a small part of a life that meant so much to so many people. Today in a Houston suburb, there stands Truitt Junior High School: an honor not only to a basketball star, but a great principal, coach, family man, and friend.

"To have a school named after you — that is truly an amazing accomplishment," said Bobby Plump.

Gene White

Milan's starting center in 1954 just can't stay away from basketball. He's tried. But after so many years of playing and coaching the game he loves, basketball runs deep in Gene White.

Clearly, Milan couldn't have won its title without Gene White. He played well as a junior at forward, and moved to center as a senior. Gene was tough, a steady force and a defensive monster. Milan fans will always remember how he shut down Aurora's Bob Fehrman in the regional finals just hours after Fehrman had set a new regional scoring record with 35 points in the afternoon game.

"He handled all those big guys, so you assume our 5'11" center could jump out of the gym, was fast as heck, and could shoot the eyes out of the bucket," said Bobby Plump. "But if you ever saw air between Gene White's shoes and the floor, it was pretty good, because he couldn't jump that high. A turtle could beat him in a race. And he averaged 16 points a game, but 14 of them were in warm-ups," said Bobby facetiously.

"But let me tell you something about Gene White. John Casterlow of Muncie Central was 6'6". Whitey took him completely out of the game. Muncie finally did take him out because Gene nullified him.

"He did that with everyone we played against. He would talk to them, harass them, same as he did as a catcher on the baseball team. He would hang onto their pants or pull the hair on their legs. He was intelligent. Also, he didn't shoot very well, so he had to pass to me."

Before winning the state title, Gene assumed he'd go to Purdue, study agriculture, and work at the family mill in Pierceville. But after winning, he decided to play ball at Franklin College, along with teammates Roger Schroder and Ken Wendelman.

Gene majored in math at Franklin. After a two-year stint in the Army, he returned to Milan High School as a math and physics teacher and coached basketball at the junior high level. He married former Milan High School classmate Anita Womack and later moved to Batesville, again teaching math and physics and even trying his hand at coaching cross country.

Around that time, Gene White became involved in politics. He served as Ripley County Republican Chairman and as a Batesville City Councilman. Indiana Governor Ed Whitcomb appointed Gene to the Indiana State School Board.

In 1971, Gene went back to Milan High School as teacher and athletic director. He also kept his hand in politics, serving on the

Planning Commission and Milan Town Board and being elected Ripley County Commissioner.

In the early 1980s, Gene White got a shot at coaching basketball. After working with the Milan freshmen, he was offered the varsity job. He held the position from 1982 through 1985, producing a sectional championship in his last season. That year, Gene had two of the state's best guards in David Voss and Pat Murphy, and might have taken his Indians further had they not run into Richmond, "the beast from the east," who beat the Indians at the regional and finally lost in the championship game to the Marion Giants — a team led by future IU players Lyndon Jones and Jay Edwards. It was, in fact, to be the first of three straight state championships for the Giants under Coach Bill Green, tying a record set by the "Franklin Wonder Five" in 1920-22.

Gene's success may have masked some turmoil in his career. Due to some concerns he had with the school administration, he began looking for another job. He found one at Franklin High School. Gene and his wife Anita moved to Franklin, and Gene taught and assisted with the girls' varsity basketball team.

While in Franklin, Gene was told of an opening as head coach of the women's varsity basketball team at Franklin College by Jenny Johnson, a former Milan High School athlete who was the school's women's athletic director. Ruth Callon, who had built a small college dynasty at Franklin with the likes of Indiana's first Miss Basketball Judi Warren of Warsaw, was retiring.

Gene was up to the challenge. He coached the team for seven years, winning more than 100 games in the process. Along the way, he ran into his old coach, Marvin Wood, three times. Woody was coaching at St. Mary's. Franklin took two of the three contests.

"He's still the best," Gene said of Woody. "He's a modern coach. He still fits into the modern game, even though he's been coaching for 40 years."

Gene's last team in the 1993-94 season was one of his highlights. The Grizzlies were 19-6 and made it to the NCAA Division III playoffs, led by Rushville's Stephanie Kramer.

Then Gene was appointed head of the math department at Franklin High School. The travel and hectic schedule of coaching would be too much. So Gene stepped down as Franklin College's coach. He's currently an assistant coach for the girls at Franklin High School.

Gene said he still is close to every member of his Milan team, especially to Bobby Plump. "I have a brother who's ten years younger, but I believe Plump and I are closer because of sports and all, and because we're about the same age. We're just like brothers. I hesitate to think that there's any other team in Indiana that's as close as we have been. I've always said that. We're the best team I've ever seen."

As for the role the Milan Miracle played in his life, Gene said he's enjoyed the ride. "It certainly has gone well beyond what I would have imagined. But, if you stop in any small town in Indiana, they had some team that was 'The Team.' The difference for us is, we won the state, so our story has lingered longer. And the bigger towns find other things to talk about. Milan hasn't come up with anything, I guess."

Gene's been worried about Bobby's health problems. "It's tough. It makes you stop and think when your buddies are going down. It made me get a check-up."

And Bobby Plump loves Gene White like a brother. "I can talk with Gene about my deep feelings, maybe to an extent greater than with anyone else except Bob Engel, but I don't live close to Bob. It seems Gene and I have the same philosophy. We've solved a lot of the world's problems together. And I've never seen Gene get down. He's a special kind of person."

Ray Craft

More than any other member of the 1954 Milan Indians, Ray Craft has stayed involved in Indiana high school athletics. As associate commissioner of the Indiana High School Athletic Association, he'd had to. In his position, Ray is in charge of monitoring high school basketball.

Ray was only one of two members of the Milan Indians who wasn't born in Ripley County. He was born in Middletown, Ohio. When Ray was in fourth grade, he moved to a farm near Milan with his parents and six brothers and sisters.

Ray's athletic career reached its zenith at the state championship game. While Bobby Plump's early shots were banging off the rim at an unusually high rate, Ray's were going through. He was four for ten from the field and four for six from the free throw line. And he nearly hit the winning shot. His missed layup late in the game opened the door for Bobby's last-ditch heroics. About his high school days, Ray said, "All the games don't stick out, but certain ones do: the regional win over Aurora, the Morton Memorial game when the clock quit, the Seymour game, and, of course, the state championship."

"Ray was a great running mate," Bobby said. "He had incredible quickness out front. And remember: he was the leading scorer in the championship game."

Ray said the Indians were successful because every player knew his job. "For instance, Gene knew he was not a scorer. He was going to get rebounds and play defense. We all knew Bobby Plump was the scorer. We all hoped to play defense and contribute offensively when the occasion arose. It was just a team that meshed together. Even today, the successful teams are teams that know their roles. If they don't play their roles, they don't win the big marble."

At Butler, Ray was a solid reserve player, a good student, and a campus leader. Like most of his Milan teammates, Ray said he would never have gone to college at all if not for basketball. "You could see right then he was going to be a leader," said Bobby. "Ray was president of the fraternity, and he was always involved on campus. I was fortunate to room with him three out of four years at Butler. We learned a lot together."

After college, he had his own shot at the marble. After graduating from Butler in 1958, Ray accepted the head coaching job at Lapel, making him the youngest coach in the state. After one season there, the head coaching job at Milan became available. Ray took the job. After four competitive seasons, differences with school board members influenced Ray to resign and take a position at Clinton Central High School, where he won one sectional title in his five years at the helm. He spent another three years as principal at Clinton Central after he resigned as coach.

Ray then moved on to Shelbyville. He was assistant principal at Shelbyville High School for three years and principal for nine before leaving to accept a position with the IHSAA. He has risen steadily through the ranks and nearly had the top spot in the organization, which went instead to Robert Gardner, a former Milan principal and current Shelbyville neighbor of Ray's.

Ray still feels a connection with his Milan teammates. "To me, it's just amazing that something that happened 40 years ago would remain important to the team, as well as the community."

Of course, he has another constant reminder of his high school glory days: Ray married Milan cheerleader Virginia "Jinky" Voss.

He also believes his small town upbringing has been a big factor in his success. "I don't think there's any doubt about it. Coming from a large family and a small community has helped me tremendously."

Bobby Plump has expressed a great deal of respect for Ray. "He's a guy who's not afraid to make decisions. Ray is a good person who wants to do right. He's done a great job."

Bob Engel

Bob Engel doesn't look like a sentimental guy. In fact, he may still be the toughest-looking guy out of the entire team of Milan Indians. But it doesn't take him long to get misty-eyed when talking about his teammates and his hometown.

"I told them all at the banquet. I told them how much I loved them. Let's forget roundball for just a minute. I am so proud of what these guys have accomplished in their lives. It was put in our minds that we were doers. We knew if we sacrificed enough, we could get the job done."

Bob Engel may have made a bigger sacrifice than anyone. After starting at guard in Marvin Wood's guard-oriented offense as a junior, Bob agreed to move to forward as a senior. "I did whatever I could do to benefit the team. We didn't have a superstar. When Bobby made that last-second shot, he came into the spotlight. But go back to the regional against Aurora. If it hadn't been for Ronnie Truitt, we would never have gotten there. Aurora was big all across the front line. We were 5'11", 5'11", and 6'2". But we controlled the boards."

Bobby Plump called Bob Engel, "the heart and soul of the ballclub. He was the never-say-die guy. He was the guy who knew we could win."

Bob was a great high school player before his back problems put him on the bench. In spite of his bad back, he was heavily recruited by the University of Cincinnati and Xavier University.

But Bob chose not to play, and not to attend college. Instead, he moved to Hamilton, Ohio, after graduating from Milan and went to work. For several years, Bob worked at IBM and attended an IBM training school. In 1965, he married his wife Saundra Hartman, who happened to be from Versailles. Later, the Engels moved to Kalamazoo, Michigan, where Bob went to work for General Motors, working his way up to a white collar job before getting frustrated and going back to work "with guys who get their hands dirty." He is now nearing retirement at GM.

Like his teammates, Bob has come a long way from the streets of Milan, where he grew up. "Right on Main Street," he said. "Right above Kirchner's Department Store." He was a poor kid who lived with his mother, his father having left when Bob was just a baby. Bob's dad showed up again during Milan's title run, but Bob didn't have anything to do with him.

Bob used to play ball games in Milan Park with his neighbors, Billy, Bobby, and Tom Voss. "Their dad, Estil Voss, put up a basketball goal out back. We used to have knock-down, drag-out games with kids who were a lot older."

It was at one of these games that Bob met Ronnie Truitt. They were to become practically inseparable.

In 1949, a Milan man named Carl Brown took Bob and Ronnie to see a semistate game at Butler Fieldhouse. "After the game, Mr. Brown took us downtown to a jewelry store where they had the championship rings on display. He put his arms around us and said, 'Now, if you boys work real hard, who knows? Maybe you can win one of those.'"

Bob credits Marc Combs with sensing the talent in these street kids and putting them on the path to greatness. "He was very soft-spoken. But when he said something, you listened. He was the one who taught us the fundamentals."

Although his friends in Michigan call him "Hoosier," Bob wasn't involved with the film. He was, however, part of another recent basketball film shot in Indiana, 1994's *Blue Chips*. Bob's brother-in-law Charlie Shorten invited him to be part of the crowd scenes shot in the gym at Frankfort. Bob can be seen sitting behind the visitors' bench.

Today, Bob still tries to get the folks in Michigan to understand the significance of the Milan Miracle. But the real significance lies in the friendships born of teamwork and triumph. "Bobby Plump is just like a brother. We're all very close. If it was three in the morning and I needed something and I had no help, I could call any of them, and I guarantee you they would be there. That's the way we are."

Glen Butte

The sophomore flash of the 1954 Milan Indians was the first member of the team to technically "retire." After more than 20 years at Batesville High School, many as athletic director, Glen is back home in Ripley County, keeping busy with his family and assisting his mother and father, who still live in the Pierceville home where Glen grew up. Many of the props of Glen's boyhood are still there: the kitchen table where he and Bobby used to devour a loaf of bread and a jar of peanut butter inside of a couple of minutes, the garage that once held up a basketball goal, out by the driveway where small town boys dreamed of glory.

"I was a 15-year-old sophomore when we won the state championship," Glen recalled. "I hadn't been out of Milan too many times. But I knew we'd accomplished a great feat. Forty years later, I'm really starting to appreciate the skill that was involved, and some of the luck."

Growing up in Pierceville, Glen was one of Bobby Plump's best friends. "We played together, ate together, camped out together. We didn't know there was another world at that time," said Glen.

"Glen and Roger Schroder and I were like the Three Muskateers," Bobby said.

He also said Glen probably turned out to be the best basketball player of the bunch. "Glen was good. He was a great shooter."

In a way, Glen's career at Milan was just beginning when the Indians won the state championship. He played on great Milan teams the next two years, advancing twice to the regional finals. In his last game, Glen scored 28 points in a defeat to Connersville, who then lost to eventual state champ Crispus Attucks.

After high school, Glen accepted a scholarship to Indiana University. He was a valuable role player for Coach Branch McCracken.

Next, like many of his Indian teammates, Glen went into teaching and coaching. His first job was as an assistant at Moores Hill under

Snort Grinstead, the coach who'd been deposed at Milan after the 1951-52 season. After two years, Glen left for Dillsboro, where he taught and coached for five years.

After one season coaching at Orleans, Glen was offered an administrative position at Batesville. He liked it so well, he stayed for two decades. It was a good place for a family man. (Glen's wife, the former Dixie Siebein, was a Milan High School classmate.)

"I wanted to raise my kids in Batesville," he said. "It's a little larger than Milan, but it's still a small town. I think my kids appreciated growing up there."

Being part of the championship team has always stayed with Glen. "I enjoy the recognition. You can say you're from Milan, and it's a magnet in Indiana. It's been a great ride."

The way Glen figures it, the legend will live on forever. "They'll probably write on our headstones, 'He was a member of the famous 1954 state champions.'"

Roger Schroder

Even today, Roger Schroder looks like he might be able to give some high school ballplayers a run for their money. More than 40 years after winning the championship, Roger is fit and youthful. Like so many of his teammates, Roger became a teacher and coach, helping other young ballplayers in their quest for achievement, but never quite reaching that pinnacle again.

Roger said that nobody was really expecting a championship from the Milan Indians in 1954. "That summer before, we played ball in the alley, went to the drive-in, went fishing. It was a simple life. I don't think anybody was sitting around saying we were going to win it all."

Although Roger didn't get a lot of playing time for the champs, his contribution was always appreciated. Bobby Plump commented that it was rugged practice sessions that kept the starters sharp. "One of the reasons we were as good as we were was that we had excellent talent to play against in practice. It's unfortunate that Roger had to play on a basketball team with two all-state guards. He and Bill Jordan could have started for anybody else in the county. Our practices were some of our toughest games."

"I ran as much in practice and took as many elbows to the head," said Roger, who usually had the job of guarding Bobby.

Roger had always planned to study engineering at Purdue after high school. But he still had basketball in his blood. Like Gene White and Ken Wendelman, Roger chose Franklin College, where he found considerably more playing time than he'd had at Milan.

After graduation, Roger took a coaching job at Indianapolis Howe High School, where he stayed for nine years. He was hired as Indianapolis Marshall High School's first varsity basketball coach when that school opened in 1967. That job, Roger held for 19 years.

Many of those 19 years were memorable for Roger and his wife, Sue Ferguson. Roger's 1968-69 team was 18-3 in the regular season, but lost to a tough Shortridge team in the sectional. Shortridge went on to play in the state championship game, losing to Gary Roosevelt. Other highlights included sectional championships in 1977, 1981, and 1983. Roger's program also produced a couple of all-state players: Larry Bullington and David "Poncho" Wright, who was also part of the University Of Louisville's 1980 national championship team.

As it happened, Roger Schroder was the first and only coach Marshall High School ever had. The school was closed in 1986, along with Crispus Attucks High School. The next season, Roger moved to Broad Ripple High School, a team that had won a state championship in 1980. He was 40-25 in three seasons as the Rockets' head coach before deciding to hang up the high tops.

Roger retired from teaching in June of 1996. His friends know him as a strong leader and devoted family man. And, after all these years, he's still amazed at how the Milan Indians took Indiana by storm.

"I remember going to play in a tournament. People would see who we were, and they'd just stop and applaud. That was the stature of this ball club," he said.

Rollin Cutter

What people remember about Rollin Cutter's contribution to the champs from Milan is that he did a great job of filling in for Bob Engel whenever Engel's bad back took him out of the action. The sophomore did an admirable job in both the afternoon and evening games on when the Indians won the championship, playing tough defense and working the Indians' offensive scheme.

What most people don't remember was Rollin's foot speed. "If there was one guy on the team slower than Gene White, it was Rollin Cutter," said Bobby Plump.

Most of all, though, Bobby remembers Rollin as an intelligent player and a hard worker. "What a job he did in the finals. It was as if we didn't miss a beat, and here we had a kid who hadn't played a whole game all year. When you can bring in somebody who hasn't played very much and nobody notices the difference, he's got to be doing a lot of things right. In my mind, it was one of the most memorable state final performances ever."

Rollin enjoyed his moment in the sun. "I had fun. As a sophomore, I was young enough that I didn't have any pressure. For most of the year, I kind of rode the team's coattails."

Rollin played for two more tough Milan Indian teams — going to the regional finals both years — before graduating in 1956 and following Bobby and Ray Craft to Butler. He played two years for the Bulldogs before knee problems ended his career.

But a bad knee didn't ruin Rollin's love of the game. After graduation in 1960, he accepted a head coaching job at Syracuse High School in Northern Indiana. Several years later, he was back in Central Indiana as head coach, and later athletic director, at Brownsburg High School.

Following Brownsburg, Rollin worked as an assistant coach at Indianapolis Arlington High School for seven years. He eventually retired as a coach and took a position at Carmel High School as a guidance counselor. Today, Rollin and his wife, former Milan classmate Maridee Smock, live in Noblesville, and Rollin is guidance director at Noblesville High School.

He still gets back to Milan occasionally, and enjoys the team reunions. "Over the years, I've become close to the guys. And I still have family in Milan. When I go there, I still see a lot of familiar faces. It makes me feel good that people remember."

And what does Rollin remember? "Other than the ball game, the celebration and the welcome we got back in Milan the next day. It was fun. The whole thing has been fun."

Ken Wendelman

Ken Wendelman is still a country boy. He lives on 48 acres in rural Ripley County, an area known as Hungry Hollar, with no other houses in sight. He loves to fish, and loves to watch deer and coyotes run across his land. Sometimes, he even watches the deer through his rifle scope. But he doesn't pull the trigger anymore. He even throws back the fish.

"Too kind-hearted, I guess," Ken said.

It fits. The big kid who spelled Gene White at center for the Indians was always a gentle soul — everywhere but on the basketball court. "I was aggressive. That was the way I played. I liked contact. I would have been more at home playing football."

"Kenny was an integral part of the ball club," said Bobby Plump. "Woody always brought him in for the press. He was a great defender, and he was quick."

Even so, Ken's best game may have been baseball. After graduating from Milan High School, he attended a Cincinnati Reds tryout at Crosley Field and was invited to spring training at Tampa, Florida. Many people who saw him play think he had the tools to play in the major leagues.

He chose instead to go to Franklin College. "I've kicked myself in the tail many times for that. I was young and stupid and let somebody talk me out of it."

Instead of playing basketball for the Grizzlies with teammates Gene White and Roger Schroder, Ken played intramural ball at Franklin. After three years in school, he decided to move back to Ripley County and started working in construction, which has been his career ever since.

Ken's had his share of health problems. In his late 20s, he was diagnosed with cancer. After beating it, he had skin cancer later in life. He also suffered a major heart attack in 1991. "Since my heart attack, the doctor says I can only have two beers a day. I asked him if I could save them all up and have 14 on Saturday, but he wouldn't let me," Ken laughed.

Ken chooses his celebrations with his Milan teammates carefully, too. Although he attended their 30th anniversary reunion, he's not a regular at team functions. "It's been 40 years. It's something I'll never forget. But it's in the past. A lot of people in Milan are like me — they get tired of hearing about it every year."

Still, Ken is proud of the team's accomplishments. "Who wouldn't be? Especially given where we came from. We were just a bunch of country boys. It is something that will probably never be duplicated."

Bill Jordan

According to his Milan teammates, Bill Jordan always looked like a movie star.

"An Adonis," said Bobby Plump of his cousin.

So it was only fitting that Bill Jordan has made a good living acting in motion pictures, television shows, and commercials.

Bill was a junior when the Indians won it all in 1954, a valuable role player who scored 15 in the sectional opener that year. The next year, he was the team's top guard, leading the Indians to the regional final.

But basketball was always secondary to Bill. Acting and music were his true passions. "He was always telling me he wanted to be an actor," said Milan teacher Corinne "Corky" Denari Casey. "I told him I could only teach him so much in speech class, but if he wanted to be an actor, he'd just have to go out and be an actor and work hard."

He did. Even during high school, Bill played piano and saxophone in a band that worked at dances all across Ripley County. "He was multi-talented. He was an excellent basketball and baseball player, and an excellent musician," Bobby Plump said.

After graduation, Bill attended Indiana University and the University of Vienna. The acting bug was still strong, so he moved to California to try to make it in films. The business was tough. But Bill was able to land a spot on a country music radio show. He also found success on the opposite coast, on Broadway, appearing in such productions as *Wait Until Dark* with Lee Remick, *The Lion in Winter* with George C. Scott, and *Who's Afraid of Virginia Woolf?* with Shelley Winters. Following these jobs, Bill landed roles on such 1960s TV favorites as *Bonanza* and *Rat Patrol*. He also had a regular part in the television series called *Project UFO*.

Over the years, Bill's film credits have included roles in *The Buddy Holly Story* and *A Man Called Horse*. But it is the movie Jordan did not appear in that has been a great disappointment. He always thought he should at least have been consulted about the making of *Hoosiers*.

"I never watched it all because it was so distorted. It sort of rubbed me the wrong way. Why should I watch it? I lived the story? I wouldn't want to hear what Hollywood had to write about it.

"But they got it made. It was a stroke of hard work and talent. But it had very little quality to it in terms of my experience of being on the ball team."

These days, Bill stays busy with commercial work — including a spot for AT&T that took him back to his old stomping grounds to play a basketball coach with a sought-after recruit. The spot, which featured Georgetown basketball coach John Thompson, ran during the NCAA Finals in 1995.

It was a great trip home for Bill. "I love it there now. It's so wonderful. It has really changed. When I was a kid, you couldn't even get a radio station. Now it's civilized."

It was those trips to Indianapolis with the Milan Indians that first opened Bill's eyes to some of the more glamorous things in life. "I remember the hotels, eating big steaks, thinking, 'My gosh, what are we doing here?' It gave me a little idea that there were lots of things out there — a lot of glory to be passed around. It appealed to me, the perks you got when you achieved something."

Bill's also achieved something even more important recently. Diagnosed with prostate cancer in the fall of 1996, he has come through treatments and is currently in good health.

A lot of his teammates think Bill might have some resentment about his lack of playing time with the 1954 Indians, and that he doesn't come around much because of it. But Bill said it's his schedule that has kept him away. "It's a really tough business. I've had to be really focused and devoted to make it. There's a lot of competition, a lot of ups and downs. You have to be driven."

And Bill wants his teammates to know how much he admires them.

"I think more fondly of the guys than the actual event. The event is foggy in my memory now; by virtue of living out here (in California), I don't have the opportunity to relive the dream that much. But I cherish those memories."

Ken Delap and Bob Wichman

Ken Delap and Bob Wichman were the odd men out in the Milan story — boys who made the Indians' 12-man regular season roster, but sat out the tournament because IHSAA rules permitted only 10 to dress for tournament games. When the Indians were on the floor, Ken and Bob were in the stands — in a way, the most difficult assignment anyone had to accept.

But Ken and Bob were definitely integral parts of the team and the team's success. They were two of the players who helped make practices harder than most games for the Indians, paving the way for the championship run. As far as their teammates were concerned, they were star players who could have started for hundreds of other teams in the state.

Today, Bob is a vice president at Pioneer Hi-Bred International, the world's largest seed corn company, based in Des Moines, Iowa. He married Milan High School classmate Libby Kohlmeier. Bob still remembers his high school days and the championship run with much fondness.

"When we played at some of the larger schools during the regular season, we'd fill 4,500-seat arenas. You really got caught up in the hysteria. Everyone who played high school ball thought of only one thing — the state championship," he said.

Ken lives on an 80-acre farm near Milan. In one of those "it's a small world" coincidences, Ken's daughter Stacey is married to Steve Cox, the son of Bobby Plump's Butler teammate Wally Cox. Stacey is a nurse who happened to help care for Marvin Wood when he was receiving cancer treatments at Methodist Hospital.

The memories of Milan's championship run are bittersweet for Ken Delap. He and Bob Wichman didn't receive championship rings as the others did. "At the time, it was a disappointment, but through the years, you learn to live with things that happen. Still, it was a great experience. I think about it every once in a while. They were a great bunch of guys."

The next year, Ken and Bob would get their chance to play. They joined Bill Jordan, Rollin Cutter, and Glen Butte in the Indians' starting line-up and were still the best team in Southeastern Indiana. "It was great. Everybody wanted to beat us because we won the year before," Ken said.

The Indians won their sectional and beat Connersville — the only team to beat Crispus Attucks in the regular season — in the first round at the regional. They lost the regional final to Rushville.

It was a good run. But the championship team of 1954 is still the one Ken Delap remembers most. "It was hard to believe. It was a dream come true, a fairy tale. For a little school like Milan, it was just unreal."

Ralph Preble and Jim Wendelman

Milan's 1954 championship run probably wouldn't have been possible without the experience they gained in their Final Four appearance in 1953. And that Final Four appearance certainly wouldn't have been possible without seniors Ralph Preble and Jim Wendelman.

Today, the Plumps and the Prebles are especially close. Ralph met his wife Sally at Miami of Ohio, where they both went to school. Sally and Jenine Plump are best friends. Ralph is a businessman who owns several pieces of property in Versailles.

Jim Wendelman is a truck driver for Hill-Rom Incorporated of Batesville. After high school, he had intended to accept a scholarship to the University of Florida — but, while working at Chris Volz's auto dealership, met and fell in love with a young woman from Sunman. He and Nicki were married and have raised their two daughters and one son in Ripley County.

Dale Smith and Jim Call

Just as Bob Wichman and Ken Delap were not allowed to dress for the state tournament in 1954, Dale Smith and Jim Call were on the Indians' taxi squad in 1953. Both were disappointed that they couldn't dress for the tournament. But both know they were looked upon as equal parts of the team. Their teammates and the people of Milan will never let them forget it.

Jim Call is recently retired from his job at the Seagram Distillery in Lawrenceburg. He was married to Zelpha Lewis, and is now a widower. Jim was a senior in 1953 and was thrilled when the Indians won the tournament the next year. "They had a good coach and a good team and everybody played together. There was a certain amount of surprise, but I knew they were good," Jim said.

Dale Smith was just a junior in 1953, but failed to make the team as a senior. Nevertheless, he was there when the Indians won it all. "I was the first guy out of the stands and on the floor. A cop tried to stop me, but I just showed him my letter jacket and he let me go. Coach Wood grabbed me and gave me a big ol' whirl!"

Dale still owns a home in Milan, but he and his wife, the former Claudia Toney, spend part of every year at their home in Florida. He finds that Milan follows him everywhere he goes. "You mention Milan, and you have to stand there and tell 'em all about it. I tell them I was part of the team. I wasn't out on the floor, but I was there. It was great."

A COMPENDIUM
OF QUOTES

Over the years, there's been a lot written and reported about the Bobby Plump, the Milan Miracle, and the great impact they had on basketball, not only in the State of Indiana, but across the nation. Here are some of the most memorable:

John Wooden, former Indiana Mr. Basketball and ten-time NCAA Championship coach at UCLA: "I was not in Indiana when Milan won it, but I did know Bobby Plump was the star of that team. Once when I was speaking at an insurance convention at the Palms Springs Marriott Hotel, a fellow came up to me and said, 'I'm from Indiana, and you and I were both part of basketball there.' I said, 'That's not unusual if you're from Indiana.' Then he asked, 'You ever hear of Milan?' I said, 'You're Bobby Plump!' I knew it was him."

Oscar "The Big O" Robertson, former Indiana Mr. Basketball and NBA Hall-Of-Famer: "His shot was historic, and I'm happy for him. But most of all, that shot sent a message to all young athletes that no matter what color your skin, how tall you are, how big your school is, what it all comes down to is one thing: whether or not you're a winner. Bobby saved high school basketball in Indiana for many years. My family and I will also always remember him and thank him for serving as a pall bearer for by brother, Bailey Robertson, Jr. Bobby is loyal and honest, a friend and a winner."

Gene Keady, head coach of the Purdue Boilermakers men's basketball team: "What Bobby did in basketball was unique. He hit the shot heard 'round the world. Bobby is as common as an old shoe, and what you see is what you get. To this day, he's still giving something back to the game of basketball. Where I come from, we call that a 'class act.'"

Bob Collins, late sports editor of The Indianapolis Star: "I saw many exciting moments in sports — some great Indianapolis 500s, like the one with (Rick) Mears and (Gordon) Johncock, or the one where Little Al (Unser) beat Scott Goodyear. I saw two Super Bowls. I saw the World Series game in which Bob Gibson struck out 18 batters, and the 1975 World Series between Cincinnati and Boston. I saw the impossible shot Tom Watson hit to beat Jack Nicklaus in the U.S. Open at Pebble Beach. I saw the Masters when Ben Hogan shot a 30 on the back nine and literally made the crowd cry. I saw Muhammed Ali fight. Plump's shot ranks in the top five great moments in sports I ever saw."

Bob Williams, former Indianapolis Star *sportswriter and IHSAA sports information director:* "Bobby Plump is one of the best ambassadors for basketball Indiana has ever had. He's always in demand as a speaker. A lot of your better ballplayers aren't very active after they're through playing, but Bobby's still active. He's been a big asset to the game."

Jimmy Angelopolous, who covered sports for The Indianapolis Times *and* The Indianapolis News *for 44 years:* "Plump was very cool. He was tuned into the fundamentals of basketball. He understood his coach and the game plan quite well. It was small schools like Milan that built this tournament, and their story was great for the press."

Herb Schwomeyer, coach, official, broadcaster, author, and Indiana high school basketball historian: "It's something nobody will every forget. It was wonderful. Bobby was a member of a real fine ball club that was very disciplined. That's how they won, and won consistently."

Bob Hammel, sports editor of the Bloomington Herald-Times: "One of the things that's been nice is that Bobby Plump has lived up to his aura. He has always been accessible and kind with his time. I'm sure it's fun for him to go back over it, but at some point, it has to have gotten old. But he hasn't ever let that come through."

Ray Crowe, who won two state championships as coach at Crispus Attucks: "Bobby was a great basketball player. But I've gotten to know him since those days, and I can say that he's also a great person. I think the world of him."

Bobby "Slick" Leonard, former IU star and coach of the Indiana Pacers: "That shot made Plump's life. It got him a scholarship, and he went on from there. What he did gives kids a dream that they can come from a small town and make it to the big show."

Jerry Sichting, former star of Martinsville, Purdue, and the NBA, ex-Boston Celtics broadcaster, and current Minnesota Timberwolves executive: "I remember my dad talking about Milan. I was a big student of the game myself. I read all the stories about all the championships. It's Milan that sets Indiana apart. It was unbelievable."

Tom Carnegie, Hall-of-Fame broadcaster and announcer: "Thank goodness Bobby Plump and Milan won that game, because, for a long time, it helped still the feeling among educators that we should be divided into classes based upon enrollment. The team itself was a group of fine young men. We can continue to admire them years later. And, with all the dramatic moments in my career, that ranks as one of the best."

Bill Green, who won a record six state championships as coach at Marion and Indianapolis Washington and was named USA Today's *1987 Coach of the Year:* "He was a great player in his time. He is just a super, super guy, a very successful businessman and a hard worker. He proved to a lot of kids in small schools that you can win it, and you can be successful."

Joe Sexson, star of Indiana high school and Purdue basketball and former Purdue University assistant and Butler University head coach: "Bobby Plump is one of the finest guys I know. He was a great player, too, the guts and nuts of that team. They talk about certain people being able to bring other players' games up. Bobby Plump was like that."

Howard Sharpe, former Terre Haute Gerstmeyer coach whose 753 wins are the most in Indiana high school basketball history: "We should never have lost to them. To this day, I can't believe it. But Bobby Plump was a real Indiana high school basketball player. He could dribble and shoot, and he was a good team player. That's why they won."

Hilliard Gates, who broadcast the 1954 championship game: "He's a legend. He played in perhaps the most exciting tournament game I ever telecast. And he's still the same guy. Bobby is a wonderful gentleman who will be remembered forever."

Marvin Wood, coach of the 1953-54 Milan Indians: "Bobby Plump is special. He's a remarkable individual. He was when he was young, and he's become even more remarkable. But I always knew he was great. When things were tough, he was always at his best."

Clarence Kelly, Jr., Milan assistant coach: "What Milan did will never go away, not in Indiana. It was fantastic."

Ed Whitcomb, Governor of Indiana from 1969-73: "The first time I ever heard of Bobby Plump was when he made the big shot. I was in Indy that day, and I saw him do it. What he did still captures the imagination of a lot of people. It may be the most spectacular thing that's every happened in our state."

Bob Fehrman, former Aurora and Purdue star: "Plump ran that ballclub like a finely tuned watch. It was probably the most perfect mix of players and coaches I've ever seen."

Nick Iaria, owner of Iaria's Italian Restaurant in Indianapolis: "In our restaurant, we have over 300 pictures of personalities, but the one customers ask most about is Bobby Plump. I have never met a more loyal, honest person than Bobby in my lifetime. It's a pleasure to call him my friend."

Don Server, former Gimbel Award winner at Madison: "The game was a classic. It will
never be duplicated. And Bobby Plump's name will always be there."

Joe Wolfla, long-time friend: "If there is anybody in this world who understands how honest and sincere Bobby Plump is, it's me. Even though Bobby is a basketball legend, everyone who knows him knows two things about him: his head is the same size it always was, and his heart is enormous. Bobby is to basketball and Indiana what John F. Kennedy was to the world. He's a winner and a class act, and I'm honored to have him as a friend."

Morry Mannies, veteran Muncie Central play-by-play announcer: "Most people in Muncie would like to forget that year, but I respect Bobby Plump for what he did and what he has done. He's a great guy. He has held the championship well."

Willard Kehrt, former coach and scout at Milan: "Bobby Plump was an excellent shooter and the engineer of the basketball team. He was a smart ballplayer who led the team in playing to the weakness of their opponents. If they had to play fast, they played fast. If they had to play slow, they played slow."

Chuck Harmon, who played on two state championship teams at Washington High School in Washington, Indiana, and, in 1954, became the first African-American to play for the Cincinnati Reds: "I heard about the Milan victory at spring training in Florida. Whenever I saw someone from Indiana, I'd ask how the tournament was going. I was amazed. I remember going through Milan that year when I was headed home to Washington."

Harley Andrews, former IU player who was famous for teaming up with his twin brother Arley and uncle Harold at Terre Haute Gerstmeyer: "Bobby is one of the better examples of what a person can achieve in Indiana high school basketball if he has the desire and the work ethic. He's also a good, warm, complete human being, a very genuine person."

Eddie Bopp, Trester Award winner and star for Indianapolis Washington's 1965 state champs: "In 1954, I was a little kid watching the game on TV in my basement. It was the first game I remember, and it was a heart-stopper."

Al Busching, Pierceville friend and Ripley County politician: "Bobby could have been good in politics. I don't see why he couldn't be governor. He'd have no trouble getting elected, that's for sure."

Genevieve White, mother of Gene White: "I just like Bobby so well. He's just like one of mine."

Ralph Preble, 1953 Milan Indian teammate: "Bobby is honest. He's a friend forever."

Don "Foozy" Voss, Milan fan who saw all of Bobby's high school games: "He was outstanding. He was smart, and he could see things nobody else could see, like Larry Bird."

Kenneth Bockhorst, another Milan fan who saw the shot: "As soon as someone finds out you're from Milan, they point at you and say, 'Bobby Plump! Do you know him?'"

Dave McCollum, Bobby's business partner for 25 years: "I've heard all the Milan stories a million times. He loves to talk about it. But he's never forgotten where he came from. I've never seen him say no to an autograph seeker. He'll always be remembered for the shot. But he'll also be remembered for the type of person he was — congenial, willing to help people. He's a very caring person."

Chris Theofanis, former Butler sports information director: "Bobby is an outstanding individual. He achieved a lot of fame and glory, but never let it go to his head. Bobby has always been Bobby. He had ability, and he had ice in his veins."

George Theofanis, former head basketball coach of the Butler Bulldogs: "He had a great attitude and a lot of confidence. He knew he could do the job. But he wasn't conceited. He was always willing to help and to give others credit. He's one of a kind."

Howard Catt, former president of the Indiana Basketball Hall of Fame: "Bobby is one of the immortals of basketball. He has done so much working with young people. He's one in a million."

George Durham, former Phillips 66ers publicity director: "If someone were to ask me to list Bobby's faults, I couldn't think of any. He was a straight arrow, right down the middle."

PLUMP'S LAST SHOT

Looking for more information about Hoosier basketball? Want a chance to chat with a basketball legend? Here's the place:

> Plump's Last Shot
> 6104 Cornell Street
> Indianapolis, Indiana, 46220
> 317-257-5867

Stop by for a nostalgic look at the Indiana game, a heaping helping of Hoosier hospitality, and some great home cooking!

INDIANA DREAMIN'
(ON A FINAL FOUR WINNER'S DAY)

I took my family to the Final Four
An event I attend every year,
To be with friends, to share the thrill
Of the Hoosier Basketball I hold so dear.

The Dome was filled with excited fans
Cheering their team to "No. 1."
The game was close. The fever was high.
They cut the nets when they were done.

My kids, they had a coke or two,
Their throats parched from hollering & braying
They had to bounce that ball before bed that night,
Pretending they were the ones that were playing.

As I tucked them in their beds
And kissed their cheeks so tender,
I wondered if they would cherish this night
And the games I hoped they'd remember.

'Cause the end of an era has come to pass.
Class Basketball is the new mission.
No longer will a single champion be.
No longer sweet tradition.

My dreams swept me away that night.
My thoughts turned to those on high.
I dreamt of standing at the Pearly Gates,
That "Big Dance" in the sky.

My Lord emerged affront a shining light,
Too blinding for my eyes.
But as I turned my eyes from Him,
Tom & Dick appeared by His side.

As the twins bore me thru those gates,
An opportunity did arise.
"The final game has begun," they said.
"But we need one more on our side"

Eagerly, I laced my hightops up,
So proud to be part of the chosen few.
But my heart jumped to my throat
When I viewed the heavenly team across the room.

There was Oscar Robertson leading that team.
He is pretty tough any day . . .
Big George was driving the lane.
No one would get in his way.

Rick Mount was swishing jumpers,
The kind that would make Hades hot.
And Bobby Plump was standing by,
Plotting his "Final Shot."

As I surveyed this wondrous team,
My ego was dealt a heavy blow.
My shot was off, I couldn't jump.
My feet were kinda slow.

Where would I find the proper tools
To compete with this almighty team?
Who could help me guard
These gentlemen I hold so high in esteem?

Then God smiled and picked me up
And whispered in my ear.
"Chin up, old friend. You're part of the elite!
There's just one Class up here.

Greg Maci
March 24, 1997